India – Studie
History of an Idea

What India means may elicit different answers from people today. The answers that might have been given a thousand, tow thousand or three thousand years ago would have been possibly quite different. This volume explores how notions of India have grown: even as a geographical expression the notion (under whatever name) took time to form. Political factors and cultural diffusion both helped in the formation. Nor is the role of outsiders in looking at India as country with some identifiable features of custom, belief, and language, to be ignored. The different contributions in this volume bring out how the idea of India has changed as Indian civilization has developed and received various cultural streams. The contributors also essay the issue of India's transformation into a nation under the stresses generated by the colonial conquest, resistance and the influx of modern ideas. The volume closes with discussions how the future of the nation was conceived in the past and what message this has for the people of India today.

The editor of this volume, Irfan Habib, was formerly Professor of History at Aligarh Muslim University, and is author of *Agrarian System of Mughal Empire*, An *Atlas of the Mughal Empire*, and *Essays in Indian History: Towards a Marxist Perception*. He is currently editing *A People's History of India* four parts of which have been published.

India - Studies in the History of an Idea

Edited by
Irfan Habib

Aligarh Historians Society

Munshiram Manoharlal
Publishers Pvt. Ltd.

ISBN 81-215-1152-6 (HB)
ISBN 81-215-1153-4 (PB)
First published 2005

Typeset by Aligarh Historians Society, Aligarh
Printed and published by
Munshiram Manoharlal Publishers Pvt. Ltd.,
Post Box 5715, 54 Rani Jhansi Road,
New Delhi 110 055.

Contents

Preface

The idea of India is a phrase of relatively recent use — much credit for this being due to Sunil Khilnani — but the substance of it has an old history. This volume is, first, about how the notion originated and evolved in the minds of both its own inhabitants and outsiders, and about what it conveyed to them in terms of geography and civilizational traits. The substance of the notions of India altered too as Indian culture itself evolved and its own contours changed. The volume is, therefore, concerned with how from being a country, whether as an essentially geographical expression or as a cultural entity, India became, or came to be regarded as, a nation. Finally, it touches on the contesting visions of the India of the future, developed within and outside the National Movement.

The Aligarh Historians Society asked a number of distinguished scholars to contribute papers on the different aspects of the theme. These papers were presented and discussed at a panel organised by the Society at the Guru Nanak Dev University, Amritsar, 28-30 December 2002. Professor Irfan Habib, who has edited the volume, contributes an introduction which, in its earlier version, had been presented as a key-note address at the panel.

The panel and the publication of the volume have been supported by grants from the Indian Council of Social Science Research, New Delhi, and the Sir Dorabji Tata Trust, Mumbai.

I should like to thank all contributors to the volume for their willing cooperation and for sending us their revised versions.

I am most grateful to my old friend, Mr P.N. Sahay, for compiling the index, which we hope readers will find convenient.

Mr Muneeruddin Khan has processed the final press-copy, while Mr Arshad Ali has kept our records and accounts. Mr Idris Beg has carried out other onerous duties.

Mr Devendra Jain of Messrs Munshiram Manoharlal Publishers has placed us greatly in his debt by agreeing to publish the volume.

Aligarh
December 2004

Shireen Moosvi
Secretary
Aligarh Historians Society

Contributors

1. ADITYA MUKHERJEE: Professor of History, Jawaharlal Nehru University, Delhi

2. ANIRUDDHA RAY: Former Professor of Islamic History and Culture, Calcutta University, Kolkata

3. GAUTAM CHATTOPADHYAY: Former President, Banga Itihas Samsad, Kolkata.

4. IMTIAZ AHMAD: Director, Khuda Bakhsh Oriental Public Library, Patna

5. INDU BANGA: Professor of History, Punjab University, Chandigarh

6. IRFAN HABIB: Former Professor of History, Aligarh Muslim University, Aligarh

7. ISHRAT ALAM: Senior Lecturer, Department of History, Aligarh Muslim University, Aligarh

8. IQTIDAR ALAM KHAN: Former Professor of History,Aligarh Muslim University, Aligarh

9. J.S. GREWAL: Chairman, Indian Institute of Advanced Study, Shimla, H.P.

10. KAMLESH MOHAN: Professor of History, Punjab University, Chandigarh

11. KESAVAN VELUTHAT: Professor of History, Mangalore University, Magalagangotri, Karnataka

12. MRIDULA MUKHERJEE: Professor of History, Jawaharlal Nehru University, New Delhi

13. NAJAF HAIDER: Reader in History, Jawaharlal Nehru University, New Delhi

14. OM PRAKASH: Former Professor, Delhi School of Economics, Delhi

15. SHEREEN RATNAGAR: Former Professor of History, Jawaharlal Nehru University, New Delhi

16. SYED ALI NADEEM REZAVI: Reader in History, Aligarh Muslim University, Aligarh

17. UDAI PRAKASH ARORA: Professor of History, M.J.P. Rohilkhand University, Bareilly

1

India: Country and Nation — An Introductory Essay

IRFAN HABIB

There will hopefully be not much objection to the statement that in history nothing has existed from all times; and countries form no exception to this rule. Even where geographical features set seemingly natural limits to a territory, the latter's recognition as a country has not automatically followed. The many indigenous communities inhabiting what is now Australia did not know, because of lack of sufficient mutual communication and exploration, that they were all placed on the same island; they were also not aware, since they did not know of any people outside Australia, that they were themselves distinct from inhabitants of other countries in important cultural ways. There was thus no country like Australia before the nineteenth century.

We can see from this example that geographical knowledge was also a pre-requisite before the concept of India as a country could arise. We do not at all know what the extent of the geographical knowledge of the people of the Indus civilization in the late third millennium BC was, although we may suppose that they had a name for the region in which their own culture prevailed, with its several uniformities.[1] Was it something like 'Meluhha', the name in use for it in contemporary Mesopotamia? As Shireen Ratnagar (chapter 2 in this volume) shows in her detailed study of the use of this name in Mesopotamia, a considerable amount of haziness was created around it by the ideological and political environment of the scribes who composed the texts in which Meluhha is mentioned. Nevertheless, the entire theme is of value because it represents the earliest instance of a territorial name for India or a part of it, and its history is interesting too as showing how geographical concepts become subject to different cultural influences.

In the *Rigveda*, whose compilation can roughly be placed within the range of 1500-1000 BC, there are hardly any territorial names, even 'Sapta Sindhava' meaning still the Seven Rivers

[1] See Irfan Habib, *Indus Civilization*, New Delhi, 2002, pp.14, 60, for a listing of these remarkable uniformities in script, artefacts and structures over such a large area.

rather than their region, the Punjab. The first evidence of the "idea of India" (courtesy, Sunil Khilnani)[2] is, perhaps no older than Gautama Buddha's time, some two thousand five hundred years ago (*c*.500 BC), when we first have lists of the "Sixteen Mahājanapadas", which together comprised Northern India and parts of Afghanistan.[3] There was yet no name given to this collection of regions, though a cultural unity of some sort seems to be assumed. It is with the Mauryan emperor Aśoka's inscriptions found all over India, datable to around 250 BC, that we find one of India's early names, "Jambudipa" (the Prakrit form of "Jambudvipa"), used in his Minor Rock Edict I, for the country as a whole.[4] The fact that this advance followed a political unification of the country under India's first empire is surely not without significance.

The cultural affinities of the Indian people, isolated from others by high mountain ranges of the north and by the Indian Ocean in the south, could only be marked more certainly, when there was knowledge of other people outside of these borders, people, that is, who could be seen as culturally different. This barrier must have been broken by the Achaemenid dominance over the Indus basin in the late sixth, fifth and fourth centuries BC, and the breach must have become still wider when Alexander conducted his lightning campaign in 327-25 BC, defeating and subjugating tribe after tribe in the Punjab and Sind. The Mauryan empire, as it expanded into this territory, came into close contact with Iranian and Greek communities and officials: nothing attests to this more than Aśoka's own edicts in Aramaic and Greek found inscribed in Taxila, Kandahar and other places in Afghanistan.[5] Such close contacts must have generated an appreciation of cultural differences between Indians and foreigners — and so a recognition of Indians as, in some respects, a distinct people. Thus Aśoka says in his Rock Edict XIII that the "Yonas" (Greeks)

[2] Sunil Khilnani, *The Idea of India*, first pub., London, 1997; updated Indian paperback ed., New Delhi, 1999. Part of our volume may, however, be regarded as analogous to Gherardo Gnoli's *The Idea of Iran: an Essay on its Origin*, Rome, 1989.

[3] For a detailed discussion of the Buddhist and Jain lists of the *mahājanapadas* and the location of the territory of each, see Hemachandra Raychaudhuri, *Political History of Ancient India*, with Commentary by B.N. Mukherjee, New Delhi, 1996, pp.85-135.

[4] The doubt must, however, remain that Asoka here meant not India, but the earth: see Beni Madhab Barua, *Inscriptions of Asoka*, part II, Calcutta, 1943, pp.338-41.

[5] See B.N. Mukherjee, *Studies in Aramaic Edicts of Aśoka*, Calcutta, 1984, which includes a study of Asoka's Greek inscription at Kandahar with text and translation (pp.35-39).

were different because they had no Brahmans and Śramanas (Buddhist priests) among them.[6] Thus a cultural distinction could reinforce a territorial one. A similar distinction occurs in the reference made in the *Manusmriti* (*c*.100 BC) to foreigners (*mlechchhas*), though in a much more hostile manner: theirs are lands where Brahmans do not perform sacrifices nor the "twice-born" dwell. The latter can dwell only in Āryavarta, that is defined as lying between the Himalayas and the Vindhyas (*Manu*, II, 22-24).[7]

It is debatable how far in the succeeding centuries the notion of Āryavarta or Bhārata-varsha (Prakrit: Bharadvasa, used in Khāravela's Hathigumpha inscription, Orissa, first century BC)[8] gained currency as the name of the country. The latter name undoubtedly acquired its popularity due to the *Mahabharata* epic, which centred on the feud between two sets of Bharata cousins, that involved in its story all the tribes and peoples known to the epic composers. The epic seems to have been composed and enlarged in its present form over a long period, possibly 200 BC to 400 AD; and it is likely therefore that its listing of peoples participating in the battle was based on a perception of India as a country.

As Ishrat Alam shows in chapter 3 of this volume, references to the territories that constitute India occur more frequently in the inscriptions and texts of the first millennium AD than those to the country itself. In a way Samudragupta's Allahabad inscription (*c*.350 AD) composed by Harishena, paved the way for subsequent *praśastis*, down to the Palam Baoli Sanskrit inscription (1276) in praise of Sultan Balban, in which various territories belonging to India are named, though India itself remains usually unnamed.[9] This conforms to the comment made

[6] Literally translated, the Edict says, "there is no locality (*jonapade*) other than that of the Yonas where there are no Brahmans and Sramanas" (cf. Barua, *Inscriptions of Asoka*, part II, p.192).

[7] G. Buhler (tr.), *The Laws of Manu*, Oxford, 1886, p.33.

[8] A transcription, 'Sanskritized' text and summary translation of the Hathigumpha inscription will be conveniently found in K.G. Krishnan, ed., *Uttankita Sanskrit Vidya Aranya Epigraphs*, II: *Prakrit and Sanskrit Epigraphs, 257 BC to 320 AD*, Mysore, 1989, pp.151-58. 'Bharadhavasa' occurs in the account of the 10th regnal year.

[9] [J.F. Fleet,] *Corpus Inscriptionum Indicarum*, III: *Inscriptions of the Early Gupta Kings*, revised by D.R. Bhandarkar, ed. B.C. Chhabra and G.S. Gai, New Delhi, 1981, pp.203-220, for the Samudragupta inscription; and Pushpa Prasad, *Sanskrit Inscriptions of Delhi Sultanate 1911-1526*, Delhi, 1990, pp.3-15, for the Palam Baoli inscription. See also D.C. Sircar, *Studies in the Geography of Ancient and Medieval India*, 2nd ed., Delhi, 1971, pp.4-16.

by the famous Chinese traveller, Yuan Chwang in the seventh century that the people of India "use local appellations for their respective countries" or regions, suggesting that they had themselves little occasion to use a name for the country as a whole.[10] Professor Veluthat examines in chapter 6 the particular case of the formation of Kerala as a region in its inhabitants' consciousness and its relationship with the broader concept of India.

This fact suggests to us that at times the outsiders' recognition of a country, based on their sense of India's distinct cultural and social features, might sometimes have been stronger than that of its own inhabitants who took these institutions and features for granted. Professor U.P. Arora in chapter 4 discusses how the Greeks from the fifth century BC onwards had a gradually expanding perception of India; and Professor J.S. Grewal in chapter 5 shows how the Chinese pilgrim Yuan Chwang (Hiuen Tsiang) in the seventh century AD offers us a coherent and detailed account of the geography and culture of this country together with a detailed description of its regions, which is the first of its kind found in any language (including Sanskrit).

It should not, therefore, surprise us that foreigners also gave to us one of the names for our country that we came in time to use ourselves, and, along with it, the name too for the principal religious community in India, which had none previously for itself. To begin with, the Iranians had long extended their version of the name of the Sindhu river, which they called "Hindu" ('h' in early Iranian standing for 's' in Indo-Aryan), to the country lying along and beyond that river.[11] Whence came the name 'India' given by the Greeks; and the Chinese `Yin-tu', representing 'Indu' in actual pronunciation.[12] In post-Hellenistic Iran territorial names began to be given the suffix *-stān*, so that `Hindu' would become `Hindustān', on the analogy of other Iranian territorial names (such as Sakastān [=Seistān], Gurjistān,

[10] Thomas Watters, *On Yuan Chwang's Travels in India 629-645 A.D.*, London, 1905, I, pp.131-2.

[11] Cf. Sudhakar Chattopadhyaya, *The Achaemenids and India*, 2nd ed., Delhi, 1974, pp.15-17, 23, 33, 44-45.

[12] 'Yin-tu' was also the Chinese transcription for the Sanskrit word *indu*, moon, which establishes the pronunciation of the characters when they came into use for India in the early centuries of the Christian era. This name for India came to China from Central Asia, where it must have been adopted from Eastern Iranian (see Watters, op.cit., I, pp.131-2).

Khuzistān, etc.).[13] Thus Hindustān, just like the name 'Hind', is an entirely Iranian word. The style of writing 'Hindusthān', as if it is a Sanskrit word meaning 'land of the Hindus' is a modern invention: the word in this form is unknown to classical Sanskrit. The word 'Hindu' too is of purely Iranian origin, meaning an inhabitant of "Hindu" or India. It was taken from the Iranians by the Arabs and Muslims in general, among whom uptill the time of Alberuni there was little reason to distinguish between those who were Indians, and those who in India followed religious sects other than Islam.[14] Once the Muslims established themselves in large parts of India, especially from the thirteenth century onwards, the latter restrictive meaning of the word began to predominate, and 'Hindū' assumed a religious colour. But by the Hindus themselves the name was not accepted before the latter half of the fourteenth century, being obviously an alien imposition. Its association with Muslim usage is still shown when the Vijayanagara rulers call themselves *Hindu rāya suratrāṇa* ('Sultan over Hindu *rāys*')[15] and, in 1438-9, the ruler of Mewar is found styled 'Hindu sultan' (*Hindu suratrāṇa*).[16] At the same time, while the word 'Hindū' in Persian designated an Indian who was not a Muslim, the words 'Hindī' and 'Hindustānī' came into use for Indians in general, the designations being used by the poets Amir Khusrau (d.1324) and 'Isāmī (1350), when they spoke of both the Hindu and Muslim inhabitants of this country taken together.[17] In chapter 7 Dr Imtiaz Ahmad traces in detail the concept of India as it developed in Arabic and Persian writing

[13] Cf. Irfan Habib, 'Linguistic Materials from Eighth-Century Sind: an Exploration of the Chachnama', Indian History Congress Symposium Papers: 11, Delhi, 1995, pp.8-9.

[14] Alberuni is found using the word Hindu already in a religious sense when he distinguishes between Hindus and Buddhists at one place, though at another he holds the corresponding distinction to be between Śramanas ('Shamaniyya') and Brahmans (Edward C. Sachau, tr., *Alberuni's India*, London, 1910, I, pp.7, 21).

[15] The title first appears for Bukka I in a Kannada inscription in 1354 at Penugonda (*Epigraphia Indica*, IV, p.327 & n.) and then occurs in subsequent inscriptions, e.g. Devaraya II's Satyamangalam plates of 1424 (*Epigraphia Indica*, III, pp.38, 40.)

[16] D.R. Bhandarkar's List of Inscriptions, *Epigraphia Indica*, XIX-XXIII, pp.109-10 (no.784). The ruler was Rana Kumbha.

[17] Amir Khusrau in a verse describes himself as a 'Hindustani Turk' (see quotation in M. Wahid Mirza, *The Life and Works of Amir Khusrau*, reprint, Delhi, 1974, p.228, fn.1). For the use of 'Hindi' in the sense of 'Indian', see 'Iṣāmī, *Futūḥu's Salaṭīn*, ed. A.S. Usha, Madras, 1948, p.465, where 'Hindi' troops are shown facing Mongol troops. But Ḥājib Khairat's *Dastūru'l Afāzil* of 1342-43, ed. Nazir Ahmad, Teheran, n.d., p.247, still defines Hindūān (plural of Hindu) as 'inhabitants of Hind', thus ignoring the distinction between Hindu and Hindī.

from the eighth to the fourteenth century in the course of which the information on the country so conceived was also, stage by stage, immensely enriched.

One of the major sources of such enrichment was undoubtedly Alberuni's *Kitāb al-Hind* (*c.*1035). It was truly a unique moment in history when a great scientist of one civilization studied in so rational a fashion and in such depth a civilization of a totally different lineage. To read such a large amount of scientific, philosophical and legal literature in Sanskrit and to appraise it in so clinical and impartial a manner was an achievement that one finds hard to praise enough. Since Professor Iqtidar Alam Khan devotes chapter 8 to a study of Alberuni's perception of India, little more needs to be said about him here beyond these words of tribute.[18]

The Ghaznavid and Ghorian conquests ultimately led to the establishment of the Delhi Sultanate (1206-1526), which covered at its zenith, in the first half of the fourteenth century, the bulk of India including the peninsula. Persian being the language of the court and government, there naturally developed an increasing store of information about India and its culture in works written in Persian, with the steady expansion of the Delhi Sultanate. The political unification of the country under a regime which saw a great deal of collaboration between the largely Muslim ruling class and its Hindu allies among the merchants and agrarian potentates,[19] simultaneously helped to create the ground for a sense of a common heritage and a composite culture. If we are looking for patriotic statements about India and its natural and cultural greatness, then, surely Amir Khusrau's *Nuh Sipihr* (1318) in Persian must be identified as the earliest and clearest example of such statements. The author proudly calls himself an Indian and lauds "love for one's country" (*ḥubb-i waṭan*). India (Hind), he says, contains people speaking twelve different regional languages, which he lists — from Sindhi and Kashmiri to Kannada (*Dhaur-samanduri*), Telugu (*Telangi*) and Tamil (*Ma'bari*). All these he calls "Hindwī" (or Indian) languages, being used "by common people for all purposes." Besides them, he praises Sanskrit, the language of the learned,

[18] We are also fortunate that Alberuni's work should have been rendered into English by so competent a translator as Edward C. Sachau, whose *Alberuni's India*, 2 vols., London, 1910, remains a classic on its own.

[19] Cf. Irfan Habib, 'Barani's Theory of the History of the Delhi Sultanate', *Indian Historical Review*, VIII(1-2), pp.111-13.

for its rich literature. He notes that Persian too had become a language of India, because people had learnt it "since the coming of the Ghorians and Turks."[20] Here is then a picture of the Indian people speaking various languages and yet constituting a single whole. (A detailed treatment of Amir Khusrau's verses on India will be found in chapter 9 by S. Ali Nadeem Rezavi.)

What makes Khusrau's verses especially patriotic is his avowed argument in favour of the precedence of India over other countries. He speaks of the superiority of its products and fruits and its animals, the faithfulness of its women, and the learning and piety of the Brahmans. Of great interest is his pride in what India had given to the world, namely, the numerals, chess, and the *Panchatantra* (*Kalīla-o-Damna*).[21] Clearly, such a comprehensive picture of India and of its culture, which is seen not as being exclusive (as Alberuni had judged it to be in his own time), but as open, innovative and tolerant, has as its context a new situation that had come about as a result of the confluence of the two civilizations, ancient Indian and Islamic — a momentous confluence which the late Professor Athar Ali insightfully described as the source of our "medieval efflorescence".[22]

This conception of India and its distinct composite culture reached its high water-mark under Akbar, the great Mughal emperor (1556-1605). In his minister Abu-l Fazl's *Ā'īn-i Akbarī* (1595) a book-length description is given of the culture of India, it being the most detailed account of its society, religious sects, learning, and arts written after Alberuni. Significantly, the Muslim component is also carefully included.[23] The same reign saw the writing of the first full-scale ḥistory of India, the *Ṭabaqāt-i Akbarī* (1592), by Nizamuddin Ahmad,[24] a book which in

[20] *The Nuh Sipihr of Amir Khusraw: Persian text*, ed. M. Wahid Mirza, London, 1950, pp.147-195.

[21] Ibid., p.168-70.

[22] General President's Address to the Indian History Congress, *Proceedings of the Indian History Congress*, Gorakhpur session, 1989-90, Delhi, 1990, pp.1-17.

[23] Abu'l Fazl, *A'in-i Akbari*, ed. H. Blochmann, Calcutta, 1867-77, vol.II. A translation of this part will be found in *A'in-i Akbari*, vol.III, tr. H.S. Jarrett, ed. Jadunath Sarkar, Calcutta, 1948. Though mostly serviceable, the translation does contain on occasion serious inaccuracies. See also M. Athar Ali, 'The Perception of India in Akbar and Abu'l Fazl', in Irfan Habib, ed., *Akbar and his India*, New Delhi, 1997, pp.215-24.

[24] Ed. B. De, 3 vols. (vol.III partly ed. and revised by M. Hidayat Hosain), Calcutta, 1913, 1927, 1931, 1935. De also translated part of the work in 2 vols., Calcutta, 1913, 1927, 1936.

Persian would be followed by a succession of others. Among these the justly famous *Tārīkh-i Firishta* of Muhammad Qāsim 'Firishta' (1609-10) makes a valiant effort to furnish also a history of India before the appearance of Muslims, necessarily based on various indigenous traditions—and, therefore, alas, almost entirely wrong.[25]

This underlining of the concept of India as a country with a distinct history of its own could now be sustained by the long and stable unity given to India by the Mughal Empire—an instrument of unity visible to the non-literate and the ordinary people as well. Tara Chand (1928), indeed, argued in a much-quoted passage that such dominance by a single power gave to India "a political uniformity and a sense of larger allegiance", necessary for the sense of belonging to a single country.[26] It was not, however, political unification alone that mattered in sustaining the sense of India as a country. There was also an accompanying network of economic relationships that brought the different regions together. In chapter 10 Najaf Haider studies an important engine behind the functioning of this network, namely, the monetary unification brought about by the Mughal Empire.

How, then, did India appear to the outside world in the seventeenth century, when the Mughal Empire enjoyed its greatest stability and power? Professor Om Prakash explores the Dutch perceptions of it, mainly from the angles that commerce could provide (chapter 11). It was a Frenchman, Francois Bernier, however, who, possessed of the rational instruments that early modern Europe was creating, sought consciously to analyse the underlying malaise of the polity and society of India early in the reign of Aurangzeb (1659-1707).[27] Professor Aniruddha Ray scrutinizes in chapter 12, the influences that shaped Bernier's mind and the audience he was writing for.

We have thus seen how the idea of India was formed, and enriched step by step. The sense of a single country was undoubtedly stronger in the Mughal Empire than it had been at any earlier time, so far as the evidence of historical records goes.

[25] This portion appears in the *Muqaddima* or introduction to the work: see Nawal Kishore edition, Kanpur, 1874, vol.I, pp.5-16.

[26] Tara Chand, *Influence of Islam on Indian Culture*, 2nd ed., Allahabad, 1963, p.141.

[27] To those, like me, who do not know French, Bernier is best accessible in Archibald Constable's translation (1891), based on the old version of Irving Brock, second edition, revised by Vincent A. Smith, *Travels in the Mogul Empire, A.D. 1656-1668*, London, 1916.

However, its entity as a country did not yet make India a "nation", which it could only become when the sense of the country as a political unit became strong enough to lay claim to its inhabitants' primary loyalty. In the much acclaimed book, *Imagined Communities*, first published in 1983, Benedict Anderson has portrayed the "nation" as mainly the product of imagination.[28] So, indeed, it is; but is this not the case with all kinds of communities? The religious community, far from being natural, is even more a product of pure imagination. It is largely a question of words: historians have long spoken of "consciousness" (e.g., "national consciousness") instead of "imagination", and yet that word did not make the nation seem as imaginary as it does after Anderson's term "imagined community" caught popular fancy.[29] The special question to ask, in any case, is why countries, or, for that matter, also territories within previously perceived countries, begin to be imagined as nations at only a particular time in history.

Not long ago, the development of a common language was regarded as the most crucial element in the formation of a nation. The *Oxford English Dictionary*, in the part published in 1906, defined "nation" as containing people "closely associated by common descent, language or history". Stalin too, while defining a "nation" in 1913, insisted that the nation arises on "the basis of a common language."[30] While "common language" was certainly one instrument of bringing people together to a consciousness of their cultural unity, the British historian Eric J. Hobsbawm is surely reasonable in holding that "language was merely one, and not necessarily the primary, way of distinguishing between cultural communities".[31] India, a country of several

[28] Benedict Anderson, *Imagined Communities: Reflections on the Origin and Spread of Nationalism*, London, 1983.

[29] The influence is visibly felt among the 'Subaltern' scholars: thus Partha Chatterjee's demand that we accept that "it is the very singularity of the idea of a national history of India which divides Indians from one another" (*Subaltern Studies-VIII*, ed. D. Arnold and D. Hardiman, Delhi, 1994, p.49). From more mainstream western scholarship comes the comment: "What the Indian nationalists substitute for the transcendent divine kingship of the British raj is the equally transcendent *idea* of Indian unity" (Ronald B. Inden, *Imagining India*, 2nd impression, London, 2000, p.198: italics author's).

[30] 'Marxism and the National Question', in J.V. Stalin, *Works*, Moscow, 1952, vol.II, p.307.

[31] E.J. Hobsbawm, *Nations and Nationalism since 1780*, Cambridge, 1990, pp.58-59. See also his discussion in ibid., pp.93-100, where he says (p.97), "Nationality, it seemed evident, was too complex to be seized by language alone."

languages, could in the older definition be conceived, at best, as a country comprising several "nationalities", each based on a separate language; but we now realise that if language is not the primary criterion, but rather only one of the possible instruments in the process of nation-formation, then, India too, could emerge as a nation in due course, despite its various languages, whatever the conventional definitions of the term "nation" might be.

While modern nation-states arose first in Western Europe in the sixteenth century as capitalism began to develop in its mercantilist stage, the major impulse outside of Europe has been different. Anderson has called attention to the formation of nations in Latin America early in the nineteenth century without any such capitalistic development. He underlines the fact that these nations were the creations of the Creoles or local white settlers, who as land-holders were often involved in a major conflict of interest with the bulk of the inhabitants, whether Amerindians or African slaves.[32] The concessions made by the Creoles to the other sections of the populations as components of the same nation were usually nominal or cosmetic. If still Bolivar and San Martin are revered as nation-builders, the reason lies surely in that they liberated South America from Spanish colonialism, which was draining away a large amount of wealth from that continent.[33] Anderson does not see that it is primarily this resistance to colonialism that was the source of Latin American nationalism and of the creation of Latin American nations; the configurations of their actual boundaries, or even distinct identities, in relation to each other, are only of secondary significance.

But if resistance to colonialism was the main source of nation-formation in Latin America, that process would not have been undertaken if the rebels did not have access to ideas about nationhood. These ideas were *not* indigenous, either in Latin America or elsewhere. The Creoles, despite the limited extent of higher education among them, spoke Spanish and were directly inspired by the great slogans of the French Revolution (1789), "Liberty, Equality, Fraternity." Not surprisingly, all the nations

[32] Anderson, op.cit., pp.51-52. Creole nationalism is also studied by Anthony McFarlane, 'Identity, Enlightenment and Political Dissent in Late Colonial Spanish America', *Transactions of the Royal Historical Society*, 6th series, VIII, pp.309-35.

[33] Anderson, op.cit., p.53, himself touches briefly on this when he mentions how the Spanish crown's revenues from Mexico practically quintupled during the eighteenth century.

created out of the Spanish dominions in the American hemisphere were firmly established as republics, though behind that facade there might yet be no real democracy. In this respect, one can contrast the Latin American revolts with our own Rebellion of 1857. The latter, despite its massive scale, remained bereft of any explicit consciousness of nationhood (at even the level of the political unity of the entire country) among its leaders.[34] On the other hand, it was in Bengal, where modern ideas were diffused earlier than elsewhere in India, that Henry Derozio (d.1831) became India's first nationalist poet, and the radical Young Bengal movement was born under his tutelage at Hindu College. In chapter 13 Professor Gautam Chattopadhyay traces in some detail the urge for national freedom that thus took shape in 'the Bengal Renaissance' of the nineteenth century.

A distinguished senior contemporary of Derozio, and the father of Modern India, if there could such be any one single man, still saw certain major obstructions in India's progress to nationhood. Speaking specifically of Hindus in 1828, Raja Ram Mohan Roy held that the "distinction of castes, introducing innumerable divisions and subdivisions among them has entirely deprived them of patriotic feeling."[35] Had he spoken of all Indians, he would have perhaps added, especially if he could have known of future developments, the words, "and religious communities" after the word "castes". So long as Indians did not break these barriers of caste and religion which gave them so many different identities, the sense of attachment to the country could not obtain primacy over all other attachments. The social barriers, therefore, needed to be removed in people's minds, and the parochial identities made to recede, before true nationalism could be generated. Here the importance of democratic ideas of equality that India received from Europe cannot be overstressed. This was the basis of what Marx called the "regenerating role" of colonialism, which by forcing the pace of English-language dissemination for its own convenience, opened the doors to the entry of these ideas. Marx in 1853 even predicted how the Indians, armed with these ideas and assisted by modern material

[34] There is an excellent chapter on the mentality of the Mutiny in Rajat Kanta Ray's pioneer work, *The Felt Community*, New Delhi, 2003, pp.354-534. There is much else in Ray's book which is of relevance to the present essay and, indeed, to this whole volume.

[35] *The English Works of Raja Rammohan Roy*, ed. Jogendra Chunder Ghose, Calcutta, 1906, single volume [reprint, New Delhi, 1982, vol.IV], p.929.

circumstances, could become "strong enough to throw off the English yoke altogether."[36]

One has to recognise that the movements of social reform, directed to removing those barriers that separated vast sections of our people and bred innumerable parochial loyalties, originated from the influx of modern ideas. To portray these efforts as stemming from any past traditions in our civilization, are absolutely unhistorical, whether one has in mind the "Hindu" or "Islamic" heritages. Indeed, wherever there has been, as in the Arya Samaj, founded by Dayanand Saraswati (1842-83), or among the Wahabis, too strong an effort to go back to the religious sources, the social reform component has been correspondingly weak. This is particularly the message of chapter 14, where Professor Indu Banga writes on Dayanand.

The concept of "nationhood", which is, in essence, the primacy of the national identity over all other caste, community and local identities, could come into being only once the social barriers were forced to loosen their vice-like grip over people's minds. For this reason, the social reform movements, initiated by Ram Mohan Roy (d.1833) and given their strong orientation by Keshav Chandra Sen (d.1884), in respect of both caste disabilities and women's rights, may be seen to have provided the necessary building blocks for constructing the Indian nation. In chapter 15 Professor Kamlesh Mohan, taking the cases of two women from early nationalist days, shows how women themselves began to grope for a juster India of the future. In 1909 in his *Hind Swaraj*, Gandhi applauded the institutions of old India, and was very casual about their defects.[37] But upon his return to India from South Africa in 1915, the fight against caste disabilities and for women's equality became an ever-growing part of his endeavours; and he showed by his own

[36] 'The Future Results of British Rule in India', in Karl Marx and Frederick Engels, *Collected Works*, XII, Moscow, 1979, pp.217-22 (the quoted words are on p.221). It is worth mentioning, in view of the extensive readership that Edward W. Said's *Orientalism* has come to enjoy that his remarks on Marx's ideas on India (*Orientalism*, Indian reprint, New Delhi, 2001, pp.153-56) are quite misleading. Even more misleading is his use of a quotation from Marx ("They cannot represent themselves, etc."), ibid., p.xiii, as if Marx is speaking here of Asian peoples in the context of colonialism, whereas Marx's words are actually about the French peasants in the context of the politics of mid-nineteenth century France.

[37] A recent edition of the English version of this book, originally written in Gujarati, is the one edited by Anthony J. Parel, *Hind Swaraj and Other Writings*, New Delhi, 1997.

practice, as no other individual Indian leader did, that this fight was inseparable from the struggle for national independence. Incidentally, this was at the root of the discord between him and the forces that came to adopt the "Hindutva" signboard.

While the social reform movements took the initial steps towards making the people counscious of unity across the barriers created by our past culture, India's transformation into a nation received impetus from yet another and more deliberate source: the vision of the national destiny as one of deliverance of the masses from exploitation and impoverishment. This notion of economic liberation too had its external sources: it received its earliest inspiration, again, from the French Revolution; and both the economic nationalism of Friedrich List and the socialism of Karl Marx would in time exert their influences on the minds of Indian nationalists.

One of the important features of Indian nationalism from its very early stages was thus the criticism of Britain's economic exploitation of India. The "Grand Old Man" of the National Movement, Dadabhoy Naoroji, drew attention constantly from the 1870's to the impoverishment imposed on India as a result of this exploitation. The very title of his book, *Poverty and UnBritish Rule in India* (a collection of papers, the first dating to 1876, the final volume published in 1901),[38] called attention to the fact that the greatest victims of British rule were the poverty-stricken masses of India. In his two-volume *Economic History of British Rule in India* (1901, 1903), constituting a detailed critique of the British economic performance in India, the redoubtable R.C. Dutt took a similar position. "Every true Indian hopes", he said at one place, "that the small cultivation of India will not be replaced by landlordism",[39] as if it was the small peasant for whom the patriotic heart must beat. It was not that these early nationalists were unmindful of the interests of the small, emerging middle classes and capitalists. That these were often at the centre of their attention becomes clear from

[38] It was published by Swan Sonnenchien & Co., London, the same firm which had published the English translation of Karl Marx's *Capital*, vol.I, in 1887. An Indian reprint of Naoroji's book was published by Publications Division, Government of India, Delhi, 1962.

[39] R.C. Dutt, *The Economic History of India in the Victorian Age* [being vol.II of the work], 7th edition, London, 1950, pp.518-19. The author himself appears to have issued in his lifetime only the second editions of both volumes, which came out in 1906. Since then the work went into several reprints.

Bipan Chandra's detailed work on the early history of Indian economic nationalism.[40] This concern for the middle classes was, indeed, not concealed, but proclaimed by the nationalist spokesmen: their argument was that the educated middle classes not only represented their own cause, but also that of the unlettered masses, who could not represent themselves. Despite the limitations of this position, the fact that the nationalists made the conditions of the poor a critical element of their arguments against colonialism assumed cardinal importance in the later popularisation of nationalist ideology. Simplified versions of the economic critiques of colonialism, appeared in pamphlets and booklets in practically every Indian language. As these ideas became more widespread, these helped to open the doors to mass participation in the National Movement itself.

This participation came with Gandhi's own experiments with mass mobilization (beginning with the Champaran peasants' *satyagraha*, 1917), the Non-Cooperation and Khilafat Movement, the emergence of the Left in the 1920s, and the heavy peasant and women's participation in the Civil Disobedience of 1930-31. This transformation of the Movement demanded a more specific delineation of the nation's future, when the freedom being striven for was attained. Neither a modern capitalist state, the dream of the Moderates, nor a reformed Old India of Gandhiji's *Hind Swaraj*, could meet the aspirations of the classes that had now emerged as the main force behind freedom struggle. This new situation became the basis for one of the most important documents of the Indian National Congress, the Karachi Resolution on Fundamental Rights, March-August, 1931.[41]

This resolution began by declaring that "political freedom must include real economic freedom of the starving millions." It envisioned India as a democratic state, with full adult suffrage, equality of women with men, constitutional observance of "neutrality" in matters of religion, and protection of minorities. Provisions were to be made for protecting labour and for securing land to the tenant, rent reduction and relief from indebtedness.

[40] Bipan Chandra, *The Rise and Growth of Economic Nationalism in India*, New Delhi, 1966.

[41] The original text of the Resolution, was passed at the Karachi session of the Congress on 29-31 March 1931, but was amended and elaborated by the All-India Congress Committee on 6-8 August 1931. Its final text is not now often easily available; and SAHMAT has done useful service by reprinting it in its publication, *Indian People in the Struggle for Freedom: Five Essays*, New Delhi, 1998, pp.132-135.

Capitalism too would be restricted: "The State shall own or control key industries and services, railways, waterways, shipping and other means of public transport." It thus envisaged a strong Public Sector to sustain industrial growth in the interest of the country as a whole.

The Karachi Resolution represented the common vision for a free India shared by all sections of the National Movement, from the Gandhians to the Communists. It was a pledge, repeated in the Congress manifesto for the 1937 elections, on the basis of which the people were asked to give their support to the National Movement.

There were two streams, however, which were fundamentally opposed not only to the principles of the Karachi Resolution, but also to the very idea of a democratic, secular nation. These were the Hindu and Muslim communalists.

At an early stage of the development of freedom struggle religion played an undeniable part as an instrument of mobilization. The appeal to religion by the rebels of 1857 (beginning with the issue of greased cartridges) is part of every school-textbook account of that great event. In the 1890's Bal Gangadhar Tilak invoked religion to develop a nationalist ideology, which sometimes seemed as anti-Muslim as it was anti-British. Aurobindo Ghosh provided a philosophical basis for this "Hindu nationalism." On the other hand, Jamaluddin Afghani, who also spent some years in India (1877-82), developed his theory of Pan-Islamism, to unite peoples of all Muslim countries against Imperialism. Clearly, while radically anti-imperialist, such communal versions of nationalism could only help to divide the Indian people. Jamaluddin Afghani had himself been acute enough to realise that Hindus and Muslims must remain united in India in order to oppose the British, and therefore he asked an audience of the young Muslims of Calcutta in 1882 to be proud of their Indian heritage; and his pan-Islamic "nation" did not therefore include India.[42] Tilak too, in his later days, shifted more and more to an accommodative position, making Hindu-Muslim unity his special object: he was the main architect of the Congress-League Pact of 1916, where the Congress accepted separate electorates for Muslims, and the Muslim League adopted

[42] Raj Kumar Trivedi, *The Critical Triangle: India, Britain, and Turkey, 1908-1924*, Jaipur, 1993, pp.9, 24n., citing Nikki R. Keddie, *An Islamic Response to Imperialism: Political Writings of Jamaluddin al-Afghani*, Berkeley, 1968, pp.101-2, et passim.

the ideal of "Home Rule" (*Swaraj*) for India. This was a major act of recognition of India as a nation equally composed of all its religious communities, as the founding fathers of the Indian National Congress, to their honour, had always insisted.

As the National Movement grew in scale and began to assume a truly mass character, its mobilization of peasants and workers, and women and other socially and economically oppressed strata on the basis of increasingly radical set of promises for "the 98 per cent" (C.R. Das, 1922) grew apace. This resulted in a growing inclination of propertied interests, especially landlords, to shift to communal positions in order to oppose the freedom struggle. Such a shift received due encouragement from Imperialism, and the Simon Commission Report (1930) laboured to deny, on the basis of the country's religious and linguistic diversities, that India was a nation at all.[43] The ground was thus being created for a full-blown "two-nation" theory.

It is often supposed that the "two-nation" theory was a product only of Muslim communalism. The fact, however, is that the slogan "Hindu, Hindi, Hindustan" has a much older history than of "Pakistan", a term coined by C. Rahmat Ali in the 1930s, and adopted by the Muslim League only after its Lahore Resolution of 1940. The Rashtriya Swayamsevak Sangh (RSS), founded in 1925, openly espoused the ideal of a "Hindu Rashtra" (Hindu Nation), which, by excluding Muslims (and other minorities), necessarily implied that there are two or more nations in India. In Chapter 16 in this volume Professor Mridula Mukherjee underlines how V.D. Savarkar had explicitly propounded the Two-Nation theory well ahead of the Lahore Resolution of the Muslim League. Hindu communalism thus had essentially the same aim of breaking the nation's unity (and so undermining the National Movement) as had Muslim communalism. It is thus no accident that the RSS throughout its existence stood consistently aside from the freedom struggle.

The Partition of 1947 was a great test for the Indian people. Despite Pakistan having been founded as a Muslim state, the people of India decided to retain for the Indian Republic a democratic and secular character. It was a decision that communal forces in India have never accepted. Gandhiji's assassination (30 January 1948) was a brutal crime committed

[43] For a trenchant critique of the Simon Commission's Report see R.P. Dutt, *India Today*, Bombay, 1947, pp.237-41.

solely to proclaim that opposition.

Secularism was one of the strong pillars on which Indian nationhood was sustained. Not only the political participation of the masses (secured through an unqualified adult suffrage, but the process of agrarian reform, an effort to develop an industrial base through building a large Public Sector, some amount of labour legislation, can all be seen as steps in partial fulfilment of the Karachi pledges of 1931. Professor Aditya Mukherjee in chapter 17 examines the economic vision of Jawaharlal Nehru (Prime Minister, 1947-64). It was perhaps more the vision of a welfare state than of a socialist society that Nehru sought to realise, despite the use of 'socialism' as a slogan. Prime Minister Indira Gandhi (assassinated, 1984), especially in the early 1970's also pressed forward on the same road.[44] Critics who today denounce the entire 'Nehruvian' or 'socialist' period as one where dogma overruled economic pragmatism should ask themselves why, if Free Trade is an answer to all problems of backwardness, India was not already an industrial power in 1947. After all right from 1813 Britain had been extending to us the benefits of Free Trade, and then had built an extensive railway system to integrate us with the world market. And yet in 1947 India had no industries of any significance except for a second-rate textile industry run on imported machinery.

There is undoubtedly a question-mark over the entire legacy of the National Movement and over India's entity as a nation now that those who acclaim Savarkar and his "Hindutva" philosophy have become such a powerful force in the country, irrespective of whether they are in or out of government. Many factors may be invoked to explain how this has come to pass: the failure of the Congress over the long period it governed to fulfil its economic and social pledges; its own passivity in the face of communal carnages such as the mass killing of the Sikhs in 1984; the setbacks to socialism on the world scale received in recent years; the failure of the secular parties to unite at crucial moments; and, not the least, the shift of Big Business patronage

[44] Two books where political, economic and other developments after 1947 are critically assessed at two distinct points of time are Charles Bettelheim, *India Independent*, London, 1968, written a little after the close of the Nehru era, and Jean Drèze and Amartya Sen, *India: Development and Participation*, 2nd ed., New Delhi, 2002. The entire period since Independence is covered by Bipan Chandra, Mridula Mukherjee and Aditya Mukherjee, *India after Independence, 1947-2000*, New Delhi, 1999.

to BJP, as a party far more pliant to its interests (as the RSS Swadeshi expert, Mr Guruswamy learnt the other day). The costs to the nation of this development are already enormous. If the demolition of the Babri Masjid at Ayodhya in 1992 was not enough to humiliate and defame India throughout the world, the orchestrated attacks on Christians and the Gujarat massacres are adding a new dimension to the undermining of our secularism. While public attention is often riveted to the successive Parliamentary crises and public scandals, the insidious work of dismantling the secular structure, using the media for communal propaganda, promoting communal and chauvinistic myths in the name of history, and changing syllabi and text books to accord with "religious values", sanctified by the Supreme Court,[45] went on unabated. Despite the setback to the communal forces in the 2004 General Elections, the long-term threat to the Indian national entity remains grave. This is one major reason why the present volume dedicated to a study of the idea of India has been compiled.

[45] To what lengths falsification of History has gone in the new saffronized text books for the central school system, issued by the NCERT, can be judged from the quotations and extracts from them given in the Indian History Congress Report, *History in the New NCERT Text Books*, Kolkata, 2003.

2

The Earliest Notions of India: 'Meluhha' in Mesopotamian Records

SHEREEN RATNAGAR

The Harappan world, comprising the Indus basin and parts of Gujarat and Baluchistan, was one of the areas that provided certain resources to Mesopotamia in the third millennium BC. Open on all sides except in the west and southwest (where the desert formed a geographic barrier until the dromedary was domesticated),[1] the valley of the lower Euphrates and Tigris, since the time pastoralism became a specialized subsistence activity, saw seasonal rounds of ingress of sheep and goat herders from the steppe and the Zagros ranges to the north and the east. The navigable Euphrates provided a route to and from Syria, and thence to Anatolia and the Mediterranean coast. The wealth of Mesopotamia also provoked countless invasions through history.

Because of its unmatched agricultural productivity, this land had the largest cities of the Bronze Age 'world'. Moreover, in the third millennium BC, there was a phase in which the rulers of Mesopotamia exercised military control over places on the upper Euphrates and its tributary, the Habur. As far as we can tell, Mesopotamia, with its high population density and its developed state institutions, was a major consumer of the mineral resources of a large region between the Anatolian plateau and the Indus valley.

The artefactual evidence of Mesopotamia's exchanges with South Asia is slender because the trade was mainly in perishable articles and raw materials. Scholars have therefore explored the cuneiform texts that refer to the land of Meluhha, as the Harappan world was called.[2] The texts testify to trade in wood, stone, metals, cereals, oils, and other items that do not survive at ancient sites.[3] Here, I may mention only briefly the oft-

[1] This was after 1000 BC.

[2] This identification was first made by A.L.Oppenheim, in 'The Seafaring Merchants of Ur', *Journal of the American Oriental Society*, 54 (1954), pp.6-17.

[3] Details on the archaeological evidence and the archival references to materials going to Mesopotamia from Meluhha were given in my *Encounters*, 1981. A radically revised edition of this book is now in press

suggested link between *Meluhha* and Pali *Milakkhu* or Sanskrit *Mleccha.* (Mesopotamian languages lack the sound *ch*, so that its replacement by a hard *h* is not impossible.) In Sanskrit texts *mleccha* meant people who spoke corrupt languages, or non-Sanskrit speakers. *Mleccha* was in many contexts the antithesis of *Arya* or "noble". It is not impossible to surmise that Sanskrit speakers were using a gentilic that had been long current but one that was not originally a derogatory label. In any case, the fact remains that 'Meluhha' is the first name for India, or any part of it, that has come down to us.

How was Meluhha or the Harappan world perceived in Mesopotamia? Very little of significance, I am afraid, can be said on this matter.

Among the genres of Sumerian and Akkadian texts that mention the world outside, are myths, poems lamenting the destruction of major cities, temple hymns to particular deities, commemorative royal inscriptions, lexical compendia, and the economic records of temples, palaces, and, occasionally, of private merchants. There are incidental references also, in administrative texts, to people of foreign origin or foreign connexion residing in Mesopotamia. A brief survey of the world as conceived, and of what we know about the literary modes of expression in Mesopotamia, is necessary in order to place the references to Meluhha in their proper context.

Foreigners and exotic creatures

As the prosperous plains and cities of Mesopotamia were repeatedly attacked, conquered, and raided by peoples of the surrounding desert, steppe, and mountains, groups like the Guti and Lullubi of the Zagros were, in the Mesopotamian scribal convention, stereotypically evil. In addition, the literature, according to modern scholars, reveals a set of cultural dichotomies concerning settled city life *versus* pastoral nomadism of the steppe. Pastoralists who were peripatetic, worshipped strange gods, and did not bury their dead, were the antithesis of settled Mesopotamian townsmen. (Interestingly, the literature does not contrast life and culture in the city with village life.) At the same time, this land of large cities and numerous city-states, with its highly productive agricultural, pastoral, and fishing systems, lacked fine wood for building or boat, stones, and metal. Its high culture, therefore, was sustained only by the flow of these materials from outside (Moorey 1993:31). Thus, as Limet (1972) shows, all people of the world outside were not necessarily regarded with a hostile eye and there were other sorts of perceptions as well.

In a poem known to us as 'The Curse of Agade', which bemoans the destruction of the capital of the legendary dynasty of Agade (believed to be the first emperors of Mesopotamia and the world), it is said that Agade city owed its prosperity to the restless labour of its patron deity, Inanna, who kept its storehouses full. In those days, "acquaintances ate together and outsiders circled around like strange birds in the sky" (Jacobsen 1987:361). In this poem, then, the prosperity and greatness of the city was obviously connected with the sojourn of foreigners.[4]

Archival texts of several periods in the third millennium refer to a Meluhha village, also to a Magan village, and to one or two men as natives of Meluhha. Parpola *et al.* (1977), Zadok (1994:50), and Glassner (1996) have dealt with these few and passing references. An Akkadian period text, for example, refers to a Meluhha settlement and names three of its residents—the names themselves are ordinary Sumerian ones. Were they, in that case, Sumerianized South Asian names? Or were the residents acculturated members of a long-existing diaspora? There is also a third possibility: that a place name like this reflected no actual connexion with Meluhha and is like the modern Parsi surname, Frenchman.

Yet, there is also the testimony about a translator of the Meluhha language (Edzard 1968; Collon 1996:215, fig.12): an early Akkadian period cylinder seal is inscribed, 'Shu-ilishu [an ordinary Mesopotamian name] *eme.bal* ("dragoman") of Meluhha'. The carving shows a seated horned deity clad in a fleecy kaunakes, and two supplicants, one carrying an animal, plus other Mesopotamian elements. This interpreter, it would thus appear, was a local person rather than a man from South Asia. Why was he required to have a seal? There is no extant reference to an interpreter of Magan or of Dilmun, other regions to the southeast and east with which Mesopotamians traded. If there were a true Meluhhan 'diaspora' in Sumer, besides, one would expect the existence of a bilingual resident community rather than the need for an official local interpreter. The *eme.bal* evidence, then, together with other kinds of data, seems to point to state organized exchanges between the two urban socieites.

[4] In an alternative translation, "foreigners would cruise about like unusual birds in the sky" (Cooper 1983 :51).

R.M.Boehmer (1975) has discussed the depictions of the water buffalo on some seals of the Akkad period. No buffalo bones have ever been found at Mesopotamian sites, and the animal is not shown in art after the Akkad period. It is not an original native of Iraq, even though buffaloes today abound on the banks of the Euphrates.[5] This led Boehmer to the conclusion that water buffalos probably arrived in Akkad on a Harappan ship, and were bred there for some time, to the end of the dynasty. What gives strength to this conclusion is a reference in the "Curse of Agade" poem to "monkeys, huge elephants, water buffaloes, beasts of faraway places jostl[ing] each other in the wide streets" during the heyday of the city. (Jacobsen 1987:361). Boehmer suggests that just one such shipload could have come, as a gift suitable for a great king, on board a Meluhha ship, and that it is of this that Sargon wrote in his famous inscription commemorating the arrival of ships of Dilmun, Magan, and Meluhha at the quay of his capital. On the seals of the late kings of Akkad, Naram Sin and Sharkalisharri, water buffaloes are carved together with bearded heroes and the waters of Ea.

The world outside

Yet, the Mesopotamian scribes were not particularly well informed about regions abroad. Foreignness was routinely associated with mountains or with the east. In the third millennium, *shadium,* a word that literally meant 'east' or 'eastern wind', was also used as a gentilic meaning 'foreigner', in much the same way as the English word 'Oriental' was used not so long ago (Steinkeller, 1980). It could be used in a way as vague as the statement that a sea merchant had brought lapis lazuli and silver from the eastern mountains (Moorey 1993:37). The association of the east with foreignness is vividly illustrated by some phrases in a proverb that mention the donkey of Anshan (southwestern Iran), the bear of Marhashi (southern Iran), the cat of Meluhha, and the elephant of the land of 'Shatium' (Steinkeller 1980:9)!

Not surprisingly, and in very general terms, the ancient Mesopotamians perceived the world as a series of places at graded distances from the homeland. The latter was, of course, the centre of their world. Modern scholars read varying nuances in the relevant texts, which are of different genres and periods.

[5] In my student days I was charged by a herd at Babylon.

Thus Glassner (1987) perceives, in the tradition about the empire of Agade, the idea of a centre surrounded by four outer regions; Naram Sin, its last great ruler, called himself "King of the Four Quarters" and only when he had conquered these latter did he put the divine determinative before his name. The Sumerologist Averbeck (1987: 136-141), in his turn, finds a continuum that runs from profane and chaotic foreign space, native human space, and thence to divine sacred space (the temple being the exemplar of the last).

Around the land of greater Mesopotamia lay the rest of the world, conceived sometimes as a central land mass or continent, beyond it the sea, and then lands beyond the seas (Berlin 1983; Horowitz 1998: 320-1). The central continent in some second-millennium texts stretched from the Cedar Mountains (Syria-Lebanon) in the north to Anshan (southern Zagros) in the south, and from Egypt in the west to Marhashi in the east. Or else the world lay between the Upper Sea (the Mediterranean) and the Lower Sea (the Gulf) or from the land of the sunset to that of the sunrise.

Geographic orientations and perceptions, and the place of Meluhha

Mesopotamian literature did not always give literal attention to the location of places or the distances between them, even in the home country. Rarely was literal geographic information the point of a 'historical' or 'geographic' text. We see this in second- and first-millennium tablets that embody the historical tradition about Sargon, the founder of the empire of Agade. Over the centuries Sargon's fame and empire became legendary, and it was thought to cover the known world. Thus the first-millennium 'Sargon Geography', drawing on several historical sources, delineates this world as starting with the 'border of the road to Meluhha' in the northwest; it lists several lands including Sumer, Agade, Mari, Zagros regions, etc.; it ends, strangely, with Magan and Meluhha lying '120 *beru* from the mouth of the Euphrates' (Horowitz 1998:67-87)! It is well known that Meluhha by this time had come to mean northeastern Africa between the Nile and the Red Sea. But the self-contradiction still requires explanation. This is, according to Horowitz, that the scribe's interest lay in the sweep of the military power of Sargon and not in geography. And so there is little value in analysing literary passages to see the place of Meluhha in a sequence of geographic names; not only is this variable and often contradictory, it tells us little about conceptions of Meluhha in the minds of the scribes.

That Meluhha was vaguely understood to lie somewhere on the horizon is also brought out in a highly crafted temple hymn known as the 'Cylinder A' of Gudea, a post-Agade ruler of the Mesopotamian city-state of Lagash. This is the first part of a long Sumerian poem that Averbeck (1987) calls a "literary masterpiece". It is an involved narrative about the construction of, and sacred installations in, a temple to the city god of Lagash. This god, Ningirsu, appears to Gudea in a dream and says,

> Great fear of my House hovers over all the lands. All these lands will gather
> on its behalf from *as far as where heaven ends*—Magan and Meluhha will descend from their mountains.... (Edzard 1997:75—emphasis added).

We find here not only a vague notion of the location of Magan and Meluhha (at the end of the world) but that, in the emphasis on the unchallenged power of Ningirsu the deity, the inhabitants of Meluhha and Magan are seen as subordinated and tributary peoples. That seems unlikely to have been the literal truth. Yet, what we need to bear in mind is that this was a text about a myriad temple rituals (sacrifices, libations, incense offerings, food offerings, cleansing with fire, anointing with scented oil, prayer, prostration, music) and on another plane a hymn exalting a temple, not a text of ethnography or geography. In this passage the intention may have been to emphasize the place of Ningirsu as the war god of the Sumerian pantheon. Ritual, as Averbeck (1987) puts it, was a frame in which cultural institutions were anchored. Additionally, there is a possibility that the building of the temple was an act of legitimation of power.

Problems of interpretation

Because regions abroad were mentioned in the interests of extolling the power of a king, such texts reveal more about the cultural understanding that the scribes and their patrons had of kingship and the state, than knowledge about the distant lands and their inhabitants. Michalowski suggests (1986) that often the references to such lands are metaphors: Aratta, for instance, is the cultural and political antithesis of Uruk, and one cannot take the epics about it and Enmerkar as historical truth. Aratta may have been a historical reality, but for the poets it symbolized certain values (albeit negative ones) — and the fact remains that it never occurs in any administrative text (Berlin 1983:22).

Establishing military domination was essential to kingship; enemies like the Guti or the Lullubi on the borders of Mesopotamia became ethnic stereotypes and proverbially evil because of this. One can thus infer that legends and traditions about the wide reach of the Agade polity encouraged a perception of Mesopotamia as the centre of the world.

Again, many archaeologists at one time emphasized the exceptionally large number of burial mounds on the island of Bahrain, and linked their presence with the portrayal of Dilmun in a myth, 'Enki and Ninhursag', as a paradise land and also with the reference in the Sumerian version of the epic of Gilgamesh to Dilmun as the abode of Ziusudra, the Sumerian Noah who was immortal. Archaeologists went so far as to suggest that Mesopotamians were brought to Dilmun-Bahrain for burial because of its religious importance. However, Alster (1983) pointed out that Sumerian cosmogony has no place for a paradise, and that what the poets were portraying was a stage when the world as we know it had not been fully formed—Dilmun had no water, no cawing crows, no old people who realized that they were old, and so on. Alster suggests that the theme of 'Enki and Ninhursag' in fact embodies the establishment of the cult of the god Enki, and the extension of that cult to Dilmun at the head of the Gulf.

Aside from political and cultic preoccupations, we need to take into account literary modes. Sumerian poetry at its highest stylistic level is known for its lavish use of metaphor or imagery. For instance, the language is short on adverbs: a man does not run swiftly, but 'like a gazelle'. There is a rich repertoire of 'indirect signals' which create difficulties for the modern cuneiform scholar; texts appear vague or extravagant (Black 1998: 8-10, 170). Black points out that this preference did not transfer to Akkadian poetry, so that many metaphors in the Sumerian versions of bilinguals are replaced by ordinary epithets (ibid: 17-18). Lines lose their 'image-value' in the process. In addition, the anonymity of the poetry makes it difficult for us to tell whether a passage reveals an individual idiosyncracy or a stylistic tradition. For its part Akkadian poetry (Foster 1993:1-29) is marked by the structure of its lines or couplets that incorporate parallelism and balance. In prose, sentences tend to have several and long clauses. Certain literary conventions, such as contrasting the city with the steppe, or depicting the nature of winds or rivers, are rarely expanded on. And so, we cannot take (the English translations of) the texts at face value, much less use them in a positivist manner.

The maritime outreach of Mesopotamia

Mesopotamian communications with the inhabitants of Dilmun, Magan, and Meluhha (which, incidentally, were not the only foreign regions that were sources of goods: there were also Elam, Marhashi, Tukrish, the Cedar Mountain, and other regions) took place by sea. This is indicated in several references to boats from these lands coming to Ur and Lagash on the lower Euphrates (and also to Akkad) and to merchandise being carried to them by boat. It is thus clear that these regions were reached by way of the Gulf. Not only that, Meluhha was a land of seafarers: its boats are mentioned by Sargon (UM XV: 4, Hirsh 1963: 37; Sollberger and Kupper 1971: IIA 1b); in an Akkad period text (BIN 8, 238) which refers to 'a . . . man of the Meluhha ship' (Leemans 1968: 220-1); in HAR.ra=*hubullu* IV; and in a vocabulary text (Jaritz 1968: 213). There are also administrative texts naming men who were officials connected with Meluhha boats (Glassner 1996:236).

In 'Enki and Ninhursag', in a passage in which the gods bless Dilmun and its trade, the boats of Meluhha are 'large'. In 'Enki and the World Order', four lines speak about Dilmun-, Magan- and Meluhha boats, the latter being a *magilum* boat that carries silver and gold (Benito 1969:120; Jacobsen 1987: 184). According to Glassner (1989: 182), *magilum* meant 'something like' a cargo boat.

Meluhha and its produce

While Mesopotamian trade with Dilmun (the upper Gulf, Kuwait to Bahrain) appears in the cuneiform documents in the ED (Early Dynastic) period,[6] it is only thereafter that Magan and Meluhha also find mention in cuneiform tablets. Sargon of Agade moored the boats from Meluhha, Magan, and Dilmun at the quay of Agade (Hirsh 1963: 37-8; Frayne 1993: 27-29). This claim is

[6] Ur-Nanshe of Lagash (ED IIIa) repeatedly refers in his dedicatory inscriptions to the temples he constructed, and to Dilmun boats bringing cargoes of wood (Sollberger and Kupper, 1971: 1C3a, d, e); ED IIIa Fara texts make allusions to Dilmun merchants; texts of the reign of Lugalanda of Lagash (ED IIIb) enumerate imports, mainly of copper, from Dilmun, for which barley, flour, cedar wood and other items were exchanged (Lambert 1953b: 60-3); and texts of all the late rulers of the first dynasty of Lagash, to the reign of Urukagina, refer now and again to imports of copper from Dilmun,

made by the emperor in a bilingual temple inscription which mentions victory in numerous battles, the destruction of city walls, and military campaigns up the Euphrates to the 'Cedar Forest and Silver Mountain', ending with a statement that thousands ate with Sargon in his palace on a daily basis. We can infer that Sargon, on acquiring political pre-eminence, claims to have received tribute (or, just wealth in general) from foreign peoples—we recall Boehmer's interpretation of the buffaloes portrayed on royal seals — which in turn would have further enhanced his reputation in the world.

Sargon's successors actually ventured out into the Gulf or the 'Lower Sea'. In a standard inscription on several artefacts, Manishtusu recorded his defeat of southwestern Iran and of 'thirty-two cities' across the Lower Sea, after which his troops plundered as far as 'the Silver Mines' and quarried black stone from the mountains (Frayne 1993: 75-77). Naram Sin, the last powerful king of the dynasty, claims to have crossed the Lower Sea and defeated the ruler of Magan; on a statue he recorded the name of the ruler of Magan as 'Manium'; booty from that campaign, mainly stone statuary and containers, is also so inscribed (Frayne 1993:95-117).

As the city of Agade has not been located, leave alone excavated, we have comparatively few administrative tablets of that realm and thus there is no satisfying match of palace/temple documents with the royal inscriptions, which in their tone tend to be boastful—although they cannot be pure fiction, as testified by the inscriptions on vessels made of imported stone. This is a serious handicap, as we need to know whether Meluhha was a trade partner on the same level as Dilmun, or whether it remained a vague region whence the occasional shipment of exotica arrived. In this context it is of great interest that many Harappan-type seals have been unearthed at Mesopotamian sites, but not a single Mesopotamian cylinder seal has ever been found at Harappan sites (or in the Gulf for that matter). One would be tempted to assert that it was the people of Meluhha who ventured abroad while Mesopotamia did not develop its own maritime tradition; yet, it also has to be said that weights of Mesopotamia occur in a few houses of Harappa, Mohenjo-daro, and Lothal.

In the temple hymn inscribed on 'Cylinders A and B' (Jacobsen 1987:386 ff) Gudea of Lagash describes the acquisition of materials for the Eninnu, the temple of Ningirsu.

The Elamite came to him from Elam,
the Susian from Susa.

Magan and Meluhha in their mountains
loaded wood upon their shoulders for him
And gathered to build Ningirsu's house. (Jacobsen 1987:406.)

In another portion of the text, we are told of 'carnelian they were lavishing on him from Meluhha' (ibid: 408). After the temple was built and the deity took possession, gifts were placed therein: a chariot, a special mace, ceremonial weapons.

Besides copper, tin, slabs of lapis lazuli, refined silver and pure Meluhha
carnelian, he set up a huge copper pail.... (ibid: 437.)

The deity showered elaborate praise on the structure, and on Gudea who built it. So too, on his Statue A this king states that after building a temple in Lagash for his god and goddess, he brought down diorite from the mountain of Magan from which a statue of himself was carved (Edzard 1997:29-30). In the Statue B inscription, however, diorite is also stated to be brought from Meluhha, together with 'gold in its ore' (ibid: 30-37). On Statue D, it is said that Magan, Meluhha, Gubin and the Land Dilmun supplied Gudea with wood. One wonders if geographic accuracy varied according to the scribe or to the historical occasion that called for the dedication of a royal statue.

Several tablets in the records of the kingdom of the Third Dynasty of Ur testify to trade with Dilmun and Magan, financed and organized by the temple (UET III: Leemans 1960: 18-22); in these the produce of Meluhha is also mentioned. The founder, Ur-Nammu (Jacobsen 1960: 184-5), says he restored the sea trade of Magan (after the Gutian interregnum): he 'rendered safe the sea trade; he restored to the god Nanna the Magan boats.' (Sollberger and Kupper 1971:136.) We do not know how this affected links with Meluhha, further south on the sea route.

There are also religious texts and lexicons of the same (or subsequent) period, such as 'Enki and Ninsikal/Ninhursag', 'Enki and the World Order', HAR. ra = *hubullu* (Landsberger 1962; Reiner 1956: 146-7); and *lipsur* (Reiner 1956). HAR.ra =*hubullu* is a bilingual (Sumerian and Akkadian) lexicon of terms for plants, trees, stones, minerals, lands, etc. *Lipsur* is a text with formulaic lines on the pattern, 'May Meluhha (a land) absolve, the land of carnelian (a product or characteristic).' These latter texts indicate that Magan and Meluhha were sources of several valuable materials. Occasionally tablets contain references to a place blessed with the wood of Meluhha (Michalowski, 1988).

(Dilmun was not just a source of things, it had, as we have seen, a special cultic significance in the culture of Mesopotamia.)

In some lexical texts (Hh VIII, 320, XVIII, 20), the *dar*-bird of Meluhha is mentioned (Landsberger 1962: 148; Salonen 1973: 156). The Akkadian for *dar.musen* is known to be *ittidu*, and other synonyms for the same bird are *burrumtu* (multicoloured bird), and *darru/tarru* (Salonen 1973: 139). This bird has been identified as the black partridge, more accurately *Francolinus francolinus* L. (CAD: sub *ittidu*). Significantly, the Akkadian for the *dar* bird of Meluhha (*dar.me.luh.ha.mushen*) is *sulamu* (Salonen 1973: 155), The root *s l m* means 'dark' or 'black' (CAD: sub *sallamu* b). It is thus reasonable to assume that the *dar.meluhha* was a dark or black variety of partridge or hen. Bones of the black partridge, *Francolinus francolinus* l. have been identified at Harappan levels at Ropar (Nath 1968: 5). But we cannot be certain that some other black variety of bird was not intended.

Texts dating to the earlier part of the Isin-Larsa period reveal that seafaring merchants of Ur sailed to Dilmun to procure copper, bronze, carnelian, agate, shell, ivory, antimony, and other materials (Leemans 1960:23 ff.). Some of these items, such as ivory and carnelian, could only have originated in South Asia. Thus the absence of cuneiform text references to Meluhha after 2100 BC need not be taken as evidence of an absence of contacts.

The historiographic poem, the 'Curse of Agade' (Jacobsen 1987:359 ff), laments a calamity which befell this capital of the dynasty of Sargon when the gods turned against it (Enlil frowned, Ishtar abandoned her sanctuary, Enki dammed up the waters of the Euphrates and Tigris, etc.) and appears to have been particularly popular among the literati in Nippur (Cooper 1983:7-8). It says that when Agade enjoyed the gods' favour, it was prosperous. 'Its city wall touched heaven like a mountain'. The goods of Sumer flowed upstream —

From Sumer's own stores
barges were towed.
The Martu of the highland,
men who knew not grain,
Were coming to her with perfect bulls,
perfect kids;
The Meluhhans, men of the black mountains,
were bringing down
Strange goods to her from them.
The Elamites and Subareans....(Jacobsen 1987: 363.)

We see that the Meluhha people come from a region of 'black' mountains or a black land. (How could a land be described as black?) They contribute to the prosperity and glory of Akkad. And they seem to be classified together with Sumerians, subjects of Akkad; with the pastoral nomadic Amorites of the west; and also with the militarily defeated Elamites. This passage ends with the statement that all the officials were bringing in regular supplies. The flow of goods, thus, appears more like tribute — or perhaps royal gifts — than exchanges with regular trade partners. This issue, however, may never have been addressed by the scribe, for the text appears to be pre-occupied with Naram Sin's deeds that antagonized the Sumerian deities and the priests of the respective temples and caused a dramatic reversal of fortunes for the dynasty.

Later memories of Meluhha

While the 'Curse' was probably composed not long after the fall of Akkad, say 2150-2000 BC, numerous later literary works preserve the memory of the dynasty of Akkad and its outstanding achievements. We have already referred to one of these, the 'Sargon Geography', that recalls the immense sway of that—by now legendary — king and in that context makes reference to Meluhha. Presumably by then Meluhha too had receded into the realm of legend.[7] Another kind of cultural memory is attested in a group of texts that narrate the great rebellion against Naram Sin. In one of these versions, one '...*ibra*' is named as the 'man' (or ruler) of Meluhha (Grayson and Sollberger 1976; Westenholz 1997: 251). Considering what we have said, it would be foolish to take this as actual testimony of the existence of kings or states in Meluhha or the Indus region.

Finally, in this body of legends there are narratives about Naram Sin fighting foreign enemy hordes. It is said that he

> scattered the army of Elam and reached the flatlands. They killed those who guarded the crossing, casting them into the sea. Dilmun, Magan and Meluhha, in the midst of the Lower Sea, as many as they were, they slaughtered. Seventeen kings, with their 90,000 troops, had marched to their aid (Westenholz 1997:315).

[7] I use 'legend' (a narrative of the past for which there is no proof) as a somewhat technical term to distinguish it from archives or court chronicles, and from myth (set in a time before ours), and epic (heroic or universalizing narrative clustering around a remembered figure of the past). Legends are important not because they embody the truth, but because they are believed to be true and hence reveal a society's conception of its past.

Obviously, there remained only vague memories of Magan and Meluhha as sources of exotic goods and the prosperity of the past. And at the time of the writing of this pseudo-historical literature, the idea remained that Mesopotamia was the hegemonic centre of the world. The place-names that occur, thus, can have had only vague connotations (see Michalowski 1999).

The religious tradition

Just as the trade of Meluhha (and Magan) enhanced the prosperity and fame of Sumer, so too did it impart greatness to the land of Dilmun. In a creation myth, 'Enki and Ninhursag', which assigned much importance to Dilmun, that land is given fresh water and becomes a trading emporium 'on the quay of the land'. Enki endows it with gold from the land of Harali; with lapis lazuli; with desirable carnelian, sea wood, and *mesh*-wood loaded in large ships from Meluhha, and various stones (including diorite) and copper from Magan. In sum, 'the wide sea' will 'yield to Dilmun its wealth'.

Meluhha also features in 'Enki and the World Order' (Falkenstein 1964: 104; ETCSL 1998-), probably written in the early second millennium. This myth praises the prowess of Enki and his power of procreation; Enki creates the world as we know it. In the process of creation, the god says,

Let the lands of Meluhha, Magan and Dilmun look upon me, upon Enki.
Let the Dilmun boats be loaded with timber.
Let the Magan boats be loaded sky-high.
Let the *magilum* boats of Meluhha
transport gold and silver and bring them to Enlil....
Enlil subsequently blesses many lands in turn.
Household Sumer, may your sheepfolds be built and your cattle multiply....
May your temples reach up to heaven....
He proceeded to the land of Meluhha.
Enki, lord of the Abzu, decreed its fate:
"Black land, may your trees be great trees,
May your forests be forests of highland mesh trees!
Chairs made from them will grace royal palaces!
May your reeds be great reeds...
May your bulls be great bulls, may they be bulls of the mountains....
May the francolins of the mountains wear carnelian beards!
May your birds all be peacocks! May their cries grace the royal palaces!
May all your silver be gold! May all your copper be tin-bronze!
Land, may all you possess be plentiful....

Parallel to this is a passage in TCL XVI 64 (ibid: 74): 'the inhabitants of Meluhha, the people of the black foreign land.' Thus Landsberger (1962: 148) said, 'Meluhha does not mean simple provenance but also covers the concept of "negro" ...', and so Falkenstein (1964: 75): 'Meluhha chickens are as black as the people there.'

As for the *haja*-bird, whose call is heard in the palace, according to Falkenstein (1964: 105, 75) this bird, with its 'royal' associations, is the peacock.[8] Clay models of peacocks are known from Mohenjo-daro and Harappa, and some of the most attractive painted Indus pottery bears figures of this bird.

Interpretation

Timber, gold, ivory and carnelian are all known to have been prized products of India in the historical period. All these materials, as well as lapis lazuli, were utilized by the Harappans (and hence the identification of 'Meluhha' with the Harappan-inhabited world).[9] Of these, Mesopotamian literature appears to single out carnelian as the most desired material. In one version of the list of stones, *abnu sikinsu*, 'carnelian that is speckled with black, Meluhha carnelian is its name.' (Horowitz 1992:114) — no such black speckled carnelian is, however, reported from sites like Mohenjo-daro. Some Harappan sites have, instead, yielded a few beautifully shaped beads of translucent black carnelian.[10]

Meluhha was not for the Mesopotamians a legendary place on a par with Aratta. If we were to take the inscriptions of Sargon at face value, Meluhha was on a par with Dilmun and Magan as in some way a subordinate tribute giver. Yet, as we have seen, the propaganda value of organizing the inflow of goods was important, and these were matters viewed differently by giver

[8] We may recall the narrative in the *Baveru Jataka* (E.B. Cowell, *Jataka*, 1957: III: 83 ff) in which Indian merchants sail to Baveru (Babylonia) with a peacock trained to scream and dance.

[9] In late second and first millennium Akkadian texts, 'Meluhha' was the name for the region between the Nile and the Red Sea, equivalent to Egyptian *Medja* (Michaux-Colombot 2001:332-3). It thus appears that this place name was in course of time transferred to a different region, perhaps because the latter had begun to supply some of the same materials (for example, ivory and gold) as had been obtained from the original Meluhha.

[10] These come from different sites but have, quite unfortunately, been displayed in the National Museum, New Delhi, without any reference to provenance and as if several formed part of the same necklace.

and receiver.

The actuality of Meluhha is revealed by the existence of the dragoman, by the references to its boats, and, in administrative texts, by references to travellers on Meluhha boats (Glassner 1996:236). That at least some Akkadians or Sumerians saw the land for themselves is indicated by the occurrence of Mesopotamian weights in India. The varieties of wood said to have came from there would indicate a trader's knowledge of the resources of South Asia. Indian buffaloes were realistically depicted on the seals of the Agade dynasty. Meluhha was a souce of lapis and carnelian which Magan was not; conversely, diorite came from Magan but is not mentioned in association with Meluhha. Meluhha was a black land with large trees, large cattle, raucous peacocks, and a wealth of metals. It was a distant, but certainly not wholly imagined or unknown land, not even for the scribes who never had a chance to sail east. Moreover, memories of it persisted in the second millennium.

And yet the Mesopotamian literature gives no hint of the way Meluhha contrasted with the valley of the Euphrates. Nowhere is there mention of the vastness and greenery of the Indus plains, or the comparative thickness of the Indian forests, or of the courage of Meluhhan seafarers. Had tales of its wonders not spread across the land? We could say that Meluhha was distant for a society lacking a tradition of crossing the seas — but it was not so distant that its wares were unknown to the elite for royal display or use in sacral contexts.

References:

Alster, B., 'Dilmun, Bahrain and the Alleged Paradise Land', in D.T.Potts (ed.), *Dilmun: New Studies in the Archaeology and Early History of Bahrain,* Berlin: D. Reimer, 1983, pp. 39-74.

Averbeck, R.E., A Preliminary Study of Ritual and Structure in the Cylinders of Gudea. Ph.D. Thesis, The Dropsie College, 1987.

Benito, C.A., 'Enki and Ninmah' and 'Enki and the World Order', Ph.D. Dissertation, University of Pennsylvania, 1969.

Berlin, Adele, Enmerkar and Ensuhkeshdanna, University of Pennsylvania Ph.D. Dissertation, 1976.

Berlin, Adele, 'Ethnopoetry and the Enmerkar epics' *Journal of the American Oriental Society,* 103.1 (1983).

Black, Jeremy, *Reading Sumerian Poetry,* Ithaca: Cornell University Press, 1998.

Boehmer, R.M: 'Das Aufreten des Wasserbuffels in Mesopotamien in historische Zeit und seine sumerische Bezeichnung', *Zeitschrift fur Assyriologie,* 64 (1975), pp. 1-12.

Collon, D., 'Mesopotamia and the Indus: The Evidence of the Seals', in J. Reade (ed.), *The Indian Ocean in Antiquity,* London: Kegan Paul, 1996, pp. 209-225.

Cooper, J.S., *The Curse of Agade,* Baltimore: Johns Hopkins University Press, 1983.

Edzard, D.O., 'Die Inschriften der altakkadischen Rollsiegel', *Archiv for Orientforschung,* 22 (1968), pp. 12-20.

Edzard, D.O., *The Royal Inscriptions of Mesopotamia Volume 3/1: Gudea and his Dynasty,* Toronto: University of Toronto, 1997.

ETCSL: *The Electronic Text Corpus of Sumerian Literature,* (xxx-etcsl.orient.ox.ac.uk), Oxford, 1998 ff.

Falkenstein, A., Review of W.F.Leemans, *Foreign Trade in the Old Babylonian Period,* 1960, in ZA 21 (1963), pp. 251-3.

Falkenstein, A., 'Sumerische religiose Texte', *ZA*, 22 (1964), pp. 44-129.

Foster, B.R., *Before the Muses: An Anthology of Akkadian Literature*, Bethesda: CDL Press, 1993.

Frayne, D., *The Royal Inscriptions of Mesopotamia Volume 2: Sargonic and Gutian Periods,* Toronto: University of Toronto Press, 1993.

Glassner, J.J., *La Chute d'Akkade: L'Evenement et sa Memoire,* Berlin: D. Reimer, 1987.

Glassner, J.J., 'Mesopotamian textual evidence on Magan/Makan', in P.M.Costa and M. Tosi (eds.), *Oman Studies*, Rome: IsMEO, 1989, pp. 181-91.

Glassner, J.J., 'Dilmun, Magan and Meluhha', in J.Reade (ed.), *The Indian Ocean in Antiquity,* London: Kegan Paul, 1996, pp. 235-48.

Grayson, A.K., and Sollberger, E., 'L'insurrection generale contre Naram Sin', *Revue d'Assyriologie*, 70 (1976), pp. 103-28.

Hirsch, H., 'Die Inscriften der Konige von Agade', *AfO*, 20 (1963), pp. 1-82.

Horowitz, W., 'Two abnu sikinsu Fragments', *ZA,* 82 (1992), 112-22.

Horowitz, W., *Mesopotamian Cosmic Geography,* Winnona Lake: Eisenbrauns, 1998.

Jacobsen, T., 'The Waters of Ur', *Iraq*, 22 (1960), pp. 174-85.

Jacobsen, D., *The Harps that once...* New Haven, Yale University Press, 1987.

Jaritz, K., 'Dilmun-Makan-Meluhha', *JNES*, 27 (1968), pp. 209-213.

Landsberger, B., *The Fauna of Ancient Mesopotamia,* Rome, 1962.

Leemans, W.F., *Foreign Trade in the Old Babylonian Period,* Leiden: Brill, 1960.

Leemans, W.F., 'Old Babylonian Letters and Economic History', *JESHO*, 11 (1968), pp. 171-226.

Limet, H., 'Létranger dans la societe Sumerienne', in D. O.Edzard (ed.), *Gesellschaftsklassed im alten Zweistromland (XVIIIeme RAI),* Munich: Bayerischen Akademie, 1972, pp. 123-38.

Michalowski, P., 'Mental maps and ideology', in H. Weiss (ed.), *The Origins of Cities in Dry-Farming Syria and Mesopotamia*, Guilford: Four Quarters, 1986, pp. 129-56.

Michalowski, P., 'Magan and Meluhha once again', *JCS*, 40 (1988), pp. 156-164.

Michalowski, P., 'Sumer dreams of Subartu', in K. van Lerberghe and G. Voet (eds.), *Languages and Cultures in Contact, (XLVIIeme RAI)*, Leuven: Peeters, 1999, pp. 305-15.

Michaux-Colombot, D., 'Magan and Meluhha: A Reappraisal', in T. Abusch et al. (eds.), *Historiography in the Cuneiform World, (XLVeme Rencontre d'Assyriologie Internationale)*, Bethesda: CDL Press, 2001.

Moorey, P.R.S., 'Iran: A Sumerian El-Dorado?' in J. Curtis (ed.), *Early Mesopotamia and Iran: Contact and Conflict 3500–1600 BC*, London: British Museum, 1993, pp. 31-42.

Nath, B., 'Advances in the Study of Prehistoric and Ancient Animal Remains in India', *Records of the Zoological Survey of India*, 61 (1968), pp. 1-63.

Parpola, S., Parpola, A. and Brunswig, R., 'The Meluhha Village', *JESHO*, 22 (1977), pp. 129-65.

Salonen, A., *Vogel und Vogelfang im alten Mesopotamien*, Helsinki, 1973.

Sollberger, E, and J.Kupper, *Inscriptions Royales Sumeriennes et Akkadiennes*, Paris: Eds. Du Cerf, 1971.

Steinkeller, P., 'The Old Akkadian term for "easterner", *Revue d'Assyriologie*, LXXIV (1980), pp. 1-9.

Westenholz, J.G., *Legends of the Kings of Akkade*, Winnona Lake: Eisnbrauns, 1997.

Zadok, R., 'Elamites and Other Peoples from Iran and the Persian Gulf Region in Early Mesopotamian Sources', *Iran*, 32 (1994), pp. 31-51.

3

Names for India in Ancient Indian Texts and Inscriptions

ISHRAT ALAM

It is generally believed that the names Āryavarta and Bhāratavarsha, signify a geographical area which approximates to pre-partition India in its limits. One knows, however, that geographical concepts often evolve and territorial names transfer from one location to another. Geographical names (first of rivers rather than territories) appear in the *Rigveda* and the subsequent texts of the Vedic corpus.[1] It has been argued that Bhāratavarsha was named after a king called Bharata, and before Bharata it was called Himāhvavarsha and Haimavata-varsha,[2] but neither Bhārata-varsha nor the other two names occur in the main Vedic corpus.

In the *Rigveda,* the Aryans are supposed to follow the *āryavrata* (observance of the laws and ordinances of Aryans or honourable men) in association with the *devas* or gods.[3] It does not have any territorial significance. The *Dāsas* and *Dasyus* in the same regions are described as *anyavrata*, those who followed different practices,[4] and *ayajvan*, who did not know about sacrifices and hence were *adeva* (without gods).[5] The geographical area of the *Rigveda* is fixed by some of the major rivers mentioned in it. The Kubha, Suvāstu Krumu, Gomatī (respectively the Kabul, Swat Kurram and Gomal rivers in E. Afghanistan and Pakistan) were situated on the west, the seven rivers of the Punjab were in the centre; and the Yamunā and Gaṅgā in the east of the Rigvedic zone. In the north was the Rasā as a small tributary of the Sindhu or Indus, the *Himavant*

[1] Michael Witzel, 'On the Localization of Vedic Texts and Schools, in India and the Ancient World', *History, Trade and Culture before* AD *650*, ed. Gilbert Pollet, Leuven, 1987, pp.173-213.

[2] Nando Lal Dey. *The Geographical Dictionary of Ancient and Medieval India*, New Delhi, 1979, p.32.

[3] F. Max Muller, *The Hymns of the Rig Veda in the Samhita and Pada Texts* (henceforth *RV*, vol.II, 3rd edition, Varanasi, 1965, p.329, 10:65:11. See also Kumkum Roy, *The Emergence of Monarchy in North India*, Delhi, 1994, p.57, fn. 45.

[4] *RV.*, 10.22.8.

[5] *RV.*, 8.10.11; 9.105.6.

or the Himalayas. In the south was the ocean (*samudra*)[6] and the Bolan pass was possibly occupied by the Bhalana tribe.[7] Witzel points out that the tiger and rice are not referred to in the *RV*,[8] and this conforms to the area we have just defined. This last, however, is a doubful line of argument. Rice has now been found in Harappa (post-Indus period), not to speak of the tiger portrayed on Indus seals. The *Sapta Sindhavah* in the *RigVeda* refers to the seven rivers of the region occupied by the Aryans, and this name, occurs also in the Avesta as Hepta Hendu which is held to represent the Punjab.[9] Later on by the time the *Atharvaveda* and *Vajurveda Saṁhitās* were composed *Sapta Sindhavah* might have started signifying just 'seven streams' rather than those of a distinct territory.[10]

The geographical data available in later Vedic texts like the *Atharvaveda,* the *Yajur Saṁhitās*, Brāhmaṇas and Upanishads, and other late texts, provide a wide range of geographical data. They have been found to be restricted to northern India with some extension northwestwards into Afghanistan and the fringe of the Indian Peninsula.[11] In these late Vedic texts we have individual mentions of Balhika, Kamboja and Gandhāra, then eastwards Salva, Madra, Madra-Kaikeya, Surasena, Uśīnara, Kuru-Pañchāla, Chedi, Naishadha, Vidarbha, Aṅga, Vaṅga, Kalinga, Magadha, Mahendra (in Orissa) – Gavasa (?) or, in another series, Kāśi-Pasiyatra-Kuru-Pañchala, Magadha-Vanga-Matsya, Videha-Audumbara, Sabara-Pulinda - Chedi-Gadhi (for Magadha?), Kalinga, Kikata, Andhra.[12] But neither the word 'Āryavarta' nor even 'Madhya-deśa' occurs in any of the pre-Buddhist Vedic corpus; and some of these territories or tribes like Bahlikas, Magadhas, Aṅgas and Andhras are obviously held to be hostile or alien.

The early Buddhist text, the *Aṅguttara Nikāya* tells us of Solasa Mahājanapada (the Sixteen *Mahājanapadas*) or territories

6 Witzel suggests the Eastern Ocean of *RV* (10.136.5) was possibly a reference to the milky way rather than to the Bay of Bengal (see Witzel, op.cit., p.176, fn.1). But this seems a little far-fetched, and the Arabian Sea could be meant (cf. Irfan Habib and Faiz Habib, 'The Historical Geography of India, 1800-800 BC', *Proceedings of the Indian History Congress*, 52nd Session, Delhi, 1992, p.86).

7 Cf. Irfan Habib and Faiz Habib, op.cit., pp.72-97.

8 Wilzel, p.176.

9 I. Habib and Faiz Habib, op.cit.: see the accompanying maps on pp.95, 97.

10 M. Witzel, op.cit., pp.176-207.

11 Ibid.

12 Ibid., p.206.

of great 'tribes' or peoples which it proceeds to list. These extend from Kamboja (Kabul valley) to Aṅga (eastern Bihar), and so cover much of Northern India.[13] These traditional principalities are said to have existed in the time of Gautama Buddha (*c*.500 BC); and it may be assumed that their being grouped together meant that they were supposed to belong in varying degrees to the same cultural complex. To a limited extent the idea of a 'country' was thus taking shape, though it had yet any name of its own.

A further stage of conceptual development is undoubtedly represented by Aśokan edicts. With his empire extending from Afghanistan to Karnataka, he had a territory distinctly corresponding to India in mind when he mentioned in his Minor Rock Edict I (*c*.258 BC) 'Jambudipa' (Jambudvipa, 'the Jambolan Island') within whose limits he made people 'mingle with the gods'.[14]

The *Manusmriti*, a post-Mauryan text, composed around the second and first centuries BC, the term 'Āryavarta' was used for the land where the Brahmanical or Ārya ritual prevailed.[15] But, significantly, the limits were set at the Himalayas in the north and the Vindhyas in the south; and so the Peninsula was excluded.

The larger view of India with detailed listing of regions appears in the *Mahābhārata*, a many-layered text compiled between 200 BC and 300 AD, rightly regarded as a treasure-house by historical geographers of Ancient India. This is, perhaps, among the first texts to use the name Bhāratavarsha. It is said to have consisted of five divisions: Madhyadeśa, (2) the Udīchya or North, (3) Prachya or east, (4) Dakshiṅāpatha or south, (5) the Aparānta or West. The *Mahābhārata* has references also to the Vidhyan region and the Himalayas. Numerous peoples are mentioned, many of which demand much ingenuity from scholars to identify and locate. Though this is not without difficulty it will be fair to say that by and large they belong to Northern India and the Northwestern borderlands, and the larger part of the Deccan and

[13] For a very detailed discussion of the *Mahajanapadas* and their location and traditional history, see Hemachandra Raychaudhuri, *Political History of Ancient India*, with commentary by B.N. Mukherjee, New Delhi, 1996, pp.85-136.

[14] See E. Hultzsch, *Corpus Inscriptionum Indicarum*, vol.I: *Inscriptions of Asoka*, Oxford, 1925, pp.166, 168, 170-71.

[15] *Manusmriti*, II. 22, 23 and X. 34; transl. G. Bühler, *The Laws of Manu*, Oxford, 1886, pp.33, 410.

southern India are excluded.[16]

During the period that the *Mahābhārata* was probably compiled, the whole of India came to be covered by inscriptions, religious (votive or donative) and secular (usually on behalf of rulers), mainly in the so-called Inscriptional Prakrit. The geographical names found in the published inscriptions of these centuries (AD 200 –300) have been studied carefully, but no name for the country as a whole has been recorded, except perhaps in Khāravela's Hathigumpha inscription in Orissa, 2nd or 1st century BC, where the Prakrit form 'Bharadavasa' for the Sanskrit 'Bhāratavarsha' is met with.[17] The existence of some sense of the existence of the country may be inferred from the use of the names 'Uttarāpatha' for Northern India in the Hathigumpha inscription itself and 'Dakhinapatha' /'Dakshināpatha' for the Deccan in Siri-Pulumāyi's Nasik cave inscription (early second century AD) and Rudradāman's Girnar inscription (150 AD).[18] The so-called northern and southern parts undoubtedly presume a larger whole.

It is in the Allahabad Pillar Inscription of Samudragupta (*c*.335-376) that we first of all get an epigraphic reference to Āryāvarta. It is claimed for him that Samudragupta was one (L.21) "who abounded in Majesty that had been increased by violently exterminating Rudradeva, Matila, Nāgadatta, Chandravarman, Ganapatinaga, Nāgasena, Achuyta, Nandin, Balavarman, and many other kings of (the land of) Āryāvarta; who made all the kings of forest countries to become his servants,"[19] All these rulers have been placed within Northern India.[20] That the Aryavarta by Samudragupta's time was confined to Northern India is also shown by the fact that the rulers whom he had captured and then liberated belonged to Mahendra of [South] Kosala,

[16] See B.C. Law, *Geographical Essays relating to Ancient Geography of India*, Delhi, 1976; and Nando Lal Dey, *The Geographical Dictionary of Ancient and Medieval India*, 2nd edn., New Delhi, 1979.

[17] The most authoritative transcription of this inscription to date is that of D.C. Sircar, *Select Inscriptions Bearing on Indian History and Civilization*, I, 2nd ed., Calcutta, 1965, pp.213-21. The name 'Bharadavasa' is to be found in the narrative (much broken) of Kharavela's 10th regnal year.

[18] Cf. Irfan Habib and Faiz Habib, 'A Map of India, BC 200-AD 300, Based on Epigraphic Evidence', *Proceedings of Indian History Congress*, (Calcutta, 1990), pp.103-14.

[19] John Faithfull Fleet, *Corpus Inscriptionum Indicarum*, Vol.III, *Inscriptions of the Early Gupta Kings and their Successors*, Calcutta, 1888, pp.7-13.

[20] Raychaudhuri, *Political History of Ancient India*, pp.471-75.

Vyāghrarāja of Mahākāntāra, Maṇṭarāja of Kaurāla, Mahendra of Pishṭapura, Svāmidatta of Kottūra on the hill, Damana of Eraṇḍapalla, Vishnugopa of Kāñchī, Nīlarāja, of Avamukta, Hastivarman of Veṅgī, Ugrasena of Palakka, Kubera of Devarāshṭra, Dhanamjaya of Kusthalapura; and these and all other kings of the region of the south (*Dakshiṇāpatha*) are not referred to as rulers of Āryāvarta.[21]

Amarasimha in the renowned lexicon *Amarakośa* (4th – 5th centuries) provides a definition of *Bhāratavarsham* (also called *Jambudvipa)*, that is, Bharata's state. It specifically identifies it with *Madhyadeśa* (*madhyadeśastu madhyama*). It refers to Manu's definition, and holds *Āryavarta* to be the holy land between the Vindhyas and Himaga (Himalayas) (*Aryavarta punyabhumirimadhyam Vindhyahimagayo).* Thus even during with fifth century AD, *Āryavarta* denoted the region between Himalaya and Vindhya ranges.[22]

The *Vishnu Purāṇa*, a post-Gupta text,[23] provides information about the concept of India at three places. First, it tells us, "The *varshas* or countries between these ranges are Bhārata, south of the Himavān mountains; next Kiṁpurusha, between Himavān and Hemakūṭa; north of the latter, and south of Nishadha, is Harivarsha; north of Meru is Ramyaka, extending from the Nīla or blue mountains to the Sveta (or white moutains). Hiranmaya lies between the Šveta and Šringi ranges; and Uttarakuru is beyond the latter, following the same direction as Bhārata. Each of these is nine thousand Yojanas in extent. Ilavrta is of similar dimensions ...." It adds: "The country of Bhadrāśva lies on the cast of Meru, and Ketumāla on the west; and between these two is the region of Ilavrita."

Next, the *Viṣhṇupurāṇa* thus defines the physical boundaries and features of *Bhāratavarsha*: "The country that lies north of the ocean, and south of the snowy mountains, is called Bhārata, for there dwelt the descendants of Bhārata. It is nine thousand leagues in extent, and the land of works, in consequence of which

[21] Ibid., pp.475-80.

[22] Amarasimha, *Namalinganusasana alias Amarakosa*, ed., M.M. Pandit Sivadatta Dadhimatha, Delhi, 1997, pp.112-13.

[23] The date of *Vishṇu Purāṇa*, like other Puranic texts remains controversial. While H.H. Wilson considered it to be a work of eleventh century, other scholars put it between second century BC and ninth century AD. See Thakur Harendra Dayal, *The Vishnu Purana: Social, Economic and Religious Aspects*, Delhi, 1983, pp.21-32. I am grateful to Professor Suvira Jayaswal for drawing my attention to this important text.

men go to heaven, or emancipation."

"The seven main chains of mountains in Bhārata are Mahendra, Malaya, Sahya, Sūktimat, Riksha, Vindhya, and Pāripātra." These seven chains of mountains, also called the Kulaparvartas (family mountains) in other texts belong essentially to one system and are linked to each other. H.H. Wilson has tried to determine their location on the basis of rivers originating from them.[25] He identifies Mahendra as the chain of hills that extends from Orissa and the northern Circars (coastal Andhra) to Gondwana, part of which, located near Ganjam, is still called Mahindra Malchi or hills of Mahindra. Malaya is identified with the southern portion of the Western Ghats. Sūktimat has not been identified because of lack of information about any river flowing from it. Sahya has been identified with the northern portion of the Western Ghats i.e. the mountains of the Konkan. Riksha refers to mountains of Gondwana. Vindhya is the general name of the chain stretching across central India. But according to Wilson, the Vishṇu Purāṇa's reference is restricted to the eastern division. Pāripātra refers to the northern and western portion of the Vindhyas.

Surprisingly there is no reference to the southern or eastern mountain ranges beyond the Vindhya and the Western Ghats.

The *Vishṇupurāṇa* gives us nine divisions of Bhāratavarsha: Indradvipa, Kaserumat, Tāmravarṇa, Gabhastimān, Nāgadvipa, Saumya, Gandharba, and Varuṇa. These are yet to be identified properly.

The *Vishṇupurāṇa* provides a list of rivers and their sources. They help us in understanding the geography of Bharatavarsha. It mentions Šatadru (the Sutlej), Chandrabhāga (Chenab), "and other rivers which flow from the foot of the Himalayas". There is a reference to a river called the Vedasmriti and others rising in the Pāripātra mountains. This is possibly the Betwa. The Narmada's source is well known. But the river Surasa's origin is not certain. The river Tapi refers to the river of that name rising in Gondwana. Other rivers like Payoshnī and the Nirvindhyā flowed from the Riksha (Gondwana) mountains. The *Vishṇupurāṇa* refers to the Godavari, Bhimarathi (Bhima), Krishṇaveṇī (Krishna), Kritamala (?), Tāmraparni (Tinivelly,

[24] *The Vishnu Purāṇa, A System of Hindu Mythology and Tradition*, tr. H.H. Wilson, introduction by R.C. Hazra, Calcutta, 1961.

[25] H.H. Wilson, op.cit., p.143, note 5.

rising at the southern extremely of the Western Ghats). They all originated from the Malaya hills (southern portion of the Western Ghats). The Trisama (?), Rishikulya (the Rasikulia or Rasikoila, Orissa) originated from the Mahendra Hills.

The *Vishṇupurāṇa* is generally silent about the peoples or territories of southern India. On the other hand it refers to several tribes of northern India like the Kuru-Pañchālas as the principal tribes of Bhārata who lived in the Middle Districts. There is only one reference to *Dakshiṇatya* (i.e. the people of the South).[26]

Thus it is amply clear that while the *Vishṇupurāṇa* by its references to mountains, rivers, and tribes penetrates the western portions of the southern peninsula, its emphasis is still on Northern India. This practically conforms to the practice prevailing in the seventh century AD, when Bhaskaravarman, the King of Kāmarūpa, refers in his inscription to Harshavardhana as the emperor of Āryavarta,[27] while Harsha's dominions lay entirely north of the Vindhya range.

Hiuen Tsiang (travelled in India, 629-645) uses the Chinese characters *Yin-tu* for India, but this is obviously derived from the Iranian name for India, 'Hindu'. He writes, "We find that different counsels have confused the designations of *Tien-chu* (India), the old names were *Shen-tu* [Sindhu] and *Sien* (or *Hien*) *tou*; now we must conform to the correct pronunciation and call it *Yin-tu*. The people of *Yin-tu* use local appellations for their respective countries; the various districts having different customs; adopting a general designation, and one which the people like, we call the country *Yin-tu* which means the 'Moon'."[28] Hiuen Tsiang evidently means that the people of India had hardly an occasion to use a name for their country, and that the foreigners' name for their country was largely acceptable to them.

It is not, however, to be thought that the Indians lacked a name for the country once they had any occasion to use it — for example, in the Risthal inscription (Western Madhya Pradesh) of AD 515, where the temple built by the local ruler is said to be

[26] Wilson, op.cit., p.143. But S.M. Ali's inclusion of the peninsula south of the Satpuras as the southern regions of Bharatavarsha, *Geography of the Puranas*, New Delhi, 1966, p.132) is without any textual sanction.

[27] *Epigraphia Indica*, XII, pp.65, 71-72.

[28] Thomas Watters, *On Yuan Chwang's Travels in India, 629-645 A.D.*, ed., T.W. Rhys Davids and S.W. Bushell, vol.I, London, 1905, p.131.

a "symbol" of Bhāratavarsha.[29]

By the tenth century the conception of Bhārata embracing the Deccan as well begins to be epigraphically attested. An inscription of the Rāshṭrakūṭa King Govinda IV (918-933 AD), places the Kuntala province in the land of Bhārata (1.24.5) and places in that province the Purikara country which had two six-hundred (or perhaps sixty-two hundred) districts.[30] An inscription of Someśvara IV (1038 AD) says: "(V.9) A place of beauty is the continent of Jambudvipa, which is surrounded by the seven seas, seven continents, and seven ranges of central mountains, as in the region of Bhārata belonging to this continent there is to be seen a province [Kuntala] , a moon expanding the lotuses of the Chālukya race, an Indra of bright semblance".[31] In another inscription, after a fanciful description of the ocean we are informed that in Jambudvipa lies *Bhārata-kshetra* and in the latter the province of Kuntala:[32] 'Bhārata' occurs in the Sravana-Belagola epitaph of Mallishena (10th March 1129 AD); where too the whole of India seems clearly meant.[33] Jambudvipa itself was now thought to be a larger segment of the inhabited world.

On the other hand, a much restricted view of Bhārata is still to be found in Hemachandra (twelfth century). In his famous work, *Abhidhānachintāmaṇi* he refers to Bhārata as one of the lands of *karma* (*Karmabhumya*) along with Airavat, Videha and Kuru; the rest were considered as the 'land of *bhoga*'. It also conforms to the *Amarakosha's* definition of Āryavarta as the land between the Vindhya and Himāga. It is said to to have two synonyms: Punyabhu and Achāravedi.

Curiously enough, a narrower concept of Bhāratavarsha still appears as late as the Handala grant of Harihara (1356 AD), which refers to "the impregnable city of Vijayanagara in the Karṇāṭaka country which lying to the south of *Bhāratavarsha* excelled the city of Indra."[34]

These various references in the texts and inscriptions show that Jambudvipa, a name going back to the Aśokan inscriptons (Minor Rock Edict I) was considered to be territorially the most

[29] *Epigraphia Indica*, vol.XIII, pp.326-27.

[30] Ibid., vol.XIV, p.244.

[31] Ibid., p.282.

[32] Ibid., vol.III, pp.184, 198-99.

[33] Hemachandra, *Abhidhānachintāmaṇi*, ed. Nemichandra Sastri, with Hindi commentary by Hargovinda Sastri, Varanasi, 2nd edn., 1996, pp.57, 88.

[34] *Epigraphia Indica*, vol.XIV, p.88.

extensive in its application, the whole of the Indian world being represented by it. The position of Bhārata was more ambiguous: it was only a part of Jambudvipa, sometimes held to be identical with Northern India, but at other times also held to include parts of the Deccan as, for instance, Kuntala; at other times, it was mentioned casually as a territorial entity at par with other regional units in India. There is little evidence of "Bhārata" being the explicit object of conquest for every aspiring *chakravartin*, contrary to the general run of assumptions in many history textbooks. Still less is there much evidence of any explicit sense of patriotism called forth by Bhārata – or for that matter Jambudvipa – in the Sanskrit texts of ancient India.

4

Ideas of India in Ancient Greek Literature

UDAI PRAKASH ARORA

The Greeks' knowledge of geography during the Homeric period was rather poor and limited mostly to the Mediterranean world. The *Iliad* manifests a sense of "geographic finiteness", while the *Odyssey's* horizons widen and Odysseus' wanderings already follow a well- defined itinerary. It would be useless to attribute any measure of truth to the wanderings of the *Odessey*, but it is possible to infer from the legend the growth of frequent and lively marine activity amongst the Greek peoples, beginning around the middle of the ninth century BC

It was the emergence of the Achaemenian Empire which provided for the first time an opportunity to the Greeks, particularly those living in Ionia (Asia Minor, or modern Anatolia, Turkey), of obtaining, some knowledge of the parts of India that lay within the Achaemenian Empire, notably the Indus basin. There were under the Achaemenians well maintained 'royal highroads' linking the various territories of their Empire, from the Mediterranean to North-West India, built mainly in order to facilitate swift movement of troops. The roads also made it possible for both Indians and Greeks, as subjects of the Persian Emperor, to come into contact with one another through trade and commerce as well as through the requirements of military and administrative service. An Ionian sailor, Skylax of Karyanda, who was in the service of the Empire, was the first known Greek to produce an account of his journey to the Achaemenian satrapy of India. He was in fact sent by Darius (521-485 BC) to India, to discover a route connecting the Indus basin by sea with west Asia. He sailed down the Indus and along the coasts ultimately to reach the Red Sea and the Gulf of Suez.[1]

'F'. and 'No'. in all the references are to Fragments and number in F. Jocoby's *Fragmente Griechischer Historiker*, hrs. I-IID Berlin, 1923, 30; IIIA-IIIC, Leiden, 1954-58.

[1] Jacoby, Skylax No.709, F.I (Herod, IV, 44). There are no grounds for believing that Skylax was the leader of the expedition. Herodotus mentions that Darius "sent in ships both others on whom he could rely and also Skylax". Only Skylax was mentioned

Hekataios of Miletos (549-486 BC) reported on the races and the regions visited by Skylax. He was the first Greek author to mention the inhabitants of the country as *Indoi* or Indians. His knowledge of India was confined to the Indus basin, and he was entirely ignorant of the region of the Gangetic valley. He had no idea also of the great range of the Himalayas and the Indian peninsula to the south. Beyond the Indus he knew of the existence of a desert which he must have known from Skylax's report. This was, of course, what we today know as the Thar. As the ocean was the boundary of the 'inhabited' (*iokoumene*) world in Hekataios' map and India was believed to be situated at the eastern end of the world. Hekataios extended the Thar desert eastward from the river Indus to the ocean.

Hekataios made a distinction between the inhabitants of the Panjab and those living lower down the Indus, who were for him the Indians proper. Does it mean, then, that the Achaemenian 'Hindu' (corresponding to Sanskrit Sindhu) meant Sindh proper, distinct from the Avestan 'Hapta Hindu', which meant the Punjab? In the map of Hekataios, the river Indus flowed eastward. It may be noted here that even if Skylax had reported the Indus to have run southwards, the curvature of the Ionian map would have brought it round to a course approximating more closely to an easterly arc with the increase in the distance from the Mediterranean. In Hekataios' map, the Caspian or Hyrkanian Sea formed the boundary of India in the North. Treating it as an inlet of the ocean, Hekataios thought it to extend in the east-west direction. However, the existing fragments of Hekataios' reports are too meagre to allow us to make a fair estimate of his knowledge of India.[2]

The impact of Ionia's contacts with the East was ultimately felt in mainland Greece, while in fifth century BC its people also began to take interest in far-off lands. The long geographical passages in the plays of Aeschylos (*c*. 525/4-456 BC) bear testimony to this fact. In his play *Supplices* the Indians are

by name, because his work was the source of Herodotus' knowledge of the voyage. Presumably, the main leaders of the expedition were Darius Persian officials. On this problem see K. Varttunen, *India in Early Greek Literature*, Helsinki, 1989, pp.40-41. Also see U.P. Arora, *Greeks on India - Skylax to Aristoteles*, Indian Society for Greek and Roman Studies (ISGAPS) (Bareilly, 1996), pp.2-3, 16-18, 111-112; and L. Pearson, *Early Ionian Historians* (Oxford, 1939).

2 Jacoby, Hekataios, no.1, F.33, F.291, F.294 ab F.295, F.296, F.297, F.298, F.299. Also see U.P. Arora, op.cit., pp.3-4, 18-19, 113; L. Pearson, op.cit.

mentioned as neighbours of Ethiopians.[3] This confusion between India and Ethiopia continued to exist in Classical literature even in later periods when the greater part of the *Oikoumene* was known and voyages to India had become quite frequent.[4]

The man in whose pages the next stage in the advance of knowledge of India can be marked, is the world's first historian, Herodotus, a native of mainland Greece. Deriving his information from Skylax and Hekataios, Herodotus also thought that the river Indus flowed towards the east. Beyond that corner of India which the Persians knew fairly well, Herodotus too, like his predecessors, reported that there was nothing towards the east but a continuous desert.[5] To the north of India he spoke of a long plain, the limits of which were unknown to him. Where there was an undoubted advance over Hekataios, was in Herodotus relegating the Caspain Sea from being a gulf of the outer ocean to its proper land-locked status. The term 'Indians' was used by Herodotus as a collective name for all the peoples living east of Persia.[6] This was also a significant development over Hekataios, who had used this term in a strict sense for the groups dwelling in Sindh only.[7]

Herodotus knew the 'India' of the Persian Empire only, although he had some vague idea of the large size and huge population of India,[8] though the southern extension of India was not known to him. He thought that Arabia was the farthest of the inhabited countries towards the south.[9] We may thus say that except for his knowledge of the Indus as a great river running into the sea, Herodotus had no real idea of the physical geography of the country.

Ephoros of Cyme (c. 405-330 BC), re-establishing the old Ionian map, regarded the four most distant regions of the earth

[3] *Supp.* 284-286 (Leob edn.). The passage has been translated as follows: 'Moreover I hear tell of Indian women that go roving on camels, mounted horse-fashion, riding on padded saddles, them, that are citizens of a land neighbouring the Ethiopians'.

[4] U.P. Arora, 'India vis-a-vis Egypt-Ethiopia in Classical Accounts'. *Graeco-Arabica*, vol.I, Athens, 1982, pp.131-40.

[5] Herod. III, 98 (Loeb edn.)

[6] Herod. I, 203, 204. Herodotus' knowledge of the Caspian is one of his geographical triumphs. Even subsequent writers, except Aristotle (*Meteorologica*, II, 1, 354a 4f), to the time of Ptolemy (*Geog.* VII, 5, 4) thought that it was a gulf of the Northern Sea. Even after Ptolemy, medieval cartographers returned to the old blunder (H.F. Tozer, *History of Ancient Geography*, London, 1935, p.367).

[7] Cf. B. Breloer, *Alexander's Bund mit Poros*, Leipzig, 1941, p.11.

[8] Herod, III, 94, 98; V, 3.

[9] Herod, III, 107.

as occupied respectively by the Indians on the East, the Ethiopians in the South, the Scythians in the North and the Celts in the West. The tracts occupied by the four nations were not of equal extent, but the Ethiopians and the Scythians extended the farthest in space, so that he already regarded the inhabited world as an oblong parallelogram, having its greatest length from East to West.[10] The frame-work of his map was already obsolete by his time and it is indeed surprising that it had lasted so long.

The geographical knowledge of India was not much better even in the time of Aristotle (384-322 BC). Like his predecessors he too thought that India was the furthest land towards the direction of sunrise (east); bounded on the north by a mountain range which he called Parnassos (Paropamisos or Paropanisos of later Greek accounts, i.e. the Hindukush) and in the east and south by the outer sea, which was near enough to be visible immediately after the mountains had been crossed.[11] According to him these mountains were the highest in that part of the world and they were the source of the many large rivers of Asia, including the river Indus.[12] Aristotle was apparently confused in his ideas about India and at one time, perhaps influenced by Ochus, accepted the view expressed by Aeschylos that India was joined to Ethiopia and that the Indus was the upper Nile.[13]

All these passages clearly show how little progress had been made from the days of Herodotus to those of Aristotle in any definite knowledge of the geography of India.

Alexander's idea of India at the beginning of his campaigns was apparently based on the kind of knowledge available to Aristotle. It was probably partly the ambition of reaching the Eastern Ocean at the end of the inhabitable world that motivated Alexander to invade India. Alexander had started by believing with his teacher Aristotle that the Indus was the upper Nile, but soon learnt the truth, namely, as reported by Nearchus, that "between the Indus and Nile are great rivers and dreadful streams, ocean first, into which all the Indian rivers empty", and that there lie in between Ariana, Persian Gulf, Arabia and the

[10] Ephoros, Jac. no.70, F.30a (Strabo, I, 2, 28); F.30b (Kosmas Indikopl. *Topogr. Christ*, II).

[11] Aristot. *Meteor* II, V, 362b, 27-309; *de Caelo* II, XIV, 298a, IIf. (Loeb edn.).

[12] Aristot. *meteor*. I, XIII, 350a, 19-26. On Aristotle's geography, see Lee's note in *Meteor*. (Loeb edn.), pp.102-105.

[13] See W.W. Tarn, *Alexander the Great*, vol.II, Cambridge, 1948, p.306, n.6; *Cambridge Ancient History*, vol.VI, p.402.

Troglodyte country.[14] Alexander's expedition opened to Grecian observation that part of the Himalayas which lay near the Punjab. The Greek designation 'Himodos'[15] was derived from the Sanskrit name for these mountains, *Haimavata* or Prakrit *Haimota* (Snowy). The knowledge of the tributaries of river Indus in the Punjab and the climatic phenomenon of heavy monsoon rain were also important new additions to the Greek knowledge of India.

The companions of Alexander established a tradition of drawing analogies between Indian and Egyptian phenomena. It is a curious fact that this habit was followed by the geographers and others even under the Romans and Byzantines.[16] The summer rains of India aroused much curiosity among the Greeks, as these seemed to provide an explanation for the summer swelling of the Nile. Alexander's admiral Nearchus believed on the basis of the rise of Indian rivers that the rise in the Nile was also caused by the summer rains.[17] Onesikritos remarked that in the Indus delta there were no winds blowing from the land and that this region was subject for the most part to winds that blew from the sea.[18] This statement implied that the monsoon rains clearly set the Indus basin apart from the valley of the Nile. Although the importance of the monsoon for nevigational purpose was not understood by him, he could connect the summer rains and the fertility of the country with the phenomenon of the south-west monsoon.[19] When the companions of Alexander looked around for the distinguishing feature of the country itself, India seemed before anything else to be a land of immense rivers. The country of Indians, according to Nearchus started after crossing the Gedrosian river Arabis (modern Purali).[20]

After defeating various Indian tribes around the region of river Cophen (Kabul),[21] Alexander crossed the Indus and reached the

[14] Nearchus, Jac. no.133, F.20 (Strabo, XV, 1, 25).

[15] Onesic, Jac. no.134, F.16a (Strebo, XII, 1, 28); Aristoboulos Strabo, XV, 1, 29 (Tarn, op.cit., p.24); Baiton, Jac. no.118, F.5 (Pliny, *N.H.*, VII, 11).

[16] U.P. Arora, op.cit.

[17] Nearchus, F.20 (Strabo, XV, 1, 25).

[18] Ones, F.8 (Strabo, XV, 1, 20).

[19] L. Pearson, *Lost Histories of Alexander the Great*, New York, 1960, p.104.

[20] Nearchus, F.I (Arr. *Ind.*, VIII, 21, 8; 22, 8-10). Arabes is said to be a river of Gedrosia, which flowed from the Montes Basti (Washati), through the country of Arabii (modern Las Bela) to the Indian Ocean. The river is now called Purali. See E. Bunbury, op.cit., vol.I, p.455, 528; Smith's *Dictionary of Greek and Roman Geography*, I, p.183.

[21] Strabo, XV, 1, 26 (The passage of Strabo has been attributed to Aristoboulos by Tarn, op.cit., p.33).Also see Arrian, *Indika*, I, 4; *Anabasis* IV, 22; V, 1.

Punjab. In the Punjab on the river Hydaspes (Jhelum),[22] he defeated the brave ruler Porus. The other important rivers encountered by him in the Punjab were Akesines (Chenab),[23] Hydraotes (Ravi)[24] and Hyphasis (Beas).[25] His weary army refused to go on beyond the Beas. The fifth river Sutlej is thus not mentioned by any of Alexander's historians. In a fragment attributed to Alexander's companion Polykleitos of Larissa by Jacoby, there is a reference to the Ganges also;[26] but Tarn opines that Alexander had no proved knowledge of this river.[27]

"India formed the largest of the four parts in which Southern Asia was divided", according to Arrian's summary of

From the order in which the river is placed with others in the accounts of the Greek historians, it seems likely that the Cophen or Cophes represents the river Kabul. See Smith, op.cit., I, p.666; Bunbury, op.cit., I, p.439.

[22] Onesik, F.19 (Plut. *Alex.*, 60); Aristoboulos, Joc. no.139, F.35 (Strabo, XV, 1, 17); Nearchus, F.32 (Arr. *Anab.*, VI, 3-5). Jhelum's Sanskrit name Vitasta, which means 'widespread', appear to have been preserved in one of its modern names, 'Behut'. This last may represent the influence of Old Iranian substitution of 'h' for 's', suggesting on evolution from Vitasta to Prakrit Bitasat, whence Old Iranian 'Bitahat' (whence Greek 'Hydasphes'), ending in modern 'Bihat' (Behut). In Ptolemy's *Geography* it appears as the 'Bidaspes' - a form nearer to the original Sanskrit name, than 'Hydaspes'. See Banbury's notes, op.cit., p.499, 508-9; Smith, op.cit., I, pp.1100-1. 23. Nearchus, F.18 (Strabo, XV, 1, 18); Ptolemy, Jac. No.138, F.22 (Arr. *Anap.*, V, 20, 8).

The river Chenab during the time of Alexander joined the Indus further down, near Mithakot, whence the distance to the sea is 470 miles.

The word 'Akesines' is the Greek form of Sanskrit 'Asikni' the name under which the river is mentioned in one of Rigvedic hymns. This name appears to have been given to it on account of the dark colour of its waters. Its other Sanskrit name was 'Chandrābhaga' which would have been Hellenized into *Sandrophagos* or *Alexandrophagos* (eater of Chandra or Alexander): the followers of Alexander changed the name to avoid evil omen, the more so perhaps on account of the disaster which befell the Macedonian fleet at the turbulent junction of the river with the Indus. In Ptolemy's *Geography* it is called 'Sondabala' an obvious error for 'Sandabage'. See, Bunbury, *op.cit.*, pp.500-2; McCrindle, *The Invasion of India by Alexander the Greet*, Westminster, 1896 (reprint, Delhi, 1992), pp.112-113n.4; Smith, op.cit., Vol.I, p.12.

[24] Aristob., F.36 (Strabo, XV, 1, 21); Ptolemy, F.35 (Arr. *Anab*, V, 21, 4). Strabo's form 'Hyarotis' is closer to the Sanskrit name 'Airavati'. Its present name Ravi is an obvious abbreviation of 'Airavati'. See Smith, *op.cit.*, I, p.1101; Bunbury, op.cit., p.502; McCrindle, op.cit., p.114, n.1.

[25] Ptolemy F.35 (Arr. *Anabs*, V, 24, 8); Aristob, F.35. Hyphasis is the present Beas, the Vipasa of Sanskrit. Rising in the wstern Himalayas, this river joins the Satadru or Sutlej, but its name is given to old channels of the combined river, that lay much to the west of the present course. See Smith, op.cit., p.1105; Bunbury, op.cit., p.502, 508, 571; McCrindle, op.cit., p.9n.1.

[26] Polykleitos, Jac. no.128, F.10 (Paradox, *Vat. Rohd.*)

[27] W.W. Tarn 'Alexander and the Ganges', *Journal of Hellenic Studies*, vol.XLIII (1923), pp.93-101; also Tarn, *Alexander the Great*, II, pp.275-85.

Megasthenes and Eratosthenes.[28] According to Strabo's summary, "It was bounded on the North from Ariana to the Eastern sea, by the extremities of the Taurus, which by the natives were severally called `Paropanisos' and 'Emodos' and 'Imaos' and other names, but by the Macedonians 'Caucasus' on the west by the Indus river; but southern and eastern sides, which were much greater than the other two, extended out into the Atlantic Sea".[29]

Thus we see that in the period after Alexander, the Greek horizons of knowledge of India expanded considerably. Only the area east of the river Indus was included in the country; and area to the west of it was held to belong to a large separate region called Ariana.[30]

The contemporaries of Alexander did not attempt to give any precise statement of the dimensions of India. But the Greeks subsequently did make such an attempt. Patrokles put down the distance from the southern point of India to the Himalayas as 15,000 stadia (1724 miles).[31] Megasthenes was farther out in putting the extent from North to south, where it was shortest as 22,300 stadia.[32] What estimate Megasthenes gave of the maximum length from north to south we are not informed about, but his contemporary Daimachos affirmed that in some places it was as much as 30,000 stadia (3448 miles).[33] The distance from west to east, where it was shortest, i.e., from the Indus to the Bay of Bengal, Patrocles put at 15000 stadia (1724 miles)[34] and Megathenes at 16,000 (1838 miles).[35]

The figures ascribed to Megathenes appear to have been actually calculated by Eratosthenes, who got the figure by

[28] Meg., Jac. no.715, F.6a and Eratosthenes in H. Berger, *De Geographischen Fragmenta Des Eratosthenes* Leipzig, 1880, Frag. III B, 9, p.227 (Arr. *Anab.*, V, 6, 2).

[29] Meg. F6C and Eratosthenes in H. Berger, op.cit., Frag. III B,6, p.225 (Strabo, XV, 1, 11). Also see Eratosth. op.cit., F.III B, 9, p.227 (Arr. *Anab*, V, 62b) and Meg. F.4 (Diod. VI, 35, 1). Bunbury (op.cit., p.644) writes, "The Great mountain chain of Imaus, which Eratosthenes regarded as the continuation of the Indian Caucasus and the Taurus, descended (according to his ideas) to the shores of the 'Eastern Ocean', and he appears to have given the name of Tamarus to the headland which formed the termination of this great range."

[30] After the chapter on India, Strabo devotes a full chapter (XV, 2.1) to Ariana.

[31] Patrok, Jac. no.712, F.2 (Strabo, II, 1, 2).

[32] Meg. F.6 (Arr. *Ind.*, III, 7).

[33] Daim, Jac. no.716, F.2a (Strabo, XV, 1, 12); F.2b (Strabo, II, 1, 14); F.2c (Strabo, II, 1, 17).

[34] Patrok, F.3a (Strabo, II, 1, 7); F.3b (Strabo, XII, 1, 11).

[35] Megasth. F.6b (Arr. *Ind.*, III, 7); F.6d (Strabo, II, 1, 7).

combining 10,000 stadia of Megasthenes measured along the royal road from the Indus to Pataliputra with 6,000 stadia being the estimated distance from Pataliputra by way of the Ganges to the sea. Eratosthenes thus set 16,000 stadia as the distance from the Indus to the mouth of the Ganges. But the western side of the quadrilateral, the course of the Indus, he reduced to 13,000 stadia (1493 miles). The real projection of India to the south from the mouth of the Indus was unknown to him, and he made Cape Comarin project east of the mouth of the Ganges. India was represented by a quadrilateral whose southern side was 3,000 stadia longer than the northern and the eastern 3,000 stadias longer than the western. The shape was thus like a rhomboid.[36]

The actual distance from the Himalayas to the southern point, is about 1,800 miles, while from west to east, i.e., from the Indus to the Bay of Bengal, it is about 1,360 miles. The figure of 15,000 stadia (1724 miles) given by Patrocles for the distance from north to south is thus a happy guess. The rhomboidal form may be regarded as the result of a pioneering though erroneous attempt to work out the shape of India.

Megasthenes got from his informants a list of 58 Indian rivers, all of which were navigable.[37] At least 17 of the tributaries of river Ganges[38] and 15 of river Indus were known to him.[39] He was the first Greek to reach the banks of the Ganges and the first writer who transmitted any account of it from personal observation. To him the greatest river of India was the Ganges.[40] It was described in highly inflated terms as 100 stadia in width at its narrowest point with 20 fathoms its depth at shallower places.[41] Where its waters spread out freely, one bank could not be discerned from the other.[42] Regarding the course of this river Megasthenes said that at its source the Ganges was 30 stadia broad. It flowed from north to south, and emptied its waters into the ocean which formed the eastern boundary of the

[36] Eratosth in H. Berger, op.cit., F.IIIb 36, p.225 and Megasth, F.6c (Strabo, XV, 1, 11).

[37] Meg., F.5 (Arr. *Ind.*, V, 1).

[38] F.9 (Arr. *Ind.*, 4, 3-6). The number is given as nineteen by Pliny.

[39] Ibid., Arr. *Ind.*, IV, 8-12. Inspite of distortions, either due to the Greeks' mishearing of the native forms of these names which have come down to us, only some have been identified with their Sanskrit equivalents and/or their current names. See McCrindle, *Ancient India as Described by Megasthenes and Arrian*, Calcutta, 1877, pp.187-93.

[40] Meg. F.9a (Arr. *Ind.*, IV, 2).

[41] F.9b (Strabo, XV, 1, 35).

[42] F.9a (Arr. *Ind.*, IV, 7).

Gangaridae.[43] Probably relying on information supplied by Megasthenes, Eratosthenes pointed out that the Ganges took its rise in the Indian Caucasus (the Himalayas) and after flowing at first to the south, then turned eastwards, and pursued an easterly course as far as Palibothra (Pataliputra). It is remarkable that Eratosthenes particularly states that the Ganges had but one mouth, as distinguished from the Indus, which formed a delta.[44]

After the Ganges the Indus was regarded as the biggest river of India by Megasthenes. It had its source, like the Ganges, in the north and pursuing its course to the ocean it formed the boundary of India.[45] After these two rivers, Erannoboas (mod. Son) was erroneously reported by Megasthenes as the third greatest river of India. It united with the Ganges near the city of Palimbothra.[46]

During the period of Alexander's successors, the Greeks continued to explore or at least speculate on the routes to India. The voyage of Nearchus had established the fact that the eastern or Indian sea was continuous with the Persian Gulf. After him Patrocles speculated that the Hyrcanian sea (Caspian sea) on the other side was also similarly connected with the ocean.[47] This was unfortunately accepted as conclusive even by Eratosthenes, who never doubted that all the oceans were interconnected and that the inhabited world of Europe, Asia, and Africa formed one island.[48] So it was thought by Eratosthenes that one could sail westward from Spain to India.[49]

The earthly globe, according to Eratosthenes, was divided into five "zoros", comprising the torrid zone, the two temperate zones, and the two glacial zones. The known lands occupied a part of the Northern Hemisphere and were completely surrounded by the ocean. India took on the form of a rhomb, with the Indus to the west, the mountains in the north and the

[43] F.4 (Diod. Sic., II, 37, 2).

[44] Eratosthenes in H. Berger, op.cit., Frag. III B, 12 (Strabo, XV, 1, 13). Likewise, Artemidoras as quoted by Strabo (XV, 1, 72) very rightly pointed out that the Ganges descended from the Emodi mountains towards the south, and on reaching the city 'Gange' turned its course eastward to Palibothra and the mouth by which it entered the sea.

[45] F.4 (Diod. II, 37, 4); Meg. F.9a (Arr. *Ind.*, IV).

[46] F.18a (Arr. *Ind.*, X, 5); F.10b (Strabo, XV, 1, 38).

[47] Patrok, F.4b (Strabo, XI, 11, 6). This statement was misunderstood by Pliny, who said that Patrokles himself had made the voyage (*N.H.*, VI, 17, 58).

[48] Eratasth., in H. Berger, op.cit., Frag. II, 27, p.115 (Strabo, II, 5, 5).

[49] Ibid., Frag. I B18, p.68 (Strabo, I, 2, 31); Frag. II c18 (Strabo, I, 4, 5); Frag. IIa 6 (Strabo, I, 4, 6).

sea to the east and south.[50]

Eratosthenes' work was widely accepted during the Roman period, and was replaced only in the second century AD when Ptolemy formulated new conceptions of the world.

The first century after Christ was an era of new discoveries, enterprises and frequent voyages, for the Mediterranean world was by then under the firm rule of Rome, which politically unified the entire Hellenistic culture-area (where Greek was the literary language) as well, along with the western Latin world. The discovery of the monsoons as an aid to navigation across the Arabian Sea was probably made in the first century BC, whereafter it caused a great increase in ocean voyages. Strabo saw in Alexandria as many as 120 vessels sailing to India, whereas under the earlier Ptolemies only a few could endeavour to undertake so arduous a voyage.[51] Loukianos reported that in two olympiads a man could sail from the pillars of Herakles to India and back again from there, with leisure to explore tribes on the way.[52] Diplomatic relations also grew, for there are notices of at least eight Indian missions sent to the courts of the Roman emperors from Augustus (63 BC–14 AD) to Julian (332-63 AD).[53] The discovery of a large number of Roman gold coins from South India and various Roman artefacts, from different parts of India bear testimony to the fact of the increased interaction between India and the Graeco-Roman world throughout the earlier period of the Roman Empire.[54]

[50] Francesco Ambrosoli, *Della geografia di Strabone, libri* XVII (Milano, 1832) vol.II, pl.V. Quoted by R.M. Cimino, *Ancient Rome and India* (New Delhi, 1994), pp.5-6. The geographical ideas of Eratosthenes were widely accepted in the Roman world and can be well recognised in the Latin works of Horace, Propertius, Pomponius Mela, and Pliny. Augustus had placed the world map of Eratosthenes in the portico of Agrippa.

[51] Strabo, II, 5, 12. The figure according to J.O. Thomson (*History of Ancient Geography*, New York, 1965, p.298) 'is perhaps not entirely to be trusted'.

[52] Lucian, *Hermotimus*, 4 (Loeb edn.).

[53] For the Indian mission to the court of Augustus (63 BC 14 AD) see Nikolaos Damaes Kanos in Jacoby no.90, F.100 (Strabo, XV, 1, 73); for the one to Trajan (98-114 AD) see Dion Cassius, Roman History (Loeb edn.), LXVII, 156; to Hadrian (117-38 AD), see *Historia Augusta*, 21; to Antoninus Pius, see Aurelius Victor, *Epit.* XVI; to Elagabalus (218-22 AD), see Bardessanes in Jacoby no.719, F.1 (Stob, Flor, I, 3, 56); To Aurelian (270-75 AD), *Historia Augusta*, 33, 41, 29, 45; to constantine (306-37 AD), see Eusebius, *Vita Const.*, IV, 7, 50; and to Julian (361-63 AD), see Ammianus Marcellinus, XXII, 7, 10 (Loeb edn.).

[54] For Indo-Roman trade see mainly E.H. Warmington, *The Commerce between the Roman Empire and India*, London, 1974 (2nd revised and enlarged edition); J.I. Miller, *The Spice Trade of the Roman Empire*, Oxford, 1969; L. Casson, *The Periplus Maris*

Despite these developments the idea of India among the educated Greeks and Romans of the age did not much advance. They appear to have been uninterested in the reports which were obtained as a result of the increased trade contacts for in the works of the authors of this period, belonging to classical literary tradition, none of this information is used and their accounts are resolutely traditional. For example, when Arrian stated in his *Indica* (second century AD) that only Alexander had made an expedition against India,[55] he did not take into consideration Seleucus I, and Antiochus I, let alone the Parthians and the Kushanas. His India was thus what it was as reported by Greeks some four hundred years or so earlier to his time. Despite trade contacts and frequent communications particularly with south India, India was considered by these authors as the land of two big rivers only, namely the Indus and the Ganges. It is surprising that authors like Arrian, Srabo, Curtius, Pliny, Seneca, Dionysios Periegetes, Philostratos and many others remained oblivious to the valuable information of their own period and did not concern themselves with the opinions or reports received after the time of Megasthenes and Eratosthenes.

What restrained these authors of the age of Imperial Rome from using more contemporary information? It cannot be believed that such information was not available to them, when a great number of sailors were making the annual passage between Egypt and India and many Graeco-Roman merchants, craftsmen, etc., were doubtless visiting southern and western India. The indifference towards contemporary information shows that the reports of the common sailors and traders returning from India were not taken seriously by the educated elites of the Graeco-Roman world. In fact they were so much influenced by the accounts of Alexander's companions and Megasthenes that they could not modify their idea of India in the light of contemporary reality. The career of Alexander, the dialogues with Porus and the episode of Alexander's meeting with the gymnosophists of Taxila excited the imaginations of the Hellenistic writers no less than Alexander's other achievements. It was due to those

Erythraei, Princeton, 1989; Rosa Maria Cimino, op.cit.; Vimla Begley and R.D. De Puma (eds.), *Rome and India: The Ancient Sea Trade*, Delhi, 1992; U.P. Arora, 'Roman Age Authors on Ancient India', *Yavanika*, no.1, Journal of Indian Society for Greek and Roman Studies, Bareilly, 1991; F. De Romanis and A. Tehernia (eds.), *Crossings: Early Mediterranean Contacts with India*, Delhi, 1997.

[55] Arrian, *Ind.*, V, 4-7.

accounts that India became to them the country of a most ancient philosophy. India's literary repute almost entirely depended on Alexander and his compaign, and that is why later information, arising from increasing commercial intercourse (such as was, indeed, utilized by astronomers), was never admitted into the literary tradition. Moreover, in early Hellenistic times, the authority of Eratosthenes still reigned supreme: his geography was to influence both science and literature, since it comprehended both ethnographic description and mathematical research. India was thus the country where Alexander had fought and Megasthenes stayed and practically nothing else was of much importance. Strabo considered his contemporary travellers returning from India with newer information as credulous persons from whom serious testimony could hardly be expected.[56] Dion Chrysostom too disparaged the accounts of commercial people, for their reports were not in accordance with his own preconceived, romantic notions.[57]

It is still some matter of surprise that this should have happened in regard to India, since in dealing with lands other than India, the Graeco-Roman authors of the classical literary tradition did utilize extensively late Hellenistic, as well as the newer information reaching them through mutual contacts. Posidonios's (135-60 BC) account of the significant discovery of the direct passage by aid of the monsoons from Egypt to India by Eudoxos, occurs not in Strabo's chapter on India, but only in the introductory part of his *Geography*.[58] In the Indian part which described Nearchus' voyage of Alexander's days, the accounts of the sailors returning from India in Strabo's own days are condemned as unworthy of credit. Furthermore, we find Strabo rejecting Artemidoros (104-101 BC) who had rightly pointed out that the river Ganges descended from the Enodi mountains towards the south, and on reaching the city of Ganges (?) turned its course eastward to Palibothra and to the mouth by which it entered the sea. Unfortunately, since this statement from Artemidoros was not in accordance with the accounts of Megasthenes or Eratosthenes, it was rejected by Strabo and in the part dealing with India Artenidoros is mentioned only once.[59]

56 Strabo, XV, 1, 4.
57 Dion Chrys. *Orationes*, XXV, 22-23 (Loeb edn.).
58 Pasidonios in Jacoby no.87, F.28 (Strabo, II, 3, 4).
59 Strabo, XV, 1, 72.

There is more contemporary information in Pliny's (23/24 AD – 79 AD) *Naturalis Historia* than Strabo, but it too basically follows the description furnished by Megasthenes and Eratosthenes. Whereas Strabo had ignored the contemporary information in favour of the earlier authors, Pliny added some of the more recent reports without making any change or improvement upon the old established narrative of India.

In his geographical description of India, Pliny follows Megasthenes and Eratosthenes, but he adds the mention of the two islands called Chryse and Argyre, identified with Malaysia and Sumatra.[60] Pliny thus, added here the information of a later date, which was not available before the opening up of the Indian Ocean routes by the discovery of the monsoons. He had heard that Sri Lanka was only seven days' sail,[61] while it was twenty days from the country of the 'Prasii' at the time of Megasthenes. Pliny explained this as due to the increase in the size of the ships during his period. He was also aware of the recent embassy from Sri Lanka during the reign of Emperor Claudius. As Pliny used more recent reports his informations about South India was in general more accurate[62] than that of his predecessors. The various routes established after the discovery of the monsoons which were developed in stages, were fairly well known to him.[63]

It appears surprising that notwithstanding the knowledge of the south Indian ports and the routes across the Indian ocean in their final stage, he remained committed to the old view of India as a rhombus projecting south-east into the ocean.[64] Pliny's statement that the island of Sri Lanka begins at the Eastern Sea, and extends facing India from east to west shows that he had little knowledge of the shape of Peninsular India and the actual size and shape of Sri Lanka.

Similar combination of the old and contemporary may be seen in the work of Pomponius Mela (first century AD)[65] whose references to Chryse and Argyre, the location of Seres between the Indians and the Scythians, the sea trade and the limits of the area known, prove that he had some knowledge of the reports of

[60] Pliny, *N.H.*, VI, 77-80 (Loeb edn.).
[61] Ibid., 81-91.
[62] Ibid., VI, 23, 26.
[63] Ibid., 101 ff.
[64] Ibid., 17, 21. *Periplus of the Eryth. Sea*, 50.
[65] Pomponius Mela, *De Sutu Orbis*, Bk III, ch.7; C.H. Tzschuck, *Pomponus Mela* (Leipzig, 1806), vol.I, pp.95-99.

traders returning from India. But like Pliny, he did not improve upon Eratosthenes' and Megasthenes' concept of India and treated contemporary information merely as additional data to be fitted into the framework of the older notions of the *Oikoumene*.

Among others, authors like Arrian and Plutarch had interest in the old data only. Their accounts do not furnish even a combination of the old and new in the manner of Strabo, Pliny and Mela. Arrian's notion of India was no improvement over that of Megasthenes. Plutarch spoke about India mainly in the context of Alexander's campaigns.[66] If somehow a late Hellenistic report was incorporated in his work, it came in without a recognition of its connection with India: Plutarch speaks about the funeral of Menander, without being aware that he ruled in India. He shows him to be a king of Bactria, which did not actually belong to Menander's kingdom.[67]

Periplus Maris Erythraei[68] of an unknown author and Ptolemy's *Geographia*[69] are the only works, which show real progress in the stock of Greek information concerning the geographical knowledge of India. First of all, both refer to a large number of places in India. The *Periplus* describes the coastal routes from Egypt to India and along East Africa with detailed information about navigators and traders. His remark that the Indian coast extends from north to south, is an observation which shows him to have had a clearer idea of the configuration of the Indian coastline than any previous geographer.[70]

Ptolemy tried to locate as many as 199 inland cities and 40 coastal towns of India and his names of Indian places are closer to Sanskrit or Prakrit forms than those of any other classical

[66] Plut. *Alexander* I. Also see J.E. Powell, 'The sources of Plutarch's Alexander', *Journal of Hellenic Studies*, 59 (1939), pp.229-40.

[67] Plot, *Moralia*, 821DE. See W.W. Tarn, *Greeks in Bactria and India*, Cambridge, 1951, pp.263-264.

[68] J.W. McCrindle, *The Commerce and Navigation of the Erythraean Sea*, Calcutta, 1879; W. Schoff, *Periplus of the Erythraean Sea*, trans. and commentary, New York, 1912; L. Casson, *The Periplus Maris Erythraei*, text with trans. and commentary, Princeton, 1989.

[69] For the text of Ptolemy see *Ptolemaii Claudi Geographia*, edited by C.F.A. Niobe, Leipzig, 1843-45, reprint, 1966; McCrindle, *Ancient India as Described by Ptolemy*, Calcutta, 1885; G.E. Gerini, *Researches on Ptolemy's Geography of Eastern Asia*, London, 1909, 2nd edn., New Delhi, 1974.

[70] *Perip*, 50.

source. But his knowledge of the shape of India was much poorer than that of the author of the *Periplus*. He ignored the peninsular character of India which was already known to the compiler of the *Periplus*, and placed the southernmost point of the peninsula only four degrees south of Barygaza (Broach),[71] making India a rectangle with its main axis running from west to east. In the second century the new.geographic system, based on Ptolemy's works was established and spread through the Hellenistic world and continued to exert great influence during the Middle Ages. Mistaken calculations of degrees of longitude assigned by him caused the great geographer to consider the direction of the Indian coasts as extending from west to east, rather than north to south (this error was to persist in Europe until the sixteenth century), so that India was still not given the peninsular shope we are so familiar with today.

Despite these errors, Ptolemy had access to considerable information regarding Indian ports and the commercial activity between India and the Mediterranean World, which makes his account not only rich but also extremely significant for the historical geography of ancient India.

[71] Ptol. *Geog*, VII, 1, 9 & 62.

5

Hiuen Tsiang's India

J.S. GREWAL

Chinese interest in India began in right earnest in the early centuries of the Christian era with the spread of Buddhism to China.[1] Chinese pilgrims began to come to India, Fa-hian or Fa-hsien ('Faxian')[2] being the first major traveller (fl. AD 414), whose account of his travels in India has survived.[3] But the most detailed and influential work has been that of Hiuen Tsiang or Hsuan Tsang or Yuan Chwang ('Xuan Zhuang'), to reproduce some of the more common roman transcriptions of the name of that renowned Chinese monk (602-64). He visited India in AD 630-44, coming and returning by land through Central Asia, and leaving a splendid geographical, cultural and political survey of India, region by region, entitled *Hsi-yu-chi* or *Si-yu-ki*, literally 'Records of the Western Lands'. There is a full-scale profusely annotated translation by Samuel Beal[4] and, then, a very important summary with commentary by Thomas Watters, who used a very large number of Chinese texts and commentaries and corrected a number of slips by the earlier translators.[5]

Huien Tsiang journeyed from China proper through the territories of Xin Jiang (Western China), Tajikistan, Uzbekistan and Northern Afghanistan, the different principalities he passed through being described in order of the stages of his journey. It

[1] On the entire subject of how these relations began and developed the best survey is still that of Prabodh Chandra Bagchi, *India and China: A Thousand Years of Cultural Relations*, 2nd ed., Bombay, 1950.

[2] Spellings according to the current official Pinyin system are given within single inverted commas.

[3] For translations of Fa-hian's account, see Samuel Beal, *Buddhist Records of the Western World*, London, 1884, I, pp.xxiii-lxxxiii; and Li Yung-hsi (transl.), *A Record of the Buddhist Countries* by Fa-hsien, Peking, 1957. There are also early translations by H.A. Giles (1877, 1923) and James Legge (1886).

[4] *Buddhist Records of the Western World*, 2 vols., London, 1884. Beal followed a transcription system of his own and heavily used M. Julien's very early French translation (1857). But he did correct several of Julien's mistakes and his notes are a valuable repository of references to work done till his time in English and French. Beal's translation would henceforth be referred to in these notes as 'B.'

[5] *On Yuan Chwang's Travels in India, 629-645 AD*, ed. after his death by T.W. Rhys Davids and S.W. Bushell, London, 1905, 2 vols. It will be cited hereafter in these notes as 'W'.

was after he had crossed the Hindu Kash range through the Bamiyan Pass, visited Kapisa (Kabul territory), and then started on his journey eastwards towards Lan-po (Lamghan) and Na-kei-lo-ho (Nagarhar) (both in eastern Afghanistan), that he thought he was now entering In-tu or India. He thereupon gives a general account of India[6] before proceeding to give further accounts of individual regions.

In the opening passage of his account of India Hiuen Tsiang offers us a comment on the name of India, which Beal translates rather inexactly, but on which Watters has an illuminating commentary.[7] Hiuen Tsiang says that there have been three names for India: in olden times *Shin-tu* and *Hien-tu*, but was now *In-tu*. As Watters points out the pilgrim is here referring to Chinese names for India. People in India like In-tu, the pilgrim says, because it means the moon in their language. Beal commits an extraordinary slip when he renders Hiuen Tsiang as saying that "in Chinese the name signifies the Moon." It is in Sanskrit that *indu* (of which the standard Chinese transcription happened incidentally to be *in-tu*) means the moon; and it is this fact which makes sense of what our pilgrim is saying here. Watters rightly refers to another important Chinese traveller to India, I-tsing (Iching, 'Yi Jing') (fl.AD 700), who says that Indians call their country *Arya-desa*, which he translates as 'Noble Land', and *Madhya-desa*, 'Middle Land'. It was the "Hu" (Chinese name for Mongols and Turks) who called India "Hindu", but this designation was not often known to people in India. As for *In-tu*, he says: "Some say that Indu means the moon, and the Chinese name for India, i.e. Indu, is derived from it; although it may mean this ['moon'], it is nevertheless not the common name [in India]."[8]

I-tsing's account gives us two names used by foreigners for Indu: Hindu by the Hu, and Indu (In-tu) by the Chinese. It is clear, however, that Indu as a territorial name had nothing to do with the Sanskrit *indu*, but was derived from the Iranian name for India, which must have been passed on to the Hu from Iran. It thus belongs to the same family of foreign names for the country to which 'India' belongs.

[6] B, I, pp.69-90; W., I, pp.130-79. Here and elsewhere, when both Beal and Watters are cited, Watters' rendering is accepted in case of a difference between them. In a few cases, the differences are explicitly noted.

[7] B., I, p.69; W., I, pp.131-41.

[8] I-tsing, *A Record of the Buddhist Religion as Practised in India and the Malay Archipelago (AD 671-695)*, transl. J. Takakusu, London, 1896, p.118.

Watters also makes another significant emendation in Beal's translation. Beal translates Hiuen Tsiang as saying: "The people of In-tu call their country by different names according to their districts,"[9] as if each region gave a different name to the whole country. Watters, on the other hand, renders it more reasonably as: "The people of Yin-tu use local appellations for their respective countries", and he himself understands this to mean that "the natives of India had only designations of their own States, such as Magadha and Kausambhi, and that they were without a general name under which these could be included."[10] Hiuen Tsiang, like I-tsing, must, of course, have known that the learned people had a name for the whole country, such as Jambudvipa or Aryavarta;[11] but he has obviously in mind the common people: They had no sense of belonging to a country, and so no need to use a name for it.

Given the name for the country that the Chinese used for India, Hiuen Tsiang then sets out to define its frontiers.

On three sides, India was bordered by the great sea; on the north, it was backed by the Snowy Mountains (Himalayas). It was divided into five In-tus (Indies) according to compass directions.The north was a continuation of mountains and hills, and the ground was dry and salty. On the east were well watered valleys and plains which were fruitful and productive. The southern districts were wooded and had luxuriant vegetation. The western parts were stony and barren. The entire land was divided into about seventy 'countries'.[12] The climate was generally hot and humid, but there were six seasons in a year : the season of gradual heat, the season of full heat, the rainy season, the season of growth, the season of gradual cold, and the season of great cold. According to the Buddhists, there were only three seasons : the summer, the winter, and the rainy season. The last was regarded as the season for rest. Yet another classification was that of spring, summer, autumn and winter. The twelve months from Chaitṛa to Phalgun, being lunar, were divided into Shukla and Krishna *pakshas*. The day-and-night (*aharatra*) was divided into eight *kalas*, each of five *mahurtas*.

[9] B, I, p.69.

[10] W., I, pp.131-2.

[11] Hiuen Tsiang himself mentions that the 'Brahmans' country' (obviously a rendering of "Brahma-varta") was a popular name for India (B, I, p.69; W., I, p.140).

[12] B, I, p.70; W., I., pp.140-41.

Each *mahurta* consisted of over two hundred thousand *kshanas*. Important among the measures of distance was the *yojana* which consisted of eight *krosas*; a *krosa* was divided into 500 bows, and a bow into four cubits of 24 fingers each.[13]

The produce from land was various in character due to variation in climate and soil. There were different kinds of plants and trees, and flowers and fruits. The pear, the plum, the peach, the apricot, and the grape were to be met with in Kashmir and beyond. Pomegranates and sweet oranges too were grown everywhere. The land was ploughed and harrowed for cultivation, and crops were sown and reaped according to the seasons. Rice and wheat were the most plentiful products. Important among the edible herbs and plants were ginger and mustard, melons and pumpkins. But onions and garlic were little grown, those who ate them being ostracised. Among the mineral products of India were gold, silver, copper, white jade, and crystals. There was abundance of rare gems and various kinds of precious stones.[14] Then there is again an important correction which Watters makes to Beal's translation. Far from saying that "the Indians have no gold or silver coins, pearl shells or little pearls," as Beal has it, Hiuen Tsiang actually says: "In the commerce of the country gold and silver coins, cowries and small pearls are the media of exchange."[15] The latter statement is, of course, the true one, as India's numismatic history shows us so well.

The towns and villages had wide and high walls with inner gates. The towers on the walls were constructed of wood or bamboo; the houses had balconies and belvederes made of wood, with a coating of lime ('chunam'), and were covered with tiles burnt or unburnt. The walls were ornamented with lime and floors made of mud, mixed with cow dung for purity. The streets and lanes were tortuous and the roads were winding; the thoroughfares were dirty, but the stalls arranged on both sides of the road had appropriate signs. Outside the walled cities were the low-walled suburbs of butchers, fishermen, public dancers, executioners and scavengers who were bound to keep to the left of the road as they sneaked along within the walled city.[16]

The nobility used beautifully painted and enriched corded seats according to their taste, but other people used mats to sit

[13] B., I, pp.70-73; W., I, pp.141-47.
[14] B, I, pp.88-89; W., I, pp.177-79.
[15] B., I, p.90; W., I, p.178.
[16] B, I, pp.73-74; W., I, p.147.

or rest on. The clothes were not cut or fashioned. The men wound their garments round their middle, gathered them under the armpits, and let them fall down across the body, leaving the right shoulder bare. They wore caps, flower wreaths, and jewelled necklaces. The women covered their shoulders completely in a long robe (sari), falling down loose to the ground. They wore a little knot of hair on their crowns and let the rest of the hair fall loose. The garments were made from cotton, wild silk (*kaushaya*), linen, wool, and a sort of wool from the hair of a wild animal, much prized. The kings and their ministers wore gem-decked caps, and adorned themselves with bracelets and necklaces.[17]

The usual food consisted of milk, ghee, granulated sugar, sugar-candy, parched grain, and the oil of mustard seed. Fish, mutton, venison were occasional dainties. Forbidden for eating was the flesh of ox, ass, elephant, horse, pig, dog, fox, wolf, lion, monkey, and ape. Those who ate their flesh were universally reprobated; they lived outside the walls. Those who used onions and garlic for food were expelled beyond the walls of the town. People generally ate from one vessel; mixing all sorts of condiments together; and they ate with their fingers. They had no spoons or cups, and no chopsticks. When sick, they were fed with copper spoons. There were saucepans and stewpans but no steamers for cooking rice. Many vessels were made of dried clay but very few of bronze. The mixed classes and base-born used vessels which were very different 'both as to value and material'. There were various sorts of wines and liquors. The upper castes, especially Vaishyas used strong fermented drinks. Medicines were used in sickness only if it lasted beyond seven days of fasting. The doctors differed in their modes of examination and treatment.[18]

Hiuen Tsiang speaks of the four-fold "hereditary" classification of society. The Brahmans guarded themselves in religion, observing ceremonial purity. They were so much noted for their purity and nobility that the people generally spoke of India as 'the country of the Brahmans'. The Kshatriyas formed the governing class, and applied themselves to virtue and

[17] B., I, p.75; W., I, p.148.

[18] B., I, pp.88-89; W., I, pp.178-9. Watters renders the drink Vaishyas took as "strong distilled spirit", unlike Beal, who has "fermented" instead. One would like to know if liquor distillation was widespread in India in Hiuen Tsiang's time.

kindness. Both the Brahmans and the Kshatriyas wore wholesome dress and lived in a homely and frugal way. The Vaishyas formed the merchant class and engaged in commercial exchange, pursuing profit at home and abroad. The Shudras formed the agricultural class and laboured in ploughing and tillage. Members of each caste married within the respective caste; and relatives, whether on father's or on mother's side did not intermary. Women married only once. Besides these four, there were other "mixed" castes of many kinds that followed their several callings.[19]

People were particular about personal cleanliness. They washed before eating, and cleaned their teeth after eating; everytime they performed the functions of nature they washed their bodies and used perfumes of sandal-wood or turmeric. They did not pass dishes, and they did not eat left- overs. The pottery and wooden (bark?) vessels were destroyed after use; the vessels of gold, silver, copper and iron were rubbed and polished after every meal. The ordinary people were upright, and faithful in their promises. They were not crafty in money matters, or deceitful in their conduct. There were nine ways of showing outward respect. The most respectful was 'to make one's prostration on the ground and then to kneel and laud the virtues of the one addressed'.[20]

There were no regulations as to the dress of mourning, or its duration. It was customary to raise lamenting cries and weep together. The mourners rent their garments and loosened their hair, struck their heads and beat their breasts. The priests were not allowed to lament or cry for the dead, not even for their parents. They simply recited their prayers, recounted their obligations to the dead, and attended carefully to them. They expected by doing this to increase the mysterious character of their religious merit. There were three ways of paying the last tribute to the dead : by cremation, by water, and by desertion. In the first, the body was burnt; in the second, it was thrown into flowing water; and in the third, it was left in a wilderness to be devoured by beasts. No eating was allowed in the house till after the funeral. Those who attended the funeral had to wash themselves. No posthumous titles were given and no death anniversaries were observed. The old and infirm, and those who

[19] B., I, pp.69, 76, 82; W., I, 168-70. Beal's rendering on p.82, needs to be corrected by reference to Watters, p.168.

[20] B., I, pp.77, 83, 85; W., I, pp.152, 171, 173.

suffered from serious illness, or wanted to end their life for other reasons, drowned themselves in the Ganges in the hope of being born among the *devas*.[21]

Hiuen Tsiang states that kingship in India was confined to the Kshatriya caste. The throne of the reigning sovereign was large and high, and much adorned with precious gems. Called the lion-throne (*simhasana*), it was covered with extremely fine drapery. The footstool too was adorned with gems. Drums were struck and hymns were sung to the tune of musical instruments when the king went for his bath. The administration of the government was founded on benign principles, and the executive was simple. The people were not subject to forced labour. When required, the labour was exacted but paid for in strict proportion to the work done. Those who cultivated the royal estates paid a sixth part of the produce as rent. The private demesnes of the crown were divided into four principal parts : the first for carrying out the affairs of the state and providing sacrificial offerings, the second for providing income to the ministers and chief officers of the state, the third for rewarding men of distinguished ability, and the fourth for charity to religious sects. The governors, ministers, magistrates, and officials had each a portion of land consigned to them for their personal support.[22]

The soldiers were selected from the bravest people in the country and the profession tended to become hereditary. There were four divisions of the army : the infantry, the cavalry, the chariots, and the elephants. The infantry went lightly into action and carried a long spear and a large shield, and sometimes held a sword or sabre for impetuous attack. The cavalrymen spread themselves in front to resist an attack. The chariots had two drivers, and were drawn by four horses abreast. The commander of the soldiers remained in the chariot, surrounded by a file of guards close to its wheels. The elephants were covered with strong armour, and their tusks were provided with sharp spurs. All the weapons of war were sharp and pointed. Used since olden times were spears, shields, bows and arrows, swords, sabres, battle-axes, lances, halberds, long javelins, and various kinds of slings. The army guarded the frontiers, punished the refractory, and mounted guard around the palace. The soldiers were raised

[21] B., I, pp.86-87; W., I, pp.174-75.

[22] B., I, pp.75, 77, 82, 87-88; W., I, pp.147-8, 152, 168, 176-77.

according to the requirement of the service. They were publicly enrolled on certain promised payments.[23]

Criminals were brought to justice after careful investigation. The offenders were generally imprisoned, or cast out of society; there was no capital punishment. For violating the rules of propriety, justice, fidelity or filial piety, the nose or ears of the offender, or his hands and feet, were cut off, or he was expelled from the country. For minor crimes, a small payment of fine could redeem the offender. If an accused persisted in denial of the crime, four kinds of ordeals were used: by water, by force, by weighing, and by poison. Hiuen Tsiang explains each of these ordeals and remarks that by these four methods of trial the way to crime was stopped.[24]

Hiuen Tsiang describes the Indian script as consistingof forty-seven letters. This alphabet had spread in different directions and formed diverse branches. Middle India preserved the original character of the language in its integrity. The pronunciation of words here was clear and pure, and fit as a model for all. The people of the frontiers had contracted several erroneous modes of pronunciation. Young men were educated in the *shastras* of 'the five sciences': grammar (*shabda vidya*), the arts and mechanics (*shilpa vidya*), the medical lore (*chikitsa vidya*), ethics (*hetuvidya*), and the science of 'the interior' (*adhyatma vidya*). The Brahmans studied the four *Vedas* which, as given by Hiuen Tsiang do not accurately represent the real four Vedas. The first, he tells us, related to the preservation of life and the regulation of the natural condition. The second related to the rules of sacrifice and prayer. The third related to decorum, casting of lots, military affairs, and army regulations. The fourth related to the various branches of science, incantations, and medicine. Competent teachers taught these works to young people. There were some who remained aloof from society and searched for wisdom, relying on their own resources.[25]

Hiuen Tsiang appears to refer to the various kinds of ascetics when he talks of their dress and ornaments. 'Some wear peacock's feathers; some wear necklaces made of skullbones (the *Kapaladharinas*); some have no clothing, but go naked (*Nirgranthas*); some wear leaf or bark garments; some pull out

23 B., I, pp.82-83, 85; W., I, pp.170-71.
24 B., I, pp.83-85; W., I, pp.171-72.
25 B., I, pp.77-80; W., I, pp.154-161.

their hair and cut off their moustaches; others have bushy whiskers and their hair braided on the top of their heads. The costume is not uniform, and the colour, whether red or white, not constant.'[26]

There were eighteen schools of Buddhism, each claiming pre-eminence. The contending utterances of the different schools rose like 'the angry waves of the sea'. The Hinayanists and the Mahayanists dwelt apart. There were some who gave themselves to quiet contemplation. There were several classes of books related to the *Vināya*, the *Sūtras*, and the Buddha's discourses. The monk who could expound one class of books was exempted from manual work. The one who could expound two classes of books was given a room. The one who could expound three was attended by servants. He who could explain four classes was attended by other monks. He who could expound five was allowed an elephant carriage. He who could expound six classes of books was allowed an elephant and an escort. The renowned monks convoked assemblies for discussion. If one distinguished oneself in an assembly by 'refined language, subtle investigation, deep penetration, and severe logic', he was mounted on an elephant covered with precious ornaments, and conducted by a numerous suite to the gates of the monastery. The one who broke the rules of discipline was publicly reproved. For a grave fault, expulsion was enforced. Sometimes, the individuals thus expelled went back to their old occupations. To return from the religious to worldly life was considered blamesworthy. The monks wore three kinds of robes. The style of the robe depended on the school to which one belonged. Both yellow and red robes were used. The monasteries were built with extraordinary skill. A three-storeyed tower was erected at each of each monastery's four angles. The beams and the projecting heads were carved with great skill in different shapes. The doors, windows and the low walls were profusely painted. The cells of the monks were plain on the outside but ornamented on the inside. In the middle of the building was a wide and high hall. There were various storeyed chambers and turrets of different heights and shapes. The doors opened towards the east, just as the royal throne faced the east.[27]

[26] B., I, p.76; W., I, pp.146-47.
[27] B., I, pp.74, 76, 80-81; W., I, pp.162-68.

II

In his description of the 'countries' of India, Hiuen Tsiang talks of their political status, their chief towns, their natural and agrarian produce, the general character, condition and habits of the people, and their religion. In this process he amplifies or modifies his general observations. He has much more to say about Buddhism than about anything else. Buddhism, evidently, was his primary concern. But his evidence on the other aspects of Indian life is not without interest or significance.

Turning to polity we find that the kings were not all Kshatriyas. Hieun Tsang refers specifically to Brahman, Vaishya and Shudra kings. All the kings were not sovereign rulers. The king of Kashmir had subjugated several 'kingdoms' which were now governed either by men whom he appointed or by subordinate chiefs who were allowed to remain in position. Harshavardhana appointed the king of Jalandhara as 'sole inspector' of the affairs of religion throughout 'the five Indies'. On Harsha's instruction 'kings of twenty countries' assembled at his capital, with the most distinguished of their Shramanas and Brahmans.[28] It is interesting to note that Hiuen Tsiang uses the term 'kingdom' sometimes with reference to the past. Gandhara, for instance, was ruled by the kings of Kapisa and had no king of its own, but it is referred to as 'the kingdom of Gandhara'. Similarly, Sthaneshvara, which was a province of Harsha's empire, is called a 'kingdom'.[29]

Most of the countries and kingdoms described by Hiuen Tsiang represented administrative units. Since their number was nearly three and a half scores, their size was not very large. In fact the largest majority of these units were less than 1,000 miles in circuit. Even Kanyakubja (Kanauj) is stated to be only about 800 miles in circuit. Sthaneshvara, however, was about 1400 miles circuit. It was equal in size to Kashmir and Sindh. The largest units mentioned by Hieun Tsang are Takka and Kamarupa, each having a circuit of about 2,000 miles. The size of a country or kingdom was no indication of its political importance. In the context of suzerain-vassal polity, the most important states in the early seventh century were those of Kashmir, Kanauj, and Maharashtra.

[28] B., I, p.218. This passage seems to be omitted in Watters' summary.

[29] B., I, pp.97-98, 183; W., I, pp.198-99, 314. Where Beal has 'kingdom', Watters has 'country'.

Many cities and towns lay in ruins, suggesting de-urbanization. A few countries had no city. The walled cities in Magadha had only a few inhabitants, but some of the towns were thickly populated. Some of the kingdoms or countries had more than one city or town. Some of these were rather small, with a circuit of less than two miles. More had a circuit of two to three miles, and many more a circuit of about four miles. Even the number of cities with a circuit of five to eight miles was quite considerable. Among the largest cities was Purushapura, the capital of the kingdom of Gandhara. Kanyakubja was nearly four miles long and about a mile in width. Only in a few cases does Hiuen Tsiang refer explicitly to the economic activity of the towns. Valuable merchandise was collected at Kanyakubja in great quantities: 'The people are well off and contented, the houses are rich and well formed'.[30] In Sthaneshvara, rare and valuable merchandise was collected from every quarter, and the people of Surashtra engaged in commerce and exchange of commodities.[31]

Hiuen Tsiang's references to the produce of the countryside are far more frequent than to the merchandise of towns and cities. Gandhara, for example, was 'rich in cereals', and produced a variety of flowers and fruits; it also produced sugar-cane from which 'the solid sugar' was prepared. The land of Takshashila was 'renowned for its fertility' and produced 'rich harvests'. The soil of Takka was suitable for rice and produced much late-sown corn. The land of Jalandhara was favourable for the cultivation of cereals and produced much rice. The rich and fertile soil of Mathura was fit for producing grain, cotton, and fruit. The land of Ayodhya produced cereals and a large quantity of fruits and flowers.[32] The soil of Magadha was rich and fertile, with abundance of cultivation of grain. An unusual sort of rice was grown here; its grains were large and scented, and of an exquisite taste. It was customary to call it 'the rice for the use of the great'. The country of Kalinga was productive of fruits and flowers in abundance. The soil of Andhra was rich and fertile for the production of cereals. The soil around Kanchipura produced abundance of grain. However, this was not true of the

[30] B, I, p.206; W., I, p.340.

[31] B, I, p.183; W., I, p.314.

[32] B., I, pp.98, 137, 165, 175-6, 179-80, 223; W., I, pp.199, 240, 286, 296, 301, 355.

Chola country which was deserted and wild, and marked by marshes and jungle. There were other areas too where the soil was infertile or saline, and much of the land was uncultivated. Not only in the mountains and hills but also in the plains Hiuen Tsiang found large areas were covered by forests. Cattle and sheep were reared in some areas, as in Sindh.[33]

The kingdom of Takka (Punjab) produced gold, silver, copper, and iron. Garhwal produced copper and rock crystal. Red copper was produced in Nepal. Dravida (South India) produced gems and other articles. Great quantities of salt were produced in Sindh.[34] It is interesting to note that Hiuen Tsiang makes no mention of the Salt Range, though it was close to the capital of Simhapura.

Even outside India, in Kapisa, Hiuen Tsiang noticed naked ascetics who could have included the Digambara Jain monks who went naked. He noticed the white-robed 'heretics' in Simhapura: 'The laws of their founder are mostly filched from the principles of the books of the Buddha. These men are of different classes, and select their rules and frame their practices accordingly. The great ones are called Bhikshus; the younger are called Shramaneras. In their ceremonies and modes of life they greatly resemble the priests (of Buddha), only they have a little twist of hair on their heads, and they go naked. Moreover, what clothes they chance to wear are white. Such are the slight differences which distinguish them from others. The figure of their sacred master they stealthily class with that of Tathagata; it differs only in point of clothing; the points of beauty are absolutely the same'. There were numerous followers of the Nirgranthas in Vaishali. A *stupa* in Magadha was virtually taken over by the naked heretics (Nirgranthas) who frequented the place in great numbers to practise penance and contemplation. At another place Hiuen Tsiang refers to 'a distinguished sooth-sayer belonging to the heretical sect of the Nirgranthas'. The naked Nirgranthas were the most numerous in Bengal. The Nirgranthas were numerous in Kalinga too. There were many Nirgrantha heretics in Chola country, and in the far south there was a multitude of heretics mostly belonging to the Nirgranthas.[35] Thus, the Jain monks were

[33] B., II, pp.82, 204, 207, 209, 217, 227, 228, 272; W., II, pp.86, 198, 209, 224, 226, 252.

[34] B., I, pp.89, 165-66, 198, II, pp.66, 80, 229, 272; W., I, p.286, II, pp.83, 226, 252.

[35] B., I, 55, 144-5, II, pp.66, 158, 195, 199, 208, 227, 231; W., I, pp.123, 251-2; II, pp.63, 154-55, 178, 183, 198, 224.

found in many different parts of India.However, Hiuen Tsang does not give the same kind of information about the Jains as about the Buddhists. In fact his interest in the Jain 'heretics' was as minimal as his interest in other non-Buddhist groups in India. The use of the term 'heretic' for all of them indicates that Hiuen Tsiang looked upon Buddhism alone as the true faith.

Almost everywhere in India there were Deva or Brahmanical temples. Many of these belonged to the worshippers of a female deity and the worshippers of Maheshvara. Hiuen Tsang noticed a Deva temple outside the western gate of Pushkalavati in Gandhara. The image of the god was imposing and worked 'constant miracles'. The temple of Bhima Devi, the wife of Ishvara Deva, was on the top of a mountain about ten miles from the city. 'All the people of the better class, and the lower orders too, declare that this figure was self-wrought. It has the reputation of working numerous miracles, and therefore is venerated (worshipped) by all, so that from every part of India men come to pay their vows and seek prosperity thereby. Both poor and rich assemble here from every part, near and distant. Those who wish to see the form of the divine spirit, being filled with faith and free from doubt, after fasting seven days are privileged to behold it, and obtain for the most part their prayers'. The temple of Maheshvara Deva was below the mountain. The heretics who came here to offer sacrifice covered themselves with ashes.[36]

In Takka, many people sacrificed to Devas and heavenly spirits, and there were hundreds of temples. There were nine Deva temples in Chinapati and three in Jalandhara with 500 cinder-sprinkled Pashupatas. Hiuen Tsiang refers vaguely to an ancient battle fought near Sthaneshvara, which accounted for the country being called 'the field of religious merit'. There were a hundred Deva temples here. There were ten Deva temples in Paryatra (northern Rajasthan), with 1,000 followers of different sects. In Mathura there were five Deva temples of all kinds of sectaries. In the Rohilkhand region there were some nine Deva temples with 300 sectaries: 'They sacrifice to Ishvara, and belong to the company of "ashes-sprinklers" (Pashupatas)'. On the eastern bank of the Ganges near Kanauj was a Deva temple with towers and storeyed turrets remarkable for their skilfully carved work.[37]

[36] B., I, pp.109, 113-14; W. I, p.214-15, 221-23.

[37] B., I, pp.166, 173, 176, 179-80, 186, 200, 224; W., I, pp.291, 296, 300-01, 314-15, 331, 352.

The number of 'heretics' in Prayaga was very large and there were several Deva temples. A temple in the city was beautifully ornamented, and it was celebrated for its numerous miracles. 'If in this temple a man gives a single farthing, his merit is greater than if he gave 1000 gold pieces elsewhere. Again, if in this temple a person is able to contemn life so as to put an end to himself, then 'he is born to eternal happiness in heaven'. The people, says the pilgrim, were encouraged to practise this false custom. The sandy ground near the confluence of the Ganges and the Yamuna was used for distributing gifts and charity by the kings and noble families. 'To the east of the enclosure of charity, at the confluence of the two rivers, every day there are many hundreds of men who bathe themselves and die'.[38]

In Varanasi there were a hundred or so Deva temples and about 10,000 'sectaries'. The majority worshipped Maheshvara. Some cut their hair off and others tied their hair in a knot, and went naked. They covered their bodies with ashes and practised all sorts of austerities to escape the cycle of birth and death. In the capital itself were twenty Deva temples. Their halls and towers were of sculptured stone and carved wood. The statue of Deva Maheshvara, made of copper, was not much less than a hundred feet in height. Its appearance was grave and majestic, as though really alive.[39]

In Bengal and Kamarupa there were hundreds of Deva temples for sectaries of all kinds who lived together. There were fifty Deva temples in Utkal for sectaries of all sorts. In Kalinga there were about a hundred Deva temples with very many 'unbelievers' of different sorts. About seventy temples in South Kosala were frequented by heretics of different persuasions. In Amaravati there were a hundred Deva temples and the people who frequented them were numerous and of different beliefs. In the Chola country there were tens of Deva temples. In Dravida there were about eighty Deva temples. The heretics in Malava were very numerous, especially the Pashupatas. In Kachha there were tens of Deva temples with very many sectaries. North of Kachha, the people worshipped heavenly spirits in hundreds of temples. Sectaries of different characters congregated in these. In Vallabhi there were several hundred Deva temples and very many sectaries of different sorts. In Surashtra there were about a hundred

[38] B., I, pp.230-32; W., I, pp.361-65.
[39] B., I, pp.44-45; W., I, pp.46-47.

temples, occupied by sectaries of various sorts. Sectaries of various denominations had tens of Deva temples in Gurjara. There were tens of Deva temples in Ujjaini, occupied by sectaries of various kinds. The principal heretics in Maheshvarapura were Pashupatas and there were tens of Deva temples in the kingdom.[40]

There were eight Deva temples in Multan. The one dedicated to the sun was very magnificent and profusely decorated. 'The image of the Sun-deva is cast in yellow gold and ornamented with rare gems. Its divine insight is mysteriously manifested and its spiritual power made plain to all. Women play their music, light their torches, offer their flowers and perfumes to honour it. This custom has been continued from the very first. The kings and high families of the five Indies never fail to make their offerings of gems and precious stones (to this Deva). They have founded a house of mercy (happiness), in which they provide food, and drink, and medicines for the poor and sick, affording succour and sustenance. Men from all countries come here to offer up their prayers; there are always some thousands doing so. On the four sides of the temple are tanks with flowering groves where one can wander about without restraint.'[41]

Besides the Hinayana and the Mahayana Buddhists who were divided into eighteen schools, and the Jains who were divided mainly into 'the naked' and 'the white-robed' monks, there were 'sectaries' of 'all sorts' and 'denominations'. Among them, the Shaivas, especially the Pashupatas, appear to have been dominant, partly because they are clearly identified. There can be no doubt about the existence of the worshippers of female deities and the worshippers of the sun. But there were still other unidentified groups who added to the religious diversity in India during the seventh century. Diversity was not confined to the sphere of religion. Hiuen Tsiang refers to 'the dialects of the countries'. In Utkal, the words used by the people, and their pronunciation, were different from what he found in Central India. In Andhra too, the language and arrangement of sentences differed from those of mid-India. People differed in their moral and cultural traits from region to region as they differed in their general appearance. Two regions were remarkable for the learning

[40] B., II, pp.195-6, 199-201, 204, 208, 210, 221, 227, 261, 265-67, 270-71; W., II, pp.179, 183-84, 186-87, 190-91, 193, 196, 198, 214-19 (Watters doubts the identification with Amaravati), 224, 226, 242, 245-46, 248-51.

[41] B., II, pp.274-75; W., II, p.254.

of the people: Magadha in the east and Malava in the west.[42]

III

With his primary interest in Buddhism, Hiuen Tsiang gives more space to those regions and kingdoms which were associated with Buddhism in one way or another. Gandhara, for example, had produced many scholars of Buddhist *shastras*. Among them were Asunga, Vasubandhu, Narayanadeva, Dharmatrata, Manorhita, and Parava. The first two were regarded as Bodhisattvas. There were about 1,000 monasteries in Gandhara but all deserted and in ruins; the *stupas* were mostly decayed. A tower was associated with the Buddha's begging bowl (*patra*). All the four Buddhas were believed to have sat under the same *pipal* tree and their sitting figures were now seen there. It was believed that the remaining 996 Buddhas who were yet to appear would also sit under this tree. Its precincts were guarded by 'secret spiritual influences'. There was a *stupa* built by Kanishka for the relics of the Buddha in accordance with the Sakya Buddha's prophecy, but all his wealth and power could not make it higher than the small *stupa* already in existence which rose higher and higher supernaturally with the rising *stupa* of Kanishka. Both these *stupas* were still there and people burnt incense and offered flowers with a sincere faith to seek cures for serious illness. There were two replicas of these *stupas*, and two full-size figures of the Buddha with which a legend was associated. There was also a painted figure of the Buddha, about sixteen feet in height with two bodies from the middle upwards, and with an appropriate legend associated with it. Another figure of the Buddha in white stone, about eighteen feet high on a great *stupa*, was believed to have 'many spiritual powers'; sometimes it was seen going around the *stupa*; and it could pursue robbers and frighten them. A hundred little *stupas* were built with consummate art on the left and right of the great stupa : 'Exquisite perfumes and different musical sounds at times are perceived, the work of Rishis, saints, and eminent sages; these also, at times are seen walking round the *stupas*.' A monastery built by Kanishka had double towers, connected terraces, and deep chambers, which bore testimony to the eminence of its great *arhats*. Now there were just a few monks who studied the Hinayana. There was a tower associated

[42] B., II, pp.136, 204, 217, 260; W., II, pp.138-9 (does not agree with Beal's version), 193, 209, 242.

with Parava who had vowed not to rest until he had thoroughly grasped 'the wisdom of the three *Pitakas*' and got rid of 'the evil desire of the three worlds', obtained 'the six miraculous powers', and reached 'the eight deliverances'. An old building was associated with Vasubandhu, the Bodhisattva; a two-storeyed pavillion was associated with Manorhita, the author of the *Vibhasha Shastra*. Both of them had vanquished many a 'heretic' in debate. There was a *stupa* built by Ashoka on a spot where the four Buddhas had delivered the law. Vasumitra had composed his *Abhidharmaprakarna-pada Shastra* in this place. A few monks in the nearby monastery followed the Hinayana. Dharmatrata had composed his *Samyuktabhi-dharma Shastra* here. Another *stupa* built by Ashoka, with carved wood and veined stone, was the work of various artists. The Sakya Buddha had taken births in the country a thousand times to prepare himself as a Bodhisattva by offering his eyes each time. Two tall and grand *stupas*, built by Brahma Deva and Shakara, were in ruins. Another *stupa* was associated with the Mother of the demons who had been converted to *ahimsa* by the Sakya Buddha: 'the common folk of this country offer sacrifices to obtain children from her'. Another *stupa* was associated with Samaka Bodhisattva (known as Sarwan in Punjabi folklore) who had dedicated his life to the service of his blind parents. In two monasteries near Pushkalavati were about a hundred monks, divided equally between the Hinayana and the Mahayana. There were a few *stupas* attributed to Ashoka. Another *stupa* marked the spot where an Arhat had converted a disciple of Panini.[43]

The kingdom of Mathura was important in its own way. There were about twenty monasteries, with 2,000 monks who studied equally the Mahayana and the Hinayana. Three *stupas* were attributed to Ashoka, with very many 'traces' of the four past Buddhas. There were *stupas* to commemorate the holy followers of the Sakya Buddha, like Sariputra, Mudgalaputra, Purnamaitrayaniputra, Upali, Ananda, Rahula, and Manjushri. There were *stupas* of other Bodhisattvas too. During the three months of fasting, and during the six fasting days of each month, monks resorted to these various *stupas* with precious offerings. Sariputra was honoured by those who studied the *Abhidharma*. Mudgalaputra was honoured by those who practised meditation. Purnamaitrayaniputra was honoured by those who recited the

[43] B., I, pp.97-118; W., I, pp.198-224.

Sutras. Upali was reverenced by those who studied the *Vinaya*. All the nuns (*bhikshunis*) honoured Ananda, and all the Shramaneras honoured Rahula. The Bodhisattvas were honoured by those who studied the Mahayana. These occasions were marked by the unfurling of jewelled banners and rich parasols, the smoke of incense, and the sight of flowers. 'The king of the country and the great ministers apply themselves to these religious duties with zeal'. Upagupta had constructed cells for monks by piercing the hill sides to form a monastery. There was also a *stupa* containing the nail-pairings of the Tathagata. There was a stone house filled with small wooden tokens four inches long, each representing the conversion of a couple at the hands of Upagupta. He did not keep count of the individuals he converted to Buddhism. There was another *stupa* which marked the spot where a monkey had died to serve the Tathagata; it was then born as a man due to the religious merit it had acquired. In the midst of a great wood beside a lake there were traces of the four former Buddhas walking to and fro. There were *stupas* erected to commemorate the spots where 1,250 great Arhats, including Sariputra and Mudgalaputra, had practised *samadhi* and left traces thereof.[44]

Magadha was extremely imporant for Hiuen Tsiang. The first of its 84,000 *stupas* was built in the palace of Ashoka at Pataliputra. Its foundation wall had sunk, and it was in a leaning, ruinous condition. The crowning jewel of its cupola was intact. It was made of carved stone, and had a surrounding balustrade. 'Spiritual indications constantly manifest themselves, and a divine light is shed around it from time to time'. On a suggestion from Upagupta, who had converted Ashoka to Buddhism, the emperor ordered the 'spirits and genii' to raise *stupas* for the relics of the Buddha throughout Jambudvipa (India) to the very last house. When they completed this meritorious work and reported to Ashoka, he distributed the Buddha's relics to them to be deposited simultaneously in all the *stupas*. Ashoka had also built a monastery close to the city for 1,000 monks, but now it was in ruins. Close to it was the *stupa* he had built to commemorate his recovery from illness due to the prayers of the monks. The 'heretic' scholars of Vaishali defeated the Buddhist monks in a debate and the gong (*ghanta*) of the monastery was

[44] B., I, pp.179-83; W., I, pp.301-13.

not sounded for twelve years. Deva, a great disciple of Nagarjuna who lived in the South, then engaged the heretic scholars in debate and refuted all their arguments. A *stupa* was built to commemorate his victory. About forty miles from the city was a monastery in ruins, with a *stupa* by its side which reflected a divine light from time to time and displayed many miracles. A thousand monks studied the Mahayana in another monastery. There was an image of the Buddha, about thirty feet high; on its left was an image of Tara Bodhisattva and on its right the image of Avalokiteshvara Bodhisattva; their appearance inspired mysterious awe. In another monastery there were about fifty monks studying the Mahayana. Gunamati Bodhisattva came from the South, defeated the Brahmans in debate, and established his monastery with an endowment from the ruler. Shilabhadra established his monastery about four miles away when his merit had been recognized in a debate with a heretic of the South. Tathagata had delivered some of his *sutras* on a mountain close to Gaya. A *stupa* was built here by Ashoka. 'Divine prodigies are exhibited by it, and a sacred effulgency often shines from it'. Ashoka built *stupas* at all those spots which were believed to be associated with the Buddha. The Bodhi tree was surrounded by a strong brick wall with gates. The enclosed space contained many sacred traces. 'The kings, princes, and great personages, throughout all Jambudvipa, who have accepted the bequeathed teaching as handed down to them, have erected these monuments as memorials.' The diamond throne was in the middle of the enclosure. 'When the great earth is shaken, this place alone is unmoved.' Close to the Bodhi tree were a number of *stupas* and *viharas*, with the relics of the Buddha and the images of the Buddhas and Bodhisattvas. Then there were *stupas* and *viharas* at many other places associated with the Buddha. The monastery at Nalanda marked the place where Tathagata had practised the life of a Bodhisattva. It was purchased by 500 merchants and offered to the Buddha for preaching the law. Monasteries were built here by the rulers of the land after the Buddha's *Nirvana*. A king of Central India also built a monastery here. There were several thousand monks in Nalanda; hundreds of them had become famous. The rules of the monastery were strict. From morning till night the monks remained engaged in discussions. Learned men from different cities came here to settle their doubts. One had to study old and new books deeply for getting admission. Among the illustrious personages of Nalanda were Dharmapala,

Chandrapala, Gunamati, Sthiramati, Prabhamitra, Jinamitra, Jnanachandra, Sigrabuddha, and Shilabhadra. Each of them composed some tens of treatises and commentaries which were widely diffused. There were hundreds of sacred relics on the four sides of the monastery. Hiuen Tsiang describes only some of them, mostly *stupas* and *viharas*. Then there were many other *stupas* and monasteries associated with the Buddha and Bodhisattvas.[45]

Other 'countries' were not so important as Magadha or Gandhara. The monasteries in the Chola country were in ruins and the monks were dirty. There was a *stupa* attributed to Ashoka and associated with the Tathagata's preaching of the law to the heretics and guiding both men and Devas. An old monastery was associated with Deva Bodhisattva's discussion with a Buddhist monk who acknowledged his superiority.[46] Buddhism was no longer important in the Chola country. This was not true of Dravida in the far south which had about a hundred monasteries and 10,000 monks. They all studied the teaching of the Sthavira school of Mahayana. Tathagata was believed to have frequented this country much, and Ashoka had built *stupas* over all the sacred spots. The city of Kanchipura was the native place of Dharmapala Bodhisattva. In the south of the city was a monastery in which men renowned for talent and learning assembled and stayed. There was a *stupa* attributed to Ashoka, built on a spot where Tathagata was believed to have converted both men and Devas.[47]

There were twenty monasteries and about 3,000 monks in Andhra. A monastery near Vengi was beautifully carved and ornamented, with a figure of the Buddha portrayed with great artistic power. A *stupa* of stone was several hundred feet high. Another *stupa*, attributed to Ashoka, commemorated Tathagata's successful preaching in the region. In another *stupa* on the top of a mountain Jina Bodhisattva had composed a *Shāstra* which, as advised by Manjushri Bodhisattva, enshrined the philosophic principle of saving all in accordance with the *Yogāchārya-bhumi Shāstra* of Maitreya Bodhisattva.[48]

In Maharashtra there were about 100 monasteries and 5,000

[45] B., II, pp.82-185; W., II, pp.86-178.

[46] B., II, 227-28; W., II, pp.224-226.

[47] B., II, pp.228-30; W., II, pp.226-28.

[48] B., II, pp.217-20; W., II, pp.209-14.

monks who followed both the Hinayana and the Mahayana. Five *stupas* built by Ashoka marked the spots where the four Buddhas walked and sat. There were many other *stupas* made of brick or stone. To the south of the capital was a monastery with the image of a Bodhisattva : 'many of those who have secretly prayed to it have obtained their wishes.' In the east of the country 'in a dark defile' among hills was the famous cave-monastery now known as Ajanta. On the stone walls of the monastery of Arhat Achara were painted with the greatest accuracy and fineness different scenes in the life of Tathagata's preparatory life as a Bodhisattva. On the gate of this monastery was a stone elephant.[49]

In Sindh there were several hundred monasteries and about 10,000 monks who studied Hinayana according to the Sammatiya School. The pastoral people in Sindh wore robes of monks and, holding to their narrow views, they attacked the Mahayana.[50]

The 'countries' taken up here for illustration represent only a fourth of the total number but they indicate the nature of Hiuen Tsiang's interest : the prevalence or decay of Buddhism, its monasteries and *stupas* and their architecture and sculpture, the works of Buddhist literature and its main branches, the past and present scholars of Buddhism, the affiliation of monks to Hinayana or Mahayana, their mutual relations, the Buddhas and Bodhisattvas and the myths and legends associated with them, Ashoka and Kanishka as the legendary patrons of Buddhism, appropriation of local cults, and the superstitious lore and miracles associated with numerous Buddhist places.

IV

A review of the foregoing sections suggests, first, that Hiuen Tsiang equated India broadly with the Indian subcontinent. Significantly, however, its north-western frontier was situated in Afghanistan. It is difficult to think that his criterion for this demarcation was geographical, or even political. He seems to have been guided by cultural considerations. There were regional variations in India in terms of physical features, climate and vegetation. Geographically, the people were not conscious of a pan-India identity.

The country was divided into a large number of states. Even the most powerful rulers held sway only in a part of the

[49] B., II, pp.255-59; W., II, pp.239-41.
[50] B., II, pp.272-73; W., II, pp.252, 254.

subcontinent. There was a certain degree of decentralization of power and no uniformity of administrative practices. There is no doubt about the existence of towns and cities, or the practice of trade, but few references to manufactures. There is no indication of networks for pan-Indian or foreign trade. The economy appears to have been predominantly agrarian and pastoral. Thus, neither polity nor economy could impinge upon local or regional affiliations.

Hiuen Tsiang bears witness to social differentiation in terms of the four castes, and the outcastes. He was more interested in the social life of the Brahmans and the Kshatriyas who formed the apex of the social order. The Vaishyas, equated with traders and shopkeepers, formed the middling order. The Shudras as peasants and the outcastes formed the lower orders, and accounted for the bulk of the population. The principle of heredity and the endogamous system divided the social order into a large number of separate compartments. At the bottom of the hierarchical scale were the outcastes with their various callings. The Shudras were clearly above them but below the Vaishyas who were socially distinct from both the Brahmans and the Kshatriyas. Spirituality was not equally accessible to all classes of men. That the women were disadvantaged is evident from the statement that they could marry only once. This carries the implication of early marriage and widowhood. There is no reference to the practice of *sati*. There is a reference to Buddhist nuns.

Hiuen Tsiang tended to assume that there was only one language and one script in India but his own evidence points to regional variations in both the language and script. Concerned solely with Sanskrit, the language of the learned, he appears not to have taken interest in the spoken languages of the people. But he does talk of 'dialects'. Some of the religious systems were also pan-Indian, like Buddhism, Jainism, and Shaivism. They all existed side by side in different parts of the country, sometimes with some tension. The existence of the laity may be assumed though the pilgrim's references are mostly to monastic orders. There were religious places which attracted people from different parts of the country, like the temple of Bhima Devi, the Sun Temple at Multan, and places like Kurukshetra, Varanasi, Prayaga, and Nalanda. The river Ganges was regarded as sacred by most people. Thus, there were systems and institutions which transcended regional concerns. On the whole, however, diversities were as striking as uniformities even at the regional level.

6

Evolution of a Regional Identity: Kerala in India

KESAVAN VELUTHAT

One basic requirement of history as knowledge is that its practitioners, located in the present, must try to understand and explain the past. This may sound like a truism; but historians often tend to forget this simple nature of their business. They are sometimes given to think that they are studying the past in its own terms; some would make a plea to spurn the 'Euro-centric' approach to Indian history and adopt an 'indigenous' view. But, the reality is that the historian cannot escape familiar categories and patterns in his attempts to come to grips with the past. These categories and patterns, it must be noted, are artefacts of the present, the ones through which the present looks at itself. They are not from the past which is the historian's subject-matter; on the contrary, they belong to the present, with the help of which the historian seeks to understand, and occasionally to manipulate, the past.

Units of historical study are typical examples of choice made under these pressures. Ranging from vast entities such as the whole world itself or more romantic ones such as civilizations, they include smaller and smaller units such as regions, localities, villages or even households. It is not as if these units offer themselves as so many 'natural' objects of historical study. It is the historian, with his own agenda, who identifies his units. The constituent-constituted relationship among them is often lost sight of as also the changing nature of both. In the present chapter we seek to substantiate this argument by presenting a report on the attempt to look for the idea of India in sources from the Malayāḷam-speaking region and to examine how the two categories (the 'local' and the 'global') were constituted, and interacted with each other, from the time that evidence expressing these ideas is available in literature. We shall also see how these two changed at a particular point in time, which change was dictated by the changing socio-economic and political circumstances.

Of these units, some are larger in extent than the others and, in a geographical sense, include these others within them. The combination often makes the smaller of the two look as if it is part' of the larger one. Sometimes it is as if the number of boxes within boxes goes on increasing, as in the case of Kēraḷa in India in the early historical period. It did exist in its own way; it was included in a larger socio-cultural unit called 'Tamiḻakam'; and it was located within the geographical limits of the subcontinent that goes by the name 'India'. It can be seen, however, that these identities and affiliations were not fixed at any point in time; they underwent transformations over long or short periods. An examination of these aspects in some detail will demonstrate the essentially historical character of the process of the emergence of such identities. It was not a 'natural' process: there were forces behind such 'emergences'. This chapter will also seek to explain these forces, placing the process within the social and economic context in which the processes were taking place.

To be sure, early sources do not use the term 'Kēraḷa' to denote the land that now goes by that name. The term Cēra/Cēramān occurs in early Tamiḻ literature in the sense of a lineage of chiefs.[1] The Prakrit/Sanskrit translation of the term Cēramān, namely Ketalaputa/Kēraḷaputra, figures in the edicts of Aśōka. The Greco-Roman accounts of the early centuries of the Christian era use a Greek variant, Kerobotros/Kaelobotros.[2] Many places in the Malayāḷam-speaking region of today figure in the copious literature in Tamiḻ produced in this period; and many lineages of that region are mentioned in this literature. But there is no notion of Kēraḷa as a geographical unit. Tamiḻakam is the land south of Vēnkaṭam, north of Kumari (Cape Camorin) and bounded by the seas on either side: This was the Tamil homeland, which subsumed present-day Kēraḷa as its integral part. Nor does the Malayāḷam language or even its name figure in any of the sources of this period. There are occasional references to variations in linguistic usage described as features characteristic of Malaināṭu, a purely geographical name by which the land west of the Western Ghats was known. Even these references are of a much later date, occurring in the medieval commentaries to the early Tamiḻ anthologies.

The earliest definitive reference to Kēraḷa as a separate geographical entity, with the use of that name, is arguably in the

[1] N. Subramanian, *Pre-Pallavan Tamil Index*, Madras, 1990, s.v., Chērakulam, Chēramān, several individual Chēramāns (20 entries), Chēral, Chēralan, Chēralādan, Chēran, pp. 392-5.

[2] R.C.Majumdar, ed., *Classical Accounts of India*, Calcutta, 1960, pp. 305, 312, 339, 365, 376 and 381.

Avantisundarīkathā of Daṇḍin.[3] The author, the eighth century Sanskrit poet from the Pallava capital in Kāñci, speaks of his friends including Mātṛdatta, 'the best of Brāhmaṇas from Kērala'. In the fashion characteristic of Sanskrit, Daṇḍin uses Kēraḷa in the plural (*Kēraḷeṣu*), showing thereby that it was already familiar as the name of a country. In the same century or early in the next, Śaktibhadra, a dramatist from Kēraḷa, composed *Āścaryacūḍāmaṇi*, a Sanskrit play where the author speaks of the unlikelihood of it being a composition coming from the South, demonstrating not only its distinctiveness but also its affiliation to a larger whole of a Sanskrit literary world all over India.[4] He does not, to be sure, refer to Kēraḷa by name. A junior contemporary of Śaktibhadra does it, almost with vengeance. He was Kulaśēkharavarman, a ninth-century king of Kēraḷa, and the author of *Subhadrādhanañjaya* and *Tapatīsaṃvaraṇa*, two Sanskrit plays and perhaps one more, *Vicchinnābhiṣēka*, as well as a work in prose, *Āścaryamañjarī*. He has been identified with Sthāṇu Ravi Kulaśēkhara (AD 844-883) of the inscriptions, and with the Vaiṣṇava Bhakti saint known as Kulaśēkhara Āḻvār, author of *Perumāḷ Tirumoḻi* in Tamiḻ and *Mukundamālā* in Sanskrit.[5] Kulaśēkharavarman describes himself as *Kēraḷakulacūḍāmaṇi* and *Kēraḷādhinātha* in the Sanskrit plays.[6] While the former is a reference to the Kēraḷa or Cēra lineage to which he belonged, the latter is an unmistakable reference to the Kēraḷa country of which he was the ruler. In fact, he styles himself more authentically as *Mahōdayapuraparamēśvara*, 'Supreme Lord of the city of Mahōdayapura', than as *Kēraḷādhinātha*, the 'Overlord of Kēraḷa', a statement with significant political implications. In any case, a slightly later text clarifies that the king of Mahōdayapurm protected Kēraḷaviṣaya, 'the land of Kēraḷa'.[7] So also, a contemporary of

[3] '*Mitrāṇi mātṛdattādyāḥ kēraḷēṣu dvijōttamāḥ.*' Daṇḍin, *Avantisundarīkathāsāra*, quoted in Ulloor S. Parameswara Iyer, *Kēraḷasāhityacaritram*, I, Trivandrum, 1967, pp.103-4. Kalidāsa, in his *Raghuvamśa*, has an obscure reference to Kerala, so have others. They are, however, inconsequential.

[4] There is the introduction of the play in the prologue of *Āścaryacūḍāmaṇi* where the actress says that a drama from the South is as much of an improbability as flowers from the sky or oil from sand!

[5] M.G.S.Narayanan, *Perumāḷs of Kēraḷa*, Calicut, 1996, p. 213.

[6] '*Kēraḷakulacūḍāmaṇēḥ mahōdayapuraparamēśvarasya śrīkulaśēkharavarmaṇaḥ...*', *Tapatīsamvaraṇam*, prologue. '*Kaḷamarāśipēśalakaidārika kēraḷādhināthasya kulaśēkharavarmaṇō...*' *Subadrādhanañjayam*, Prologue.

[7] '*Kēraḷaviṣayam pālikkānāy mahitamahōdayanilayē maruvum nṛpasimhasya...*', *Anantapuravarnanam*.

Kulaśēkhara describes his patron as 'ruling the earth', *vasudhām+avataḥ*, punning on which he also says that he possessed resources as well as his own city [of Mahōdayapuram] (*vasu+dhāmavataḥ*).[8] *Vyaṅgyavyākhyā*, commentaries of the plays composed during the playwright's lifetime, describes the author as a *Kēraḷaviṣayādhipa* or the lord of the Kēraḷa-*viṣaya*.[9] In short, Kēraḷa gets defined as a geographical unit with definite boundaries, and that territory also becomes the territory of a political unit by the ninth century.

Interestingly, we start getting references to Kēraḷa as a separate political unit in the records of the Cālukyas, Pallavas and Pāṇḍyas a little earlier and of the Cōḻas by the time of these plays.[10] Whether the early references are to the lineage of the Cēras or the country of Kēraḷa, the later ones, found in Cōḻa records, are certainly to the Kēraḷa country. It is significant that this coincides with the emergence of the state in what is now Kēraḷa. The Cēra kingdom of Mahōdayapuram or Makōtai makes its appearance in the records, at least from the beginning of the ninth century.[11] This kingdom is to be distinguished from the chiefdom of the Cēras found in an earlier period, evidence of which is available in ancient Tamil poetry, Aśōkan edicts and the Tamiḻ Brāhmi cave label inscriptions.[12] The rise of this later Cēra kingdom of

[8] K. Kunjunni Raja, *The Contribution of Kerala to Sanskrit Literature*, Madras, 1980, p.20, nn. 95-96.

[9] '*kulaśēkharanāmnā kēraḷādhipēna...*' *Vyaṅgyavyākhyā*, quoted by N.P.Unni, *Sanskrit Dramas of Kulaśēkhara: A Study*, Trivandrum, 1977, p.24.

[10] Kēraḷa starts figuring in the lists of conquests made by the Cālukyas, Pallavas and Pāṇḍyas from this period on. Narayanan, *Perumāls...*, op.cit., chapter on 'Early Wars and Alliances'. Much of this is conventional and it is not very clear whether Kēraḷa there stands for the lineage or the country. Other references are indefinite.

[11] The history of the Cēra kingdom of Mahōdayapuram was reconstructed only in the second half of the 20th century. The epigraphical sources were published in the late nineteenth and early twentieth centuries; but it was the work of Elamkulam P.N.Kunjan Pillai that was responsible for bringing out the outline of the history of that kingdom. Pillai wrote largely in Malayāḷam. For a summary of his more important articles in English, Elamkulam P.N.Kunjan Pillai, *Studies in Kerala History*, Kottayam, 1969. Improving upon the work of Pillai, M.G.S. Narayanan wrote a somewhat exhaustive history of this Kingdom. (Narayanan, *Perumāḷs ...*, op.cit.)

[12] This lineage of the Cēras is celebrated in several early Tamiḻ songs, the *PatihḤuppattu* being devoted exclusively for them. A few 'cave label' inscriptions from Pugaliyur near Karur mention the names of some of these chiefs. Works like K.G.Sesha Aiyar, *Chera Kings of the Sangam Period*, London, 1937, and S.Krishnaswami Aiyangar, *Śēran Vañji*, Madras, 1912, deal with the 'political history' of this early Tamil 'kingdom'. It had its 'capital'

Mahōdayapuram was not just another 'event' in the political history of this region; it represented the culmination of a series of complex processes with far-reaching consequences for economy, society and polity. The entire area covered by the modern linguistic state of Kēraḷa formed the territory of this newly formed state and a kind of uniformity, however loosely defined, is seen in this area.[13] Inscriptions from this period, discovered from the entire length of Kēraḷa, bear the stamp of a single socio-political unit, which was presided over by the Cēra Perumāḷ. The same language and script are used in these records,[14] which are dated in the regnal years of the Cēra Perumāḷ or else follow some other means of dating such as the mention of the position of Jupiter, use of the Śaka or Kali era, etc., which were known all over the region. Conventions accepted all over the area emerged, and among these there was some kind of uniformity in the matter of the organisation and functioning of the agrarian corporations of Brāhmaṇical groups.[15]

in the interior, in the Tirucchirappalli district, and it may have covered also regions on the west coast. It is important to remember that the Cēra kingdom of Mahōdayapuram has to be distinguished from this earlier chiefdom.

[13] This is not to suggest that the Cēra kingdom of Mahōdayapuram represented a uniform structure with complete political control over the entire territory of Kēraḷa from Kasaragod to Thiruvananthapuram. An earlier fashion of historiography represented by Elamkulam Kunjan Pillai, op.cit., had believed that this 'Second Cēra Empire', or 'Kulaśēkhara Empire' was a highly centralised polity. However, M.G.S.Narayanan, *Perumāḷs...*, op.cit., offered a major corrective to this. In fact, Narayanan has recently taken a position on the other extreme that the Cēra Perumāḷ had only a ritual sovereignty and the actual political power rested with 'a bold and visible brahman oligarchy' which was only 'thinly disguised as a monarchy to satisfy the sentiments of the lawgivers of India'! M.G.S.Narayanan, 'The State in the Era of the Cēraman Perumāḷs of Kerala', in R. Champakalakshmi, Kesavan Veluthat and T.R.Venugopalan, eds., *State and Society in Premodern South India*, Thrissur, 2002, pp. 111-19. While we cannot go all the way with this formulation, Kunjan Pillai's model of a highly centralised empire is not acceptable either.

[14] The political importance of the use of a uniform script and language has not been adequately recognized at least in the context of the history of Kēraḷa. Script, unless used for purposes of trade, can be one of those engines used by a political agency to impose its authority over vast areas in pre-modern contexts where the use of literacy for purposes of communication was limited.

[15] The Brāhmaṇical corporations of Kēraḷa had a pivotal role in the power structure of the power structure of the Cēra kingdom. This was adequately appreciated only in the work of M.G.S.Narayanan, *Perumāḷs...* The present writer has elaborated on this. Kesavan Veluthat, *Brahaman Settlements in Kerala*, Calicut, 1978, particularly, pp. 52-67. For a slightly different perception, Raghava Varier and Rajan Gurukkal, *Kēraḷacaritram*, Śukapuram, 1989.

It is also significant that this identity and uniformity were defined in contradistinction with what was obtaining in the Tuḷu-speaking regions to the north and the Tamil̲-speaking regions to the south and east.

The emergence of the Cēra kingdom of Mahōdayapuram marks the beginning of a new era in the history of Kēraḷa, as indeed does the emergence of the new state under the Pallavas or Pāṇḍyas in relation to the respective regions in south India. An epochal transformation has been identified in this process, and a veritable 'transition debate' has grown around it.[16] The social formation of the early historical period, described somewhat wrongly by historians as the 'Sangam Period', was characterised by a subsistence economy maintained by family labour, reciprocity and patronage. A highly differentiated economy and society, with extra-kin labour, production of surplus and its distribution and notions of pricing and profit in exchange, came to replace the older one by the time the new state, as for example the Cēra kingdom of Mahōdayapuram on the west coast, was established in south India.[17] A characteristic feature of the state that came into existence by this period, under the Pallavas, Pāṇḍyas, Cēras and Cōl̲as, is the highly Kṣatriya-ised monarchy which presided over them, answering in every detail to the model available in the *kāvya-śāstra-nāṭaka* literature in Sanskrit. In the case of Kēraḷa, there were further differences from its counterparts elsewhere in south India.[18]

One of the factors responsible for the formation of the state and the peculiar character it had as distinct from the rest of south India was the rise of Brāhmaṇical settlements in the river valleys of Kēraḷa. Although some Brāhmaṇical presence with the characteristic Paraśurāma tradition of the west coast and a Vedic sacrificial background is noticed in Kēraḷa early in the age of the Tamil̲ anthologies such as *Akanān̲ūḤu*,[19] the majority of them took

[16] For a discussion, Kesavan Veluthat, "Into the 'Medieval' – and Out of It: Early South India in Transition", Presidential Address, Section II, Medieval Indian History, Indian History Congress, 58th session, Bangalore, 1997.

[17] Ibid.

[18] For the image of royalty in south India and how it was different from what obtained in earlier period, Kesavan Veluthat, *Political Structure of Medieval South India*, New Delhi, 1993, chapter on the 'Image of Royalty'. The difference that the Cēra kingdom presented is discussed there. See also M.G.S.Narayanan, *Perumals of Kerala*, Calicut, 1996, chapter on "Nature of Monarchy".

[19] *Akanān̲ūḤu*, 220. For an analysis, Kesavan Veluthat, *Brahman Settlements in Kerala*, pp.12-20.

shape only in the period of the transition from the early historical to early medieval period.[20] These were somewhat unique in ways more than one. The Brāhmaṇas of Kēraḷa cherished the Paraśurāma tradition, something which they shared with their counterparts in the rest of the west coast but distinct from other parts of the peninsula.[21] They developed a number of unusual practices, known as *anācāras*, and these distinguished the Brāhmaṇas of Kēraḷa from those in the rest of India.[22] There was difference in the pattern of settlements, which was a function of the physiography and ecology of the region.[23] In any case, the Brāhmaṇical settlements of Kēraḷa developed certain features that were entirely different from their counterparts in other parts of the peninsula. This Brāhmaṇical character with the Paraśurāma stamp can be seen from the statement in an eleventh-century Cōḻa record, the Tiruvālaṅgāḍu Copper Plates, describing Kēraḷa as "the land created by Rāma who takes pleasure in exterminating the Kṣatriyas and where good people live with joy".[24] At the same time, they also shared, with the rest of south India or perhaps the entire country, many common features of what was laid down in the Dharmaśāstra texts in the matter of their community organisation, even when the Dharmaśāstras were flouted with impunity in the matter of many of the *anācāras* as well as other practices.

The introduction of the Brāhmaṇical element with the Paraśurāma tradition seems to be the starting point of the distinctiveness of Kēraḷa and its departure from the rest of Tamiḻakam. The Brāhmaṇical claim, that it was Paraśurāma who created *their* land and donated it to *them*, is seen all over the

[20] This transition could be located between the third-fourth and seventh-eighth centuries of the Christian era. Kesavan Veluthat, 'Into the 'Medieval' – and Out of It': ..., op. cit.

[21] For a study of the Paraśurāma tradition of the Brāhmaṇas of the west coast of India, B.A. Saletore, *Ancient Karnataka*, vol. I, *History of Tuluva* (Poona, 1936). For a recent study, Pradeep Kant Chaudhury, 'The Cult of Parashuram: A Study in the Making of an Avatara', Ph.D. thesis, Delhi University, 2001.

[22] They are called *anācāras* not because they were 'forbidden practices'. *Anyatrācaraṇābhāvād anācāra itīritaḥ.* A list of 64 of them is given in the law-book of Kēraḷa Brāhmaṇas attributed to Śaṅkarācārya. For the list, William Logan, *Malabar*, I, (Madras, 1886), pp.156-7.

[23] Joan P. Mencher, 'Kerala and Madras: A Comparative Study of Ecology and Social Structure', *Ethnology*, University of Pittsburg, Pennsylvania, V, part II, pp-135-71.

[24] "*Sarvakṣatravadhavratapraṇayinā rāmēṇa yannirmitam rāṣṭram śiṣṭajanābhirāmam atulam* ...", *South Indian Inscriptions*, III, p.398.

western seaboard in India. In the case of the south, it is the strip of land from Gōkarṇa to Kanyākumāri which is identified as the land retrieved by Paraśurāma. Gradually, even this unit disintegrates, as the land between Perumpuḷa (in Kasaragod district) and Kanyākumāri is defined as actually the Malanāṭu within the Paraśurāma-*kṣētra.* This newly defined unit was earlier a part of Tamiḻakam, but there is a conscious rejection of this affiliation in the changed context. The historical tradition of this new formation does not cherish details concerning the earlier Cēra rulers and their exploits contained in early Tamiḻ songs such as the *Patiṛṛuppattu* any more. For instance, a Malayāḷam narrative called *Kēraḷōlpatti,* concerned with the history of Kēraḷa, is totally silent about this aspect of the past. The contents of this narrative date from this period, although the date of its composition itself is problematic.[25]

This text is significant as an attempt to historicise Kēraḷa as a separate unit, with its own defined territory and peculiar institutions. It opens by giving an account of Paraśurāma's creation of Kēraḷa, the land between Gōkarṇa and Kanyākumāri, by claiming it from the Arabian Sea with a fling of his axe and settling it by Brāhmaṇas brought from the North in 64 *grāma*s, of which 32 are in Tuḷunāḍu and the remaining in present-day Kēraḷa. Speaking about the way in which Paraśurāma peopled the land of Kēraḷa after raising it from the sea, the *Kēraḷōlpatti* says that the Brāhmaṇas, who were brought and settled in the first instance, would not stay; they returned to their original home in Ahicchatra (a historical place and now also an archaeological site in Northern India) for fear of serpents in the new land. Paraśurāma brought a second wave of Brāhmaṇas, again from Ahicchatra. In order that they would not be accepted back 'home' if they returned, he had their hair style and dress code changed. He also persuaded them to accept the mother right so that he could expiate for his own matricidal sin; but only those of one village, namely Payyannūr, obliged him by following matrilineal descent. Paraśurāma also established 108 temples each for Śiva, Śāstā and Durgā. He chose 36,000 Brāhmaṇas from the different *grāmas* and conferred on

[25] The date of this text is a matter of debate among historians; nor is there agreement regarding its validity as a "source" of history. For a discussion, and a plea to look at it as an expression of the historical consciousness rather than as a source of history, Kesavan Veluthat, "The *Keralolpatti* as History: A Note on the Pre-Colonial Traditions of Historiography", Paper presented in a seminar at the Ecole des Hautes Etudes en Sciences Sociales, Paris, May, 2002.

them the right to arms (*śastrabhikṣā*), so that they could protect their land themselves.

There is the crucial difference between the situation in Kēraḷa and the land immediately to its north, viz. South Canara. It is a significant indication of the difference in the role of the Brāhmaṇical groups in the two societies. The landed wealth in South Canara was not under the control of the Brāhmaṇical groups as much as it was in Kēraḷa and, therefore, the importance that the Brāhmaṇas of Kēraḷa had in polity and society was not matched by what their counterparts in South Canara had. As it was much greater in the case of Kēraḷa, Paraśurāma is invoked as not only the creator of the land but also the donor to the Brāhmaṇa groups. So also the exceptional importance attached to the arms-bearing Brāhmaṇas called *śastra-Brāhmaṇas* or *cāttirar* and their group meetings is another instance of the use of the past in seeking validation of the Brāhmaṇical groups in Kēraḷa society. Paraśurāma established a *Brahmakṣatra* in Kēraḷa, where Brāhmaṇas looked after the work of the Kṣatriyas, with every arrangement for the welfare of the people, including religion, administration and law. The Brāhmaṇical authority in Kēraḷa was so great that it took Viṣṇu as Paraśurāma, a Brāhmaṇical *avatāra* with sufficient Kṣatriya pretensions, to legitimise it. And, that underlined the distinctiveness of Kēraḷa with reference to the Tuḷu country, too.

In the next period taken up in the narrative, the text shows that the Brāhmaṇical groups played a major role in society and politics. Representatives of the Brāhmaṇical establishment governed the land gifted to them by Paraśurāma as *Brahmakṣatra.* In course of time, however, they realised that the business of governance corrupted them, and they themselves decided to get a Kṣatriya as their ruler. Accordingly, a Kṣatriya and his sister were brought; the brother was anointed king and was made to swear habitual allegiance to them. A monarchical state was established in Kēraḷa. The sister was married to a Brāhmaṇa and it was agreed that the progeny would belong to the Kṣatriya caste according to the matrilineal system of succession. The descendants of this sister would be the successors to the throne. The conviction that government was not the Brāhmaṇas' proper occupation and that it belonged to the Kṣatriya is very much in tune with the Brāhmaṇical principles and the theory of *varṇāśramadharma.* The upper caste, Brāhmaṇical character of it all is hard to miss, both in the narrative and in other contemporary records. At the same time, there is no attempt to latch the origin of the dynasty on either to one of the reputed Kṣatriya lineages of Purāṇic fame or to those celebrated in the Tamiḻ tradition; nor is an origin myth in the tradition typical of the medieval court literature in Sanskrit invented or the heroic deeds of the ruler or his ancestors recited. All this would show that Kēraḷa had arrived as a separate political entity and that the *Kēraḷōlpatti* was historicising it.

One feature which distinguished the new formation was its 'religion'. The cults and practices of the earlier period, aimed at the propitiation of the deities of the *tiṇais*, gave way to the worship of *Āgamaic* deities consecrated in temples. The Brāhmaṇical element had a not insignificant role to play in this, for all the Brāhmaṇical settlements, which functioned as agrarian corporations controlling vast estates of land, were centred on temples. The native population was brought within their magnetic field, and this provided the necessary claims for the hegemonic elements to command the acquiescence of the hegemonized. Taking place in the period of the celebrated 'Bhakti Movement' in south India, of which at least two leaders were Cēra Perumāḷs themsleves, this religious transformation was very crucial for the realignment of identities as well. Gods worshipped by the people were part of a larger pan-Indian tradition from now on, and all the traditions of the epics and Purāṇas in Sanskrit became part of the heritage of anybody who identified himself with this 'new' religion. Sanskrit was getting precedence over Tamiḻ, the fact that literary productions of the early leaders of the 'Bhakti Movement' from Kēraḷa were in Tamiḻ notwithstanding. To be considered along with religion, if not as part of it, is caste. It is here that Kēraḷa presents its distinctiveness in the clearest manner. Interestingly, the *Kēraḷōlpatti* has a whole section giving details about the innumerable castes and the relative status of each defining the norms of purity and pollution and attributing the entire system to the inevitable Śaṅkarācārya.

The heavy Sanskritic nature of the ideas and institutions obtaining in this newly emerged political-cultural unit is obvious. Prescriptions of the *dharmaśāstras* are followed in matters of social conduct and statecraft. In fact, even in laying down the details of the organization of an urban centre under the Christian church at Kurakkēṇi Kollam, it is the model of the *Arthaśāstra* that is followed. In cultural matters, the repertoire of the Sanskrit epics, *Rāmayaṇa* and *Mahābhārata*, is used heavily as the earliest dramas such as the *Āścaryacūḍāmaṇi*, *Subhadrādhanañjaya* and *Tapatīsaṃvaraṇa* would show. The temple theatre, which had its beginning in this period, used these and other Sanskrit plays with their epic contents. Sculpture and such painting as there was drew liberally on this repertoire. Arrangements for the propagation of the epics were made through specialists such as the *Mahābhārata bhaṭṭas* who expounded the epic in temples. And, there is no evidence that the old Tamiḻ tradition was patronised any more. A comparison of the popularity of the Sanskrit works of Kulaśēkharavarman and the Tamiḻ hymns of the same author in Kērala in this and later periods will eminently prove this point. So also, themes from the equally rich treasure available in Tamiḻ are not used by authors in Kēraḷa for their compositions in Sanskrit. Even the first literary works in Malayāḷam are *Rāmacarita* and a translation of the *Arthaśāstra*, both dated to about the twelfth century. When more works were composed, the themes were either taken from the storehouse of Sanskrit epics and other literary works or invented *de novo*. Thus, the identity of Kēraḷa that was crafted in the age of the Cēramān Perumāḷs (AD 800-1124) was clearly of an upper caste, Brāhmaṇical, Sanskritic nature.

At this point, it is interesting to note a major variation in the course of history in this part of the country. While the Sanskritic tradition in literature mentioned above was matched by the production of Sanskrit inscriptions elsewhere, Kēraḷa used old Malayāḷam for inscriptions from the beginning of the ninth century.[26] Inscriptions of the Cēras of Mahōdayapuram, starting from the very first one, are in old Malayāḷam û not Sanskrit. In fact, there is only one inscription in Sanskrit from Kēraḷa,[27] and

[26] Early epigraphists and scholars of language who read the inscriptions took them for Tamiḻ records and edited them in the Tamiḻ script in the pages of *South Indian Inscriptions, Travancore Archaeological Series* and similar publications. Most of the early scholars who edited and took up a linguistic study of these records were Tamiḻ Brāhmaṇas (K.V.Subrahmaya Aiyar, A.S.Ramanatha Aiyar, L.V.Ramaswami Aiyar, Ulloor S.Parameswara Aiyar and A.C.Sekhar). Even A.R.Rajarajavarma was under the heavy influence of this Tamiḻ tradition. They, naturally, failed to appreciate the 'Malayāḷam-ness' of these inscriptions. M.G.S.Narayanan recognised it in his *Index to Cēra Inscriptions*, a companion volume to his Ph.D. thesis on "The Political and Social conditions of Kēraḷa under the Kulaśēkhara Empire" submitted to the University of Kerala, Trivandrum, 1972. The text of the thesis is available in print, although this extremely useful *Index...* is not yet published. For an argument in favour of Malayāḷam, see Kesavan Veluthat, 'Epigraphy in the Historiography of Kerala' in K.K.N.Kurup, ed., *New Dimensions in South Indian History: Essays in Honour of M.R.Raghava Varier*, Calicut, 1996.

[27] Pāliyam Plates of Vikramāditya Varaguṇa. *Travancore Archaeological Series*, I, part XII, pp.187-93.

that too from the southern extreme and not of a Cēra king — the proverbial exception which proves the rule. Thus Kēraḷa presents a deviation from the pattern which Sheldon Pollock has seen.[28] The model that he constructs, of a 'Sanskrit Cosmopolis' affiliating regional cultures to it before the 'vernacular transformation' of regions, is not empirically valid for the situation obtaining in the extreme south of the west coast. Even while inscriptions used the 'vernacular' when a literate tradition emerged there, literature used the Sanskrit language, made use of its rich repertoire and followed the science of its prosody and poetics (*alaṅkāraśāstra*) that had developed at an all-India level. In fact, contemporary as well as modern scholars have shown how even the Sanskrit dramas of Kulaśēkhara are influenced by the *dhvani* theory of the Kashmiri writer Ānandavardhana, which was barely half a century old at the time of their composition.[29] So also, compositions from Kēraḷa were lauded by poets and critics from other parts of the country not long after they were produced. Both these instances show how the 'Sanskrit Cosmopolis' did exert its influence here on written literature in Kēraḷa from the period of the Cēramān Perumāḷs.

It is this historical baggage of unity and identity that Kēraḷa carried with it in the subsequent periods, in spite of the heavy fragmentation which its polity experienced. Kēraḷa was referred to as *Cēramān nāḍu*, the 'Land of the Cēramāns' in the literature of the post-Cēra period. The ghost of the Perumāḷ haunted the land in many ways. Mahōdayapuram is still represented in the literature as the town from which the Land of the Cēramāns was still ruled — a town of cultivated gentlemen and comely ladies, an epitome of civilised life.[30] A copper plate record dated a century after the formal disintegration of the Cēra kingdom suggests a pan-Kēraḷa appeal that the town had.[31] It speaks, perhaps wishfully, of the endorsement that the important political divisions and social units had made on the grant recorded in it. Each of the large number

[28] Sheldon Pollock, 'The Cosmopolitan Vernacular', *The Journal of Asian Studies*, vol. 57, no. 1 (Feb. 1998), pp.6-37.

[29] The *Vyaṅgavyākhyā* commentaries mentioned above acknowledges this. See also, Raja, op.cit. p.15; Unni, op.cit., pp.33-8.

[30] For a detailed discussion, Kesavan Veluthat, 'Further Expansion of Agrarian Society: A. Political Forms', in P.J.Cherian, ed. *Perspectives on Kerala History: the Second Millennium*, Trivandrum, 1999, pp.62-78; Kesavan Veluthat, ''Medieval Kerala': State and Society' in J.S.Grewal, ed., *Social History of Medieval India*, in the press.

[31] *Epigraphia Indica*, IV, pp.290-7.

of principalities that came into existence on the ruins of the Cēra kingdom claimed to be not only a splinter of the old kingdom but also deriving its authority from the donation of the last Cēramān Perumāḷ. Thus Vēṇāḍ in the south and Kōlattunāḍ in the north, and all other 'kingdoms' in between, participated in the same historical tradition and the same identity. Many of these rulers also claimed to step into the shoes of the Perumāḷ in claiming to be the overlord of Kerala. Thus the ruler of Vēṇāḍ or the Zamorin or the *rājā* of Cochin staked this claim in various ways. *Māmākam*, a festival in the temple of Tirunāvāya every twelve years, was the occasion where this claim was ritually made, and contested. So also, a local era, originating in Kollam in Vēṇāḍ in the ninth century and used only locally for the next three centuries, gained acceptance as a standard for reckoning dates all over Kēraḷa. The strong Brāhmaṇical character that the earlier power structure had is not seen in most of the 'successor states' any more; but the cultural identity of Kēraḷa, which was forged in the earlier period of Brāhmaṇical hegemony, continued. Ōṇam, which began as a Vaiṣṇava sectarian festival with a strong Tamiḻ background, gets entirely 'Malayāḷamised' in this period.

All this would show that the clearly defined identity that Kēraḷa had acquired in the Perumāḷ era continued in nearly all its detail. In fact, this period looked upon itself as a continuation of the earlier period whereas the earlier one was conscious of the break that it represented. These differences, and the factors behind it, are a matter recognised by the authors of this period. For instance, a medieval Maṇipravāḷam text speaks of the speciality of the land on account of its fertility also as a gift of Paraśurāma: "the rainy season, under the orders of Paraśurāma, comes here with such frequency as if to breastfeed her children".[32] The *Śukasandēśa*, a work in Sanskrit, puts the same thing slightly differently. The messenger of love, on his way from Ramēśvaram to Guṇakā in Kēraḷa carrying the message to the separated heroine, is introduced to the land when he is to cross the Western Ghats: "Now you can see the *brhamakṣatra* land which testifies to the might of Paraśurāma's arms. This country, rich in pepper and betel vines growing on tall coconut and areca palms, is celebrated as Kēraḷa".[33]

[32] "*Sakalaphalasamṛddhyai kēraḷānām pratāpam periya paraśurāmasyājñayā yatra nityam kanivoṭu maḻa kālam pārttupārttarbhakānām janani mulakoṭuppānennapōlē varunnū*", Ibid., I, 51.

[33] "*Brahmakṣatram janapadamatha sphītamadhyakṣayēthāḥ*

The separateness of Kēraḷa, these texts imply, was a function of its geography and climate.

It is here that one sees a conscious attempt at defining Kēraḷa and its language, creating a self-image, as it were. M.R.Raghava Varier has made a brilliant analysis of a medieval text, *Līlātilakam*,[34] a manual of the grammar, prosody and poetics of *Maṇipravāḷam*, a 'union of *bhāṣā* and Sanskrit', where *bhāṣā* stands for Malayāḷam.[35] The language of this text itself is Sanskrit, not Malayāḷam, although the author exhibits his deep knowledge of literary texts in Malayāḷam as well as the literary and grammatical theories in Sanskrit, Tamiḻ and Kannada. This, or any other contemporary text from Kerala, does not call Malayāḷam by that name, it being used for the first time outside Kēraḷa, as in the fifteenth century Telugu work, *Śrībhīmēśvarapurāṇamu* of Śrīnātha.[36] Curiously, another term that *Līlātilakam* uses to denote the language of Kēraḷa is Tamiḻ, but the anonymous author hastens to explain that this Tamiḻ is different from the language used in "the Cōḷa country, etc..." A very detailed discussion, bordering on the polemical, follows in an attempt to demonstrate the distinctiveness of "Kēraḷa-*bhāṣā*" as opposed to other languages of south India; so also, the same text shows that Kēraḷa had acquired the necessary self-confidence to consider languages, people and institutions outside Kēraḷa as inferior.

darpādarśam dṛḍhataramṛṣēr jāmadagnyasya bāhvōḥ /
yam mēdinyām ruciramaricōttālatāmbūlavallī-
vēllatkērakramukanikarān kēraḷānudgṛṇantī" ॥ *Śukasandēśa*, I, 34.

[34] M.R.Raghava Varier, "*LīlātialakatthinṞe rāṣṭrīyam*", in *Mathrubhūmi Weekly*, 71, no. 43, pp.23-28 reproduced in Varier, *Vāyanayuṭe Vaḷikaḷ*, Thrissur, 1998, pp. pp. 9-19. Varier takes the formation of the identity of Kēraḷa to the post-Perumāḷ era after the twelfth century, which we do not accept here. So also he does not appreciate the heavily upper caste character of this identity. It is interesting to see how much of Varier's arguments is used by Rich Freeman, "Rubies and Coral: The Lapidary Crafting of Language in Kerala", *The Journal of Asian Studies*, 57, no.1 (February 1998), pp. 38-65.

[35] Maṇipravāḷam did exist in the Tamiḻ country, too; but it has to be distinguished from what developed in the Malayāḷam-speaking region. For a discussion of the character of Maṇipravāḷam in Kēraḷa, K. Ramachandran Nair, *Early Maṇipravāḷam: A Study*, Trivandrum, 1978. For a discussion of *Līlātilakam*, K.N.Ezhuthachan, *The History of Grammatical Theories in Malayalam*, I, Trivandrum, 1975, pp. 61-129.

[36] Śrīnātha, *Śrībhīmēśvarapurāṇamu*, I, 72, 73. Quoted in Velcheru Narayana Rao, David Shulaman and Sanjay Subrahmanyam, *Textures of Time: Writing History in South India 1600-1800*, Delhi, 2001, p.20.

At the same time, the eagerness to participate in an all-India tradition was on the increase. Identifying Kēraḷa as a *janapada* in *Bhāratavarṣa* can be seen from the period of the Purāṇas on;[37] but that is as vague as it is inconsequential. The attempt to achieve linkage to the larger unit from this side can be seen, again, in the *Kēraḷōlpatti*. One of its recensions from Kōlattunāḍ in the northern part of Kēraḷa has a pretentious beginning, with a claim to narrate *jambudvīpōlpatti* in *bhāṣā* (Malayāḷam).[38] Kēraḷa is clearly situated within the geographical horizon familiar to the *Purāṇic* world; and its 'origin', naturally, is part of the origin of *Jambudvīpa*. This attempt in a narrative that seeks to constitute Kēraḷa is extremely significant. But, it goes beyond such technical texts. One of the medieval Maṇiparavāḷam texts, the *Candrōtsavam*, has a verse which seeks to participate in this tradition and includes Kēraḷa within this geographical locus. It says that, there are seven other *khaṇḍas* around and that the southern one of Bhārata is more charming than them; even in it, the Land of the Cēramāns [is] like the auspicious mark on the forehead of the goddess of prosperity and god of love.[39] By the time we come to Pūntanam Nampūtiri, a poet who wrote in simple Malayāḷam in the sixteenth century, we see this Purāṇic geography accepted without even an attempt to bring in any distinction for Kēraḷa within Bhārata. He is happy that he was just living in Bhārata and that it was in the present age that he was doing so.[40]

The idea of Bhārata or Bhāratavarṣa, which evolved through centuries in the expressions of high culture in India, particularly in the period of and after the Guptas, was something which Kēraḷa came to know about in the age of the Cēramān Perumāḷs. To begin with, Tamiḻakam, of which present- day Kēraḷa was an inseparable

[37] Muzaffar Ali, *The Geography of the Purāṇas*, second edition, New Delhi, 1973, p. 153.

[38] M.R.Raghava Varier, ed., *Kerlolpatti Granthavari: The Kolattunad Traditions*, Calicut University, 1984, pp. 54-55. The document describes itself as "Jambudvīpōlpatti".

[39] "*Parabhṛtamoḷi cuḤḤum maḤḤu khaṇḍaṅṅaḷeṭṭuṇṭatilumadhikahṛdyam dakṣiṇam bhāratākhyam* I *vaḷarnila malarmātinnaṅgajannum trilōkī ceḤutoṭukuḤipōlē cēramānnāḍu yasmin* II", *Candrōtsavam*, 1, 46.

[40] "*Lavaṇāmbudhi madhyē viḷaṅṅunna* / *jambudvīporu yōjana lakṣavum* //
ēḷu dvīpukaḷiṅṅaneyuḷḷatil / *uttamam i sthalam ennu vāḻtthunnu* //
... ...
itil onpatu khanṇḍaṅṅaḷ uṇṭallō / *atil uttamam bhāratabhūtalam* ||..." Pūntānam, *Jñānappāna*, in Manoj Kurur, ed., *Añcaṭi, Jñānappāna, Ōṇappāṭṭu*, Changanasseri, 1996, p.96.

part, did not have much consciousness of this idea. The copious literature in Tamiḻ, although containing stray influences of the Vedic-Śāstraic-Purāṇic elements,[41] does not participate in this tradition at all. It was only in the age of transition from the early historical to the early medieval that such an idea itself makes its appearance in south India, perhaps through what Pollock has described as the 'Sanskrit Cosmopolis'. However, in spite of the knowledge of this idea of Bhārata, there is nothing in the records to show that Kēraḷa sought affiliation to it even at this stage. What it did at this stage was to wean itself away from the old affiliation to Tamiḻakam. Gradually, however, Kēraḷa began to participate in the common traditions of this larger unit of Bhārata as an affiliate. The post-Perumāḷ era in Kēraḷa thus found itself as an integral part of Bhāratavarṣa, and it was the Brāhmaṇical agency which achieved it. The land created by Paraśurāma was already part of the land of Bharata.

[41] M.G.S. Narayanan, 'The Vedic-Sastraic-Puranic Element in Tamil Sangam Literature', Proceedings of the Indian History Congress, Aligarh,

7

Concepts of India: Expanding Horizons in Early Medieval Arabic and Persian Writing

IMTIAZ AHMAD

Contact between India and the Islamic world was established in two stages: first by the Arabs, initially by trade and later by the conquest of Sindh; then by the Ghaznavids and Ghorians, initially in the north-west frontier, then over the northern part of the subcontinent. The subsequent political construct, the Delhi Sultanate, made for a constant intercourse and produced a wider range of results. The whole process was spread over a fairly long period covering over seven centuries, the seventh to the fifteenth.

The events of political and military history find a fairly detailed description in contemporary literary sources, in both Arabic and Persian. What is more interesting is the fact that as the extent of political control increases, the awareness about the country and its geography, gets more detailed and accurate, and finally a sense of belonging to the country and its culture, begins to be reflected in contemporary writings. An attempt is made here to review the idea of India — called *Hind* and *Hindostān* – and trace its expanding geographical and cultural horizons in these writings. The sources examined include general accounts, historical chronicles and travelogues. Though limited in number, these are hopefully representative in nature.They mainly include the *Chachnāma, Kitāb ul-Hind* of Alberuni, *Tabqāt-i Nāsirī* of Minhaj, *Tārīkh-i Fīroz Shāhī* of Barani, *Futūh us-Salātīn* of Isami and the *Rihla* of Ibn-Battūta.

It would be helpful to focus on three important aspects: (i) the gradual increase in geographical awareness about the country writings; (ii) examples of growing empathy with the country, its people and their culture, with the expansion of the geographical horizon; and (iii) Indian literary and other influences reflected in these writings.

A beginning may be made with the *Chachnāma,*[1] which is the most valuable source of information on the Arab conquest

[1] 'Ali Kūfi (thirteenth-century translator), *Chachnāma* (Persian version of an early Arabic History of the Brahman dynasty of Sindh and the Arab Conquest), ed. U.M. Daudpota, Hyderabad-Deccan, 1939.

of Sindh and also the earliest, among the sources under review, to use the expression 'Hind' and 'Hindustan'. Irfan Habib comments: "The word 'Hind' originated in the ancient Indian substitution of 'h'for 's' giving 'Hi(n)du' for the Vedic 'Sindhu', and was thus simply derived from the Iranian form of the name for Sind. It is, perhaps, this which explains the pairing of Hind-o-Sind... 'Hindostān' was created by the usual Iranian practice of adding the suffix – *stān* to geographical names[2] ... The Indus itself is called in the *Chachnāma* by the Iranian name 'Mihran', not Sind."[3]

Andre Wink's observations are also interesting. He writes: "The Arabic literature often conflates 'Sind' with 'Hind' into a single term but also refers to 'Sind and Hind' to distinguish the two ... Sind derived its name and identity from the river, which in Sanskrit was called *Sindhu* (meaning literally 'river' or 'stream'), i.e. the 'Indus' of the Greeks and Romans, the Mihran of the Arabs. 'The land of Sind' designated the alluvial plains created by the river on both sides in its middle and lower course, from Attock to the coast, with varying portions of the rocky uplands (Kuhistan) adjoining Baluchistan and of the sand hills of the Thar."[4] He also observes: "like Makran, Zamindawar, Zabulistan and Kabul, Sind belonged to *al-Hind* in its widest sense but also to the frontier zone between Persia and India. It is perceptible in the sources that the early Arab invaders were prone to see Sind as an extension of eastern Persia in some respects."[5]

It thus appears that in the early Arab writings the geographical limits of "Hind" are not precisely delineated. The term is used at times for the area adjacent to the river Indus, at times to the lands spreading further east of it, at times for both, and at times, even further to south-east Asia.

The other point to be noted is that detailed geographical information about the area is also not clear in the earlier texts. The *Chachnāma*, for example, refers to the boundaries of the kingdom of King Sīhars, son of Sāhasi Rāi, of Sind.[6] It states,

[2] Irfan Habib, *Linguistic Materials from Eighth Century Sind: An Exploration of the Chachnāma*, Symposia papers (II), Indian History Congress, 1994-95, pp.8-9.

[3] Ibid., p.9.

[4] Andre Wink, *Al-Hind, The Making of the Indo-Islamic World*, reprint, New Delhi, 1999, I, pp.145-46.

[5] Ibid., p.147.

[6] See Irfan Habib, op.cit., p.9, for an explanation of the names.

that the boundaries of his dominions extended "on the east to Kashmir, on the west to Makran, on the south to the shores of the Ocean and to Debal, and on the north to the mountains of Kardān and Kaikānān."[7] It is also mentioned that the King divided his kingdom into four provinces, each under a local governor, but seating himself at Aror. The names of many important towns are mentioned, a few of them difficult to identify.[8] Of the rest of the subcontinent, there is awareness only of Kashmir and Kanauj as important kingdoms, and also of Kachchh ('Qassa'). The *Chachnāma* is remarkable not only for its familiarity with Buddhism, but also for its reference to *Avadand-vihār*, the famous Buddhist monastery in Bihar. Authenticity is stamped all over the work.

Some awareness of the geography of India is noticeable in the accounts of ninth- and tenth-century Arab travellers, but these mainly relate to the coastal areas and the information is often not very accurate beyond the Indus basin. We have the description of some ports, trade and social life in the region. There is also some mention of important Indian rulers and their kingdoms, but it is often based on uncorroborated information.[9] Some of it like the remarkably erroneous number of seven for the number of Indian castes goes back to Megasthenes though the Arab geographers doubtless picked it up from the folklore of the Mediterranean world, in which bits of ancient Greek knowledge of India might have yet survived.

The campaigns of Mahmud in the first quarter of the eleventh century mark the beginning of a new phase. Virtually, the entire area now constituting Pakistan came under the rule of Mahmud and his successors. There is a perceptible increase of information on India in Arabic and Persian now, both in their number and variety. We have on the one hand, the *Tārīkh-i Yaminī* in the nature of a general historical chronicle which describes in fair detail the campaigns of Mahmud in India; on the other hand, we have the great account of India and her culture given by Alberuni

[7] *Chachnāma*, ed. U.M. Daudpota, p.15.

[8] For the identification of many of the places and territories mentioned in the *Chachnāma*, see Irfan Habib and Faiz Habib, 'From Oxus to the Yamuna, c.600-c.750', *Proceedings of the Indian History Congress*, 55th (Aligarh, 1994) session, pp.52-82.

[9] Most of the important early Arab travellers' and geographers' accounts relating to India are made available to us in English translation in H.M. Elliot and John Dowson, *History of India as told by its own Historians*, I, London, 1867, pp.1-99. Maqdisi's narrative is an important omission.

in his *Kitāb ul-Hind.* The two works, almost contemporary, differ in nature. 'Utbī treats India and the Indians with an attitude of contempt, generally displayed by an alien. Alberuni looks upon India and her people with a sense of interest and inquisitiveness. Secondly, the element of accuracy and details is missing in 'Utbī's writing. In Dowson's words, he "evidently had no knowledge of the topography of India and his statements in respect of localities are of little authority. He never mentions Lahore or Delhi, and with the exception of the title *Rāi*, no Hindi word is found in his pages. In dates, he is deficient, and far from precise."[10]

Baihaqi, in the *Tarikh-i Al-i Subktagin,* offers an interesting contrast to the narrative of Utbi. He provides information on the presence of 'Hindu' (Indian) soldiers in the army of Mahmud and acknowledges their valour and sense of fidelity.[11] This is important in indicating a different outlook, based on increased personal contcts.

Alberuni himself, one of the Islamic world's greatest scientists and polymaths, stands on a totally different plane from these authors, both in perspective and information. Firstly he shows a far better awareness of the geography of India. In fact he appears to be the first among our sources to provide a clear distinction between the terms 'Hind' and 'Sind'. He writes:[12] "the country of Sind lies to the west of Kanauj. In marching from our country [Khwarizm] to Sind we start from the country of Nimroz, i.e. the country of Sijistan, while marching to Hind or India proper we start from the side of Kabul." It appears that he uses 'Hind' as the generic name for India, synonymous with *Bharatavarsha*, but excluding Sind.[13] Alberuni is also fairly accurate in his description of the geographical boundaries of the subcontinent when he writes: "... one of these plains is India, limited in the south by the above mentioned ocean, and on all three other sides by lofty mountains, the waters of which flow down to it."[14] He also gives a fairly dependable description on the country, its rivers and major cities and the routes connecting them, etc.[15]

[10] Elliot and Dowson, op.cit., II, p.14. Dowson himself falls into a slip here: Delhi was of little importance at the time; there is no certainty even that the town's original name 'Dhilli' was in existence.

[11] Ibid., pp.59-60.

[12] Edward C. Sachau (tr.), *Alberuni's India*, London, 1910, p.198.

[13] On *Bharatavarsha*, see Alberuni's comments in ibid., I, pp.294-5.

[14] Ibid., I, p.198.

[15] Ibid., I, pp.198-203.

Secondly, he gives a fairly comprehensive account of the Hindus, or the people of India, their religion, sciences, philosophy, etc. Although an alien, coming from Khwarizm in Central Asia, then half Iranic, half Turkic, he made an extraordinarily conscientious effort to study and understand Indian culture and to convey it to the Arabic-reading public. A few examples may be cited. Referring to the religious beliefs of the Hindus, Alberuni is not very keen about showing the contrast between Hinduism and Islam; instead he identifies the similarities between the two. On the Hindus' concept of God, he states: "The Hindus believe with regard to God that He is eternal, without beginning and end, acting by free will, almighty, all-wise, living, giving life, ruling, preserving; one Who in His sovereignty is unique, beyond all likeness and unlikeness, and that He does not resemble anything nor does anything resemble Him."[16] In connection with idol-worship too, he offers a sensible explanation: "It is well-known that the popular mind leans towards the sensible world, and has an aversion to the world of abstract thought which is only understood by educated people, of whom in every time and every place there are only few ... this is the cause which leads to manufacturing of idols... but we declare at once that they are worshipped only by the common uneducated people. For those who march on the path to liberation, or those who study philosophy and theology, and who desire abstract truth which they call *sara*, are entirely free from worshipping anything but God alone, and would never dream of worshipping an image manufactured to represent Him."[17] More significant still are certain excerpts from the *Bhagavadgita*, which Alberuni places before his readers, regarding the concept of God among the enlightened Hindus.[18] He quotes Vasudeva (Lord Krishna, from the *Bhagavadgita*): "I am the universe, without a beginning by being born, or without an end by dying. I do not aim by whatever I do at any recompense. I do not specially belong to one class of beings to the exclusion of others, as if I were the friend of one and enemy of others. I have given to each one in my creation what is sufficient to him in all his functions. Therefore, whoever knows me in this capacity and tries to become similar to me by keeping desire apart from his action, his fetters will be loosened,

[16] Ibid., I, p.27.
[17] Ibid., I, pp.111-13.
[18] Ibid., I, pp.122-23.

and he will easily be saved and freed."[19] Equally interesting is Alberuni's insight into the social institutions of the Hindus. Scholars have debated the accuracy of these statements – the question whether these are merely textually derived or refer to the actual conditions – but all agree that this is the first detailed and authentic account of India and her people.[20] We have here truly the case of one of the best minds of one civilization looking deeply into the highest levels of another.

Though it is not possible to determine a direct link between Alberuni's outlook and that of some of the later medieval Indian writers, his work was, in some ways, the beginning of a new tendency that was to fructify in the later centuries. We can notice some similarity of attitude – though there is no evidence always of a direct impact of Alberuni – in the writings of Amir Khusrau (d.1325) who takes pride in his Indian birth; in the thoughts of a host of Sufi saints who assimilated Vedantist ideas and proudly identified themselves with the Indian cultural milieu; in the teachings of the Ismaili preachers on the western coast who identified themselves with Brahma, Vishnu and Indra, with ease; and in the still later examples of Abu'l Fazl, with his detailed survey of Indian culture, and of Dara Shukoh, who treats the essence of Vedanta and Tasawwuf as two sides of the same coin. It is very clear that the expansion of political control led to a better awareness of the country and its people and a tendency to accept its influences and identify oneself with it. This was the essence of the composite cultural entity that *Hindostan* or India came to represent in the medieval period.

This position becomes more unambiguous by the thirteenth century. The hold of the Sultans extended deeper into the north Indian plains and a detailed account of the rise of the Delhi-Sultanate in its first (or Turkish) phase is provided in the *Ṭabaqāt-i Nāṣirī* of Minhāj (fl. 1259). The special value of the *Tabaqāt* lies in the first-hand details it provides, especially of the geography of several areas. Almost the whole of the Gangetic basin up to Bengal is familiar ground to Minhaj, who himself travelled to Bengal in 1243.[21]

[19] Ibid., I, p.29.

[20] See for an excellent summary Qeyamuddin Ahmad, ed., *India by Al-Biruni*, New Delhi, 1983.

[21] Minhaj-i Siraj, *Ṭabaqāt-i Nāṣirī*, Eng. tr. by H.G. Raverty, Bib. Ind., Calcutta, 1873-81, II, p.548. Also see Elliot and Dowson, op.cit., II, p.260.

Minhaj is remarkably accurate about place-names, territories and political boundaries; though, as befitted a person brought up earlier in Ghor, the most detailed information is reserved for the regions of present-day Afghanistan. More important from our present point of view is the fact that in the writings of Minhaj, an awareness of *Hind* or *Hindostan* as a defined territorial entity gradually but unmistakably emerges. A few interesting examples may be cited. In his earlier chapters, where he deals with the dynasties of Central Asia, Minhaj refers to *Hindostān* essentially as the area extending from the eastern fringe of Central Asia to the banks of the Indus; the region which Arab writers preferred to call as '*Sind*' or at times conjointly as '*Sind o Hind*'.[22] In the later chapters, he refers to the territory of Delhi Sultanate as '*Hindostān*'.[23] In a still later context, he describes the precise boundaries of *Hindostan* in these words: "from the territory of Karah and Manikpur and Awadh and the district of Tirhut, as far as Badayun, and from the side of Tabarhinda as far as Sunam, Kuhram and Samạnah and the whole of the Sawalak."[24] A little later, the sub-Himalayan Tarais are also mentioned as part of *Hindostān*. Interestingly, the areas of Lakhnauti (Bengal) and Kamrud (Kamrup) are treated almost as a different 'country'; for these areas are mentioned in the same breath as distinct entities between *Hind* and *Chin* (China).[25]

By the fourteenth century, our sources become still more extensive. The most valued of these is Baranī's *Tārīkh-i Fīroz Shāhī* which constitutes our most elaborate and incisive source for the history of the Sultanate, both under Alauddin Khalji (1296-1316) and, then with fluctuating political boundaries, under Muhammad bin Tughluq (1324-51). Of special interest for our purpose are the portions dealing with the Deccan[26] which, in the fourteenth century, became a totally new area to which the Sultans' power was extended. Barani also provides some

[22] Minhaj, op.cit., tr. Raverty, I, pp.111-13, 115, etc.

[23] Ibid., Vol.I, p.248: Vol.II, p.1129, and *passim*.

[24] Ibid., II, p.830, and *passim*. Almost the whole of northern India, rather than only the territories of the Delhi Sultanate are referred to as *Hindostan*. "Sawalak" is not Siwalik, but a territory supposed to contain "1,25,000 (*sawa-lak*) villages", comprising Haryana and eastern Rajasthan.

[25] Ibid., pp.1081, 1151.

[26] The information on the campaigns in that area and more importantly on the Daulatabad project may not be very accurate for details of political history, but the geographical information is certainly significant.

interesting information on some of the frontier regions in the context of the campaigns of Muhammad bin Tughluq, the abortive one in Khurasan and the unsuccessful one in Qarachil. He also provides information on the various regions of the Punjab while discussing the conflict with the Mongols and portions of the Doab, when he gives an account of the revolts in that region, or relates the administrative measures taken there.

Of greater interest are some references made by Barani to the Hindus.[27] These are important, because they differ strikingly from the otherwise oft-quoted derogatory remarks of the historian about the Hindus. It may be added, before mentioning the relatively less-known – but appreciative – comments of Barani, that even when he speaks harshly about the Hindus, he does so either because he considers the discriminatory treatment against the Hindus a political device or a religious duty, though not necessarily a merit! If we take up the more positive comments, they show an interesting departure from derogatory remarks. To cite one example, Barani states that when Balban suppressed the revolt of Tughril in Bengal, the victorious Sultan, on his return to the capital, was felicitated by eminent persons and by 'Muslims and Hindus, Turks and Tajiks'.[28] He seems to treat the Hindus, together with the (Indian) Muslims, Turks and Tajiks, as one category, whose support and welcome were of some political significance. Similarly, when Barani narrates the details of the first campaign of Firoz Tughluq against the kingdom of Lakhnauti,[29] it transpires from his account that one of the major pretended reasons for the Bengal campaign was the fact that Ilyās Shāh, the ruler of Lakhnauti, had made encroachments upon the imperial territory and was harassing the *Muslim* and *Hindu* (emphasis added) subjects in the area. Further, he tells us that after the defeat of Ilyās Shāh and the capture of many of his nobles and other items of booty, these were paraded in the city of Delhi and the Hindus and Muslims expressed their happiness at that sight. As a third example, one may cite the incident about Jalāluddīn Khaljī praising and rewarding a Hindu chief of Kaithal,

[27] Cf. Qeyamuddin Ahmad, 'Barani's References to the Hindus in the *Tarikh-i Firoz Shahi* – Territorial and Other Dimensions', *Islamic Culture*, LVI, no.4, October, 1982.

[28] Ibid., p.295. Also see Baranī, *Tārīkh-i Fīroz Shāhī*, Persian text, Bib. Ind., Calcutta, 1862, p.108.

[29] Baranī, op.cit., pp.586-96. For a short translation of the portion into English, see, Q. Ahmad, op.cit., pp.296ff.

who had actually wounded him in a battle when, as an officer, he had used force to collect revenue from the area.[30]

Another less-noticed feature of Baranī's writing is the admiration he shows for the literary and cultural progress made in India under the Delhi Sultans. Particularly interesting are the observations made by him with regard to the reign of Alauddin Khalji. He avers that there lived at Delhi scholars who were highly learned; and of whose calibre there were to be found none in Bokhara, Samarqand, Damascus, Tabrez, Isfahan, Asia Minor or indeed any other part of the world![31] He further writes that some of these scholars were equal to Ghazali and Razi. In every branch of learning that they took up – commentaries, theology, principles of religion, grammar, explanations, discourse and logic, their researches were authentic and exhaustive. Every year a number of students graduated under their training and were able to challenge established theological opinions. He concludes by maintaining that no book was considered meritorious anywhere unless it was so recognised by Indian scholars.[32] These few examples not only show a different attitude on the part of Barani towards India and the Hindus but also a new-found pride in India.[33]

It is important to remember that there are other examples of this attitude. Amir Khusrau is well known for his love of India which is beautifully expressed in many of his writings, notably the *Nuh Sipihr.* Another example is that of 'Iṣāmī, who wrote his *Futuh us-Salatin* (1350) with the intention of immortalising the exploits of the Sultans of Delhi. The book contains several verses where 'Isami extols the glory of *Hindostan* (India) as a country. Some of these verses, in their English translation, by Sabahuddin Abdur Rahman,[34] are quoted below:

What a beautiful country India is; so beautiful indeed that even paradise is envious of her!

She is an ornament to the globe enhancing its beauty in the same manner as does a mole on the face of every sweetheart.

The rivers are seen flowing at close distances in this country and their waters are healthy and vital like the water of life; (yet) they are free

[30] Qeyamuddin Ahmad, op.cit., pp.298-99.

[31] Sabahuddin Abdur Rahman, 'National Sentiments in Indo-Persian Literature', *Indo-Iranica*, vol.XVIII, no.1, March 1965, pp.1-34.

[32] Ibid., p.9.

[33] Ibid.

[34] Ibid., pp.6-7.

from the darkness that shrouds the fabulous water of life.
Indian soil is full of the aroma of roses; and the dew, like rainwater, enhances its qualities (further).
Its soil produces such strong persons as if the foundation-stone of mankind was laid here; its breeze is pleasant and refreshing like zephyr.
Whoever came from Iraq, Sind and Arabia into this garden of pleasure became so attached to it that he ever hardly recalled his native land.[35]

One may here refer to a different example as well. From Minhaj to Isami, the historians happen to be persons who had settled in India. Their sentiments for the country and its people are understandable. But we find an identical attitude even in the writings of a foreign traveller who visited India in the fourteenth century. His example shows the extent to which Muslims, even from other parts of the Islamic world, had begun to appreciate India, her people and their culture.

It was during the reign of Muhammad bin Tughluq that the Moroccan traveller, Ibn Battuta visited India, as part of his celebrated world-wide travels. Ibn Battuta spent a fairly long time in India and he travelled over different parts of the country. These included the frontier region, Sindh, Multan, Delhi, Goa, Calicut, Tamil Nadu and Bengal. His descriptions of the capital city of Delhi, its important monuments and the architectural activities sponsored by some of the rulers, besides the abortive plan of Muhammad bin Tughluq to interlink its four major 'towns', 'Dilli, Siri,Tughlaqabad and Jahanpanah' into a single metropolis, provide interesting reading. Among other important towns he mentions Sehwan, Bhakkar, Abohar, Ajodhan, Sarsuti, Hansi, Masudabad and Amroha.[36]

Ibn Batuta's travels cover three continents, but the most interesting and elaborate descriptions given by him concern India. It is not necessary here to discuss the reasons for it. What is important is the fact that Ibn Battuta, in spite of being an alien, evinces great interest in India, her people, and their customs and shows considerable respect for them. To cite one example, he refers to the custom of *sati*, which he had personally observed. He mentions that the Sultan readily gave permission to the women desirous to observe *sati*, a clear indication of the

[35] Translation slightly modified. The original Persian verses will be found in *Futuhu-s-Salatin by Isami*, ed. A.S. Usha, Madras, 1948, p.604.

[36] Hamilton Gibb (ed.), *The Travels of Ibn Batuta*, III, Cambridge, 1971, pp.735 ff.

tolerance of Hindu practices, even if considered un-Islamic, by the Sultans of Delhi.[37] In spite of being a member of the class of the Ulema, Ibn Battuta took keen interest in the Hindus, their social customs and practices and showed a sense of appreciation for them. He admires the law-abiding Hindus who lived in towns and villages and pursued peaceful vocations. He admired them for their devotion to their faith.[38] He speaks appreciatively of the worship of cows and rivers by the Hindus, and even the practice of caste and untouchability among them. He does not even seem to mind the fact the Muslims were not allowed to enter into Hindu households or use the utensils of the Hindus. He also admires Indian flora and fauna, food and cuisine.[39]

To sum up, the gradual expansion of the Sultanate and the kind of regime it established, created greater familiarity with the country among the chroniclers, travellers and other persons writing about the country and its rulers and people. The change from a rather vague – and often changing – notion of India in the early writings to a more precise awareness of its features, represented a major transition to a closer and more detailed knowledge of the geographical regions of the Indian subcontinent and the customs of its people. The two political and cultural processes were not only inter-lined but also, at times, complementary to one another. The other, and the more important, fact was that such awareness generated a feeling of empathy with the people and an appreciation of their culture. If initially a healthy curiosity was the driving motive behind the Arabic and Persian writings on India, it subsequently gave way to a more positive sentiment of appreciation and identification.

A very definite example may be cited from the use – and assimilation – of Indian words in Persian writings. The *Chachnama* contains several references to literary, administrative and religious terms of indigenous origin to which Irfan Habib has drawn attention.[40]

In the eleventh century, Alberuni because of his knowledge of Sanskrit stands as a case apart. He mentions and explains Indian words and terms profusely in his work. These are mainly

[37] Mahdi Husain, 'Introduction', to his *Rehla of Ibn Battuta*, Baroda, 1953, p.xxxiii.

[38] Ibid.

[39] Ibn Baṭṭūṭa's description of the flora and fauna of the country forms an interesting point of similarity between him and Alberuni. To cite only one example, both have mentioned the presence of the rhinoceros in the region of Sindh.

[40] Cf. Irfan Habib, *Linguistic Materials,* op.cit.

Sanskrit words because he was writing on the basis of Indian texts and treatises which, obviously were in the language of the intelligentsia, that is, the Sanskrit language. But naturally he does not make Indian words a part of his Arabic idiom.

By the fourteenth century this stage had been reached – in the case of Persian, which began to receive and absorb a number of Indian words. Attention has been drawn[41] to the use of Hindi (Indian) words by Barani in his writings. It clearly shows the steadily growing influence of Indian spoken dialects of the Persian writers as also their urge to apply effective expressions and phrases from the Indian dialects. If is, indeed, a matter of reflection that there was no movement to purge Persian vocabulary of Indian entrants. Rather, Mahmud Shadiabadi sought to explain a number of Persian words through their Hindi equivalents in his dictionary *Miftāhu'l Fuzalā* written in Malwa in 1479.[42] Translations of Indian works on diverse subjects such as philosophy, astrology, astronomy, medicine, and music during the time of Firoz Tughluq (fourteenth century) and Sikandar Lodi (sixteenth century) followed. Such a process logically culminated in the emergence of a composite tradition in social and cultural life in the subcontinent. This was one of the most enduring and valuable achievements of medieval India. The terms *Hind* and *Hindostan*, thus, evolved fairly early both in a geographical and cultural contexts; and, over the centuries, the two names came to represent a composite rather than an exclusive entity.

[41] Sabahuddin Abdur Rahman, op.cit., p.9.

[42] The unique MS of this dictionary, illustrated in the sixteenth century in Malwa school style, is in British Library, London, No. Oriental 3299. A photographic edition of this MS is sorely needed.

8

Concept of India in Alberuni

IQTIDAR ALAM KHAN

The concept of India spelled out in the writings of men representing the mainstream of the freedom movement, may be perceived as largely rooted in the evolving cultural plurality within the Indian civilization since ancient times. Mahatma Gandhi was no doubt inclined at one stage to see Hinduism as embodying an overarching quality that cutting across sectarian divisions provided a cultural basis for religious tolerance. He could concede what Amartya Sen calls a "usurping" role to Hinduism "in the synthesis of the nation as a whole".[1] Later on Gandhi appears to have modified his position to bring it in greater agreement with the reality of persisting cultural plurality of Indian history. He is reported to have said: "Indian culture is neither Hindu, nor Islamic, nor any other, wholly. It is a fusion of all."[2] This thesis in varied forms was also presented in the writings of such nationalist historians as Mohammad Habib and Tara Chand, both of whom tend to emphasise the cultural plurality that informed the process of political unification in Medieval India.

According to Mohammad Habib, the laying of "indestructible foundations of our cultural and racial unity" was "the comprehensive work of comprehensive minds" of Ancient India. "In the Hindu institutions of pilgrimages and temples, in the fasts and ceremonies of Vedas and the folktales of the *Ramayana* and the *Mahabharata*, in the tolerant philosophy of Mahayana Buddhism and the code of Manu", Habib opines, "we see the potent influences that made the sacred land of Aryavarta one and indivisible for all time to come". He perceives the political unification as also cultural adjustments achieved under the Muslim rulers like Alauddin and Akbar deriving "moral solidity" from the fusion of cultures and races achieved in ancient times.[3] Tara Chand views the "Muslim conquest" as bringing about

[1] Amartya Sen, 'On Interpreting India's Past' in *Nationalism, Democracy and Development*, ed. Sugata Bose and Ayesha Jalal, New Delhi, 1998, p.18.

[2] As quoted in Jawaharlal Nehru, *The Discovery of India*, London, 1960, p.367.

[3] Mohammad Habib, 'Introduction to the Study of Medieval India (AD 1000-1400)', in *Polities and Society during the Early Medieval Period*, ed. K.A. Nizami, I, New Delhi, 1974, p.22.

"many political and cultural changes in the ancient societies of India" while "much of the foundation and structure of her old culture remained". The rise of a highly centralized "Mughal Empire over greater parts of India", according to Tara Chand, "gave a great impetus to the tendencies of political unification and cultural harmony."[4]

In his *Discovery of India*, Jawaharlal Nehru developed this idea of a multi-racial and multi-cultural India fused into a unified political and cultural entity, into a poetic vision of eternal India assimilating within its fold innumerable cultural streams. According to Nehru, "Ancient India, like Ancient China, was a world in itself, a culture and civilization which gave shape to all things — some kind of dream of unity has occupied the mind of India since the dawn of civilization." He perceives the cultural diversity of Indian society as superficial ("lies on the surface") which in the long run, was bound to give way to national unity promoted by "long existing Indian cultural tradition."[5] Nehru's interpretation of India's past has attracted sharp criticism from various quarters including some of the left-leaning social theorists. Brigitle Schulze characterizes Nehru's elaboration of this concept as "a concret example in concurrence to Hobsbawm's theory of invention of tradition in the context of modern nationalism." In his fascination with the oneness of India, Nehru is supposed to have invented "the civilization of ancient India" attributing a common past to all the different cultures of the subcontinent. This criticism at times comes close to debunking Nehru's concept of India as not being in consonance with the reality of cultural plurality and of regional and social divisions of Indian history.[6]

In the context of this debate on the historical viability of the concept of India, Alberuni's description of India is relevant in a variety of ways. First, as his work dates back to a period that separates the earliest Islamic intrusion into a part of North-Western India (AD 712) from the eventual conquest of the whole of North India by the Ghaurides (AD 1193-1206), it is of help in discerning the Indian response to the growing Islamic presence

[4] Tara Chand, *Influence of Islam on Indian Culture*, Allahabad, 1963, p.141, and *History of the Freedom Movement in India*, Vol.I, Delhi, 1961, pp.2-3.

[5] *The Discovery of India*, pp.61-62.

[6] Brigitte Schulze, 'The Cinematic 'Discovery of India': Mahboob's Re-invention of the Nation in Mother India', *Social Scientist*, 30, September-October, 2002, pp.74, 76-77.

in the Trans-Indus tract during the intervening period. Alberuni's description of India is also important as it represents an attempt to study Hinduism and associated sciences, by a highly cultivated mind of the era when dogmatism of the post-Ghazali (d.1112) orthodoxy had not yet become a dominant tendency in the Islamic intellectual tradition. He makes it a point to state in the very beginning of his book that his was not a polemical discourse aimed at exposing the supposed falsity of Hindu beliefs and practices.[7] His attempt throughout appears to be to sift authentic information traceable to known sacred texts as well as the writings of reputed scientists and other literary figures. On the other hand, many of the notions relating to religion as well as science that circulated and often found popular favour are contemptuously rejected by Alberuni as prejudices unworthy of serious consideration. In this respect, Alberuni had an unashamedly elitist bias which he never tires of proclaiming. But the noteworthy point is that even the information that, according to Alberuni's assessment, was not acceptable is recorded by him while he explains why he prefers to reject such information furnished orally by an informant or gleaned from a text of doubtful authenticity.[8]

Alberuni is not averse occasionally to noticing Hindu sacred dictums or achievements in particular fields with palpable sympathy and admiration. It is an aspect of his narrative that demarcates it from other accounts prior to the Ghaurian conquests. The point may be illustrated with reference to the manner in which he, in Sachau's words, "revelled in pure theories of *Bhagavadgita*" or speaks of Hindu scholars as "enjoying the help of God", which to a Muslim may mean as much as "inspired by God" or "guided by divine inspiration."[9] In this respect Alberuni may be seen as representing a tendency of Islamic learning that later blossomed in India in the writings of Amir Khusrau, Faizi, Abu'l Fazl and Dara Shukoh.

[7] *Alberuni's India: An Account of the religion, philosophy, literature, geography, chronology, astronomy, customs, laws and astrology of India*, I, translated with notes by Edward C. Sachau, (first published 1910), reprint, Delhi, 1989, p.25.

[8] As an illustration, one may cite Alberuni's comments on the information furnished by some persons hailing from Kanauj regarding a cycle of *samvatsaras* of 1248 years. He suspected them of deliberate fraud: "I used great care in examining every single-one of them, in repeating the same questions at different times in a different order and context. But lo! what different answers did I get! God is all-wise." Cf. *Alberuni's India*, tr. Edward C. Sachau, II, p.129.

[9] *Alberuni's India*, I, Edward C. Sachau's Preface, pp.xvii-xviii.

The fact that, before commencing his *Al-Hind*, Alberuni took pains to learn Sanskrit, collected Sanskrit books from distant places as well as carefully recorded oral testimony from persons representing different centres of Hindu learning, evokes spontaneous respect and admiration for his scholarship. One feels confident of accepting as authentic the information he furnishes, though his characterizations of groups and situations based on the same information may sometimes need to be scrutinised critically.

One such often cited characterization is the one where he appears to ascribe a universally dogmatic and inwardlooking tendency to the Indian scholars of his time. According to him, the Indian scholars (the reference, obviously, is to Brahman *Pandits* initially known to him) were averse to entering into a meaningful dialogue with outsiders.[10] At another place, in one of his much quoted flourishes, Alberuni gives the impression that the resentment created among the Hindus by Mahmud of Ghazni's plundering raids had led to their withdrawing to places like Banaras and Kashmir so as to avoid interaction with Muslims.[11] It is, however, possible that Alberuni formed such an impression as his experience of discussions on scientific and religious questions with the pundits present in places like Ghazni, Multan and Lahore was, to begin with, not a very happy one. The Hindu scholars present in these places being generally unsure about their position *visa vis* the men representing the newly established Ghaznavide political authority would naturally be not very forthcoming while discussing questions relating to religion and science.

Perhaps, the same set of people were Alberuni's informants regarding the situation in Kashmir, where, reportedly, all outsiders were unwelcome. One of Alberuni's statements, to the effect that the farthest point in the valley of Kashmir up to which Muslim traders travelled was Rajauri suggests that authorities in Kashmir did not allow Muslims to enter the valley down to the beginning of the eleventh century.[12] It would, however, be farfetched to imagine that this restriction on Muslims travelling to Kashmir was aimed at isolating Hindu learning from alien influences. One would, perhaps, be on surer grounds in

[10] *Alberuni's India*, tr. Edward C. Sachau, I, pp.22-23.

[11] Op.cit., I, pp.21-22.

[12] Op.cit., I, p.28. Alberuni specifies that Rajawari (Rajori) "is the farthest place to which our merchants trade, and beyond which they never pass."

attributing this to the then general fear of foreign incursions among the Kashmir rulers. Such an impression is supported by Alberuni's recording, again on the authority of the same set of informants, that even Hindus from other parts of India not already known locally were barred from entering Kashmir.

There are several passages in Alberuni's work that negate the impression created by the statements examined above. Most revealing of such passages is the one where Alberuni records the response of the Hindu scholars at Lahore upon his explaining to them the basic concept of (Greek?) astronomy. They are reported to have "flocked together round me from all parts, wondering, and most eager to learn from me, asking me at the same time from what Hindu master I had learnt those things." Again, at another place, Alberuni mentions almost gratefully the help that he received from the pundits assisting him; they are reported to have taught him Sanskrit and translated accurately Sanskrit texts into Arabic /Persian for Alberuni's use.[13] The fact that some of the scholars assisting Alberuni were capable of rendering Sanskrit texts into Arabic or Persian for him actually speaks of a situation quite different from the one he implies in his more general statements that we have just touched upon.

II

India as a geographical entity is perceived by Alberuni in two overlapping forms. At one level, he imagines it vaguely as the territory to the east of the Indus, i.e., the al-Hind of the Arab geographers' description, which perhaps, included entire South-East Asia up to the confines of China.[14] His notice of the *Bhāratavarsha* of Hindu *Shāstras*, however, tends to provide a different perspective to this image. He seems to equate *Hind* with the territorial spread of *Bhāratavarsha,* extending from mountains in the north (*Himavant*) upto the sea coast in the south. This incidentally suggests that in the south he takes the expanse of *al'-Hind* of his perception to the natural confines of the Indian subcontinent. In other words, Alberuni's *Hind* did not include South East Asia.[15] Again, while he goes out of his

[13] Op.cit., Vol.I, pp.22-23, 229.

[14] For Arab concepts of Al-Hind see Andre Wenk, *Al-Hind*, Vol.I, New Delhi, 1999, p.5. Compare M. Athar Ali, 'The Perception of India in Akbar and Abu'l Fazl', *Akbar and His India*, ed. Irfan Habib, Delhi, 1997, p.216.

[15] Cf. *Alberuni's India*, tr. by Edward C. Sachau, I, pp.196-200, 294-98. M. Athar Ali (op.cit., p.216) points out that Alberuni defines *al-Hind* more precisely, limits it in the south to the Indian Ocean.

way in refuting the shastric notion that *Bharatavarsha* represented the entire civilized world, his critical comment on the tradition that its inhabitants were the virtuous off-spring of Bharata is slightly tricky in nature. He seeks to highlight the irrationality of the concept that only one particular part of humanity, namely, the off-spring of Bharata of Hindu mythology were subject to the divine rule of *reward and punishment*. But at the same time, he refrains from challenging the identification of the inhabitants of India as the descendants of Bharata. He seems to treat this identification at par with his own perception of Hind being primarily a cultural to be entity identified with the dominant Hindu tradition.

Incidental references in Alberuni's account of different parts of India to the nature of the political authorities controlling them combined with the information on such divisions in the past reproduced by him from Sanskrit texts, enables one to form an impression in broad outline of the prevailing situation in the beginning of eleventh century. According to Alberuni, the most important component of Hind was the vast plain lying to the south of the northern mountains. He calls this region, represented by the Ganga-Yamuna Doab, with its *Puranic* name, *Madhyadesha* and identifies Kanauj as its socio-political centre. While dilating on the linguistic diversity of *Hind*, Alberuni records that this territory (of *Madhyadesha*) was some times also designated *Aryavarta*,[16] which is a very significant pointer. Evidently, according to Alberuni's informants, down to the beginning of the eleventh century, part of *Bharatavarsha* identified with an "Aryan" past, was limited to the North Indian plains of Haryana and the Ganga-Yamana Doab. From Alberuni's notice of the Sanskrit alphabet, *Siddhamtrika,* one gathers the impression that this was in use in *Madhyadesha* for writing the spoken language of the region as well.[17]

The way Alberuni explains the location of important places in the whole of Northern as well as Central India and Gujarat with reference to their distances from Kanauj, suggests that the territorial legacy of Harsha's empire was still fresh down to his time. At the same time, his incidental identification of the regions on the prephery of *Madhyadesha* as being ruled by powerful

[16] *Alberuni's India*, I, p.173.
[17] Ibid.

independent rulers, for example the territory of Dhar under Raja Bhoj or those of Ujjain and Kashmir, as well as his list of Indian scripts corresponding to linguistic divisions of the subcontinent, show that Alberuni was fully aware of the existing political boundaries as well as linguistic and cultural zones of *Hind*. Yet he treats the entire country as representing a single cultural tradition carrying within its folds a variety of faiths, languages, and social formations. It is noteworthy that he includes the scripts of the regions falling outside the confines of *Aryavarta*, including "*Andhri*" (Telugu), "*Kanari*" (Kannada) and "*Dravidi*" (Tamil) in the list of the then known Indian languages. This should indicate the extent to which the process of the absorption into India of the regions outside the core territory of *Aryavarta* had progressed by the beginning of the eleventh century.

III

Of the caste-system Alberuni gives us two distinct impressions. One reflects the *shastric* rhetoric of his texts and of his informants most of whom were possibly learned Brahmans. This impression ascribes a sanctified rigidity to the caste taboos which, in all likelihood, were much looser in actual practice. The other impression represents the caste system in a state of continuous flux and change. This second impression may be related to information based on his personal observation or obtained from persons not committed to reproducing shastric pronouncements. This is, for example, illustrated by his remarks on the caste status of a person falling prisoner into the hands of Muslim invaders. He was told by his learned informants that once a person was taken prisoner or enslaved, he was "never allowed to return into those conditions of life in which he was before he was carried off as a prisoner." On the other hand, popular gossip indicated that a regaining of caste status was possible for such persons provided they went through a cleansing ritual after returning to their country.[18] Similarly, Alberuni's reference to the rise of the Brahmanical ruling dynasty of Hindu Shahiyas clearly reveals his knowledge that the functions assigned to the twice-born Kshatriyas and Brahmans were not always adhered to in practice.[19] Yet while describing the functions Brahmans were

[18] Ibid., II, p.163.
[19] Ibid., II, p.13.

obliged to perform, the only role he assigns to them is that of priests.[20]

In the light of there examples, one may suggest, that Alberuni's qualitative statements about the caste system, though representing a significant pool of contemporary information, cannot always be accepted at face value. They need to be checked with other sources, as well as with Alberuni's own statements on the theme in other contexts.[21]

Alberuni's account tends to indicate a slow change in the religious beliefs of the people during his time. As is known, the process of displacement of Buddhism and Jainism by Brahmanical cults all over North India had been progressing steadily since the seventh century.[22] By the time Alberuni wrote his account, Buddhism had already been reduced to the status of a small sect in some parts of India. It was almost entirely represented by the Mahayana sect, which had already incorporated in its system many of the beliefs and practices of the Brahmanical cults. Referring to them as *Shamaniyya* (red-robed monks), Alberuni makes the acute observation that "though they cordially hate the Brahmans, [they] still are nearer to them than to others."[23] It is, perhaps, keeping in mind this situation of Brahmanical-Buddhist relationship, that Alberuni opines: "there is very little disputing about theological topics" among Indians. "At the most", he writes, "they fight with words, but they will never stake their soul or body or their property on religious controversy."[24] This observation, however, was true only for the North-Western parts of India where Buddhism had been reduced, by Alberuni's time, to the position of an insignificant sect. The situation in the eastern parts was quite different. Antagonism

[20] Ibid., II, pp.130-35.

[21] An illustration of the uncritical acceptance of Alberuni's statements leading to erroneous conclusions is provided by K.A. Nizami's (*Some Aspects of Religion and Politics in India during the Thirteenth Century*, Aligarh, 1961, p.69) reference to limits imposed on the Brahmans. He cites Alberuni's statement: "The Brahmana is obliged to dwell between the river Sindh in the north and the river Carmavati in the South. He is not allowed to cross either of these frontiers so as to enter the country of the Turk or of Karnataka" (*Alberuni's India*, II, pp.133-134). Nizami, however, fails to note that this statement is negated by Alberuni's own mention of the Brahman dynasty of Hindu Shahiyas of Kabul who were ruling there down to 1026 (op.cit., II, p.13).

[22] Tara Chand, *Influence of Islam on Indian Culture*, p.5.

[23] *Alberuni's India*, I, p.21.

[24] Ibid., I, p.19.

between Buddhists and followers of Brahmanical cults often led to violent clashes down to the time Bengal was overrun by Bakhtyar Khalji (1203).[25]

It is apparent that the two facets of Brahmanical faith more familiar to Alberuni were its Vaishnavite and Shaivite versions. Between them the former appears to have become more popular. In Alberuni's perception, the *Bhagavadgita* was the most important religious text of the Hindus. He frequently reproduces passages from an early version of the book with admiration and unconcealed sympathy.[26] It is an indication that Vaishnavism with its emphasis on *bhakti* was emerging as the more popular cult during the eleventh century.

That the Vaishnavism of Alberuni's perception was still in its formative stage is borne out by his inadequate notice of the beliefs and values that surround the legends of Rama and Krishna. He was, no doubt, aware of the story of the *Ramayana* as "immortalized" in Valmiki's "books",[27] but most probably, the text was not available to him for a closer study. Again, his references to the legend of Rama do not mention Ayodhya, which, like the Chinese traveller Yuan Chwang (629-45), he places on the Ganges somewhere between Kanauj and Varanasi.[28] It seems that his entire information on Rama's legend was derived from the *Vaishnavapurana*.

Some of the popular beliefs and attitudes that became central to Vaishnav ethos by the sixteenth century were thus yet to be clearly defined. This also applies to the legend of Krishna and Radha.[29] Although, Alberuni's perception was that Hindus generally venerated the cow and that its killing was strictly forbidden, there is no hint of the cow being an object of worship. On the other hand, he records some of his Hindu informants telling him that eating of cow's flesh is forbidden "because it is essentially cold" and thus harmful to the health of human beings. There were others among his Hindu informants who came forward with the information that before the time of the legendary king Bharata "there existed sacrifices, part of which was killing of

[25] Cf. Tara Chand, *Influence of Islam on Indian Culture*, pp.215-17.

[26] Cf. Sachau, *Alberuni's India*, Preface, p.xlvii. See tr. of Alberuni's text, II, pp.27-30, where the Hindu concept of God is explained by quoting from the *Bhagavadgita*.

[27] *Alberuni's India*, tr. Edward C. Sachau, II, p.3.

[28] Ibid., I, p.200.

[29] The legend of Krishna and Radha is not noticed by Alberuni, nor does he mention places like Mathura, Vrindraban and Dwarka in its context.

cows."[30] This evidence confirms that some of the popular Hindu beliefs and cultural traits that came to be firmly established in North India with the growing impact of Vaishnavism during the succeeding centuries, were as yet in their early formative stage in the beginning of the eleventh century.

IV

The response of the Hindu rulers to the intrusion of the Ghaznavides (AD 997-1001) into Trans-Indus region the was, apparently, on the same pattern as discernible later in the case of the Delhi Sultanate. They offered fierce resistance to initial acts of conquest but once the invaders had established their military pre-eminence in the region, the defeated Hindu rulers would be inclined to come to terms with them in the same manner as they would have done in the case of a Hindu superior power. This is illustrated by Alberuni's notice of the relations between Sultan Mahmud of Ghaznin (997-1030) and the Hindu Shahiya ruler of Kabul, Anandapala. According to Alberuni, Anandapala offered to assist Mahmud militarily against the "Turks" of Khurasan at a time when the relations between the two were very strained. Anandapala is reported to have written to Mahmud "I do not speculate on the impression which this will make on you. I have been conquered by you, and, therefore, I do not wish that another man should conquer you."[31] The sentiment permeating this message, much lauded by Alberuni, is obviously the one that would ideally be perceived as informing the relations between two Hindu rulers. There is nothing in Alberuni's account to suggest that Hindu Shahiya resistance to Ghaznavides was viewed by either side as a part of a larger "civilizational" conflict. This impression seems to agree with the general picture of Ghaznavide-Hindu Shahiya relations, based on a more comprehensive survey of contemporary evidence.[32]

Another important aspect of the Ghaznavide state system was the presence of several highly placed Hindu military officers in Mahmud's service. The most famous of them, Tilak played an important role in controlling the situation in the Punjab after

[30] *Alberuni's India*, I, pp.60, 151-53.

[31] Ibid., I, pp.13-14.

[32] Cf. Mohammad Habib, *Sultan Mahmud of Ghazni*, reprint, Delhi, 1967, pp.23, 27, 33, 34-39.

Mahmud's son Mas'ud's accession.[33] From Alberuni, one comes to know that some of the Hindu troops serving in the Ghaznavide army were of *Kanara* origin.[34]

There is also a strong probability of the lower rung of Ghaznavide administration, particularly in the Punjab, being manned by elements of the dispossessed Hindu aristocracy. Alberuni's statements implying the presence of a large number of educated Hindus at Ghaznin, Multan and Lahore point to such a likelihood; this would also have been in accord with the practice of Arab rule in Sindh and Multan during the preceeding two centuries.[35]

One might suggest that the general hostility of the Hindus towards Muslims, resulting from Mahmud's plundering raids,[36] was a temporary phenomenon. Cordial treatment of Muslims settled in different parts of India by the Hindu rulers appears to have continued during the eleventh and twelfth centuries.[37] This impression is supported by inscriptions as well as by recorded traditions. For example, a tradition recorded in the sixteenth century credits a Pandiya ruler with building a large mosque at the village Goripaleiyan near Madurai during the eleventh century.[38] And the construction of the Somnath-Veraval mosque by Arjunadeva of Gujarat in 1262, as attested by a bilingual Sanskrit-Arabic inscription, has long been known to epigraphists.[39]

33 *Mahmud of Ghazni*, pp.96-97: Abu'l Fazl Baihaqi (*Tarikh-i Al-i Subuktigin*, ed. Morely, Calcutta, 1862) is cited as stating that "kettle-drums were beaten in his quarters according to the customs of Hindu chiefs." He is reported to have taken over the command of "the Indian troops" from a certain Sonyad Rai at the time of Mas'ud's accession.

34 *Alberuni's India*, I, p.173.

35 Cf. Andre Wink, *al-Hind*, Vol.I, p.155, for the incorporation of "native aristocracy" in the Arab "power centres".

36 For Alberuni's statement to this effect, see *Alberuni's India*, tr. Edward C. Sachau, I, p.21.

37 Cf. Tara Chand, *Influence of Islam on Indian Culture*, pp.40-48.

38 See Tara Chand, op.cit., p.40-41.

39 E. Hultszsch, 'A Grant of Arjunadeva of Gujarat dated 1264 AD', *Indian Antiquary* , XI, pp.241-45; D.C. Sircar, 'Veraval Inscription of Chaulukya-Vaghela Arjuna, 1264 AD', *Epigraphia Indica*, XXXIV, pp.141-50.

9

The Idea of India in Amir Khusrau

SYED ALI NADEEM REZAVI

It appears that by the thirteenth century, the concept of India as a distinct geographical entity, came into Indo-Persian literature along with an understanding of a composite culture, and, also with it, a sense of love of the country. The most prominent examples of such patriotism and ideas of a common heritage appear in the writings of Amir Khusrau, the poet-laureate of the Delhi Sultanate.

Amir Khusrau was born at Patiali in the modern district of Etah in Uttar Pradesh in 1253. His father, Amir Saifuddin Mahmud was a Turk who had migrated to India during the reign of Iltutmish, some years prior to Khusrau's birth, from the city of Kush (now known as Shahr-i Sabz) in Uzbekistan. His mother was the daughter of 'Imādul Mulk, a noble from Delhi.[1] Khusrau was a prolific writer and has left behind important works like *Qirānu-s Sa'dain, Miftāhu-l Futūh, Shīrīn wa Khusrau, Hasht Bihisht, Masnavi Dewal Rānī wa Khizr Khān, Matlau'l Anwār, I'jaz-i Khusravī, Khazāinu-l Futūh* and *Nuh Sipihr*.[2] Although in almost all these works Khusrau has left behind statements which help us understand his vision and concept of India, the *Nuh Sipihr* appears to be the most prolific in the outflow of patriotic statements.

The *Nuh Sipihr* is a *masnawī* which was completed by Khusrau in 1318 and eulogises Mubarak Shah Khalji. It appears to reflect most perfectly the ideas of Khusrau about India which he had tried to develop in his earlier works. This work is divided into nine chapters which correspond to the nine skies or spheres (*sipihr*) of the heavens. It is in the third chapter of this work that we find a long and detailed eulogy of India. Amir Khusrau proudly asserts:

[1] For a life history of Amir Khusrau see, Muhammad Wahid Mirza, *The Life and Works of Amir Khusrau*, Calcutta, 1935; Mohammad Habib, 'Hazrat Amir Khusrau of Delhi', *Politics and Society During the Early Medieval Period, Collected Works of Professor Mohammad Habib*, ed.K.A. Nizami, Aligarh, 1974, I, pp.291-355.

[2] For a full list of authentic writings of Khusrau, see, Wahid Mirza, op.cit.; For an exhaustive listing of Khusrau's patriotic verse see, S. Sabahuddin Abdur Rahman, *Hindustan Amir Khusrau ki Nazar Mein*, Azamgarh, n.d. (Urdu).

If my adversary taunts me as to why I prefer (*tarjih*) *Hind* over other lands.
(I would say:)There are two reasons for this assertion (*hujjat*):
The first reason is that this land since time immemorial (has been destined)
To be the place of my birth (*maulud*), abode (*mawa*) and motherland (*watan*).[3]

He further justifies the praise and precedence which his motherland deserves by citing a well known tradition of the Prophet: "the love of motherland is an essential part of the true faith (*hub al-watan min al-īmān*)".He asserts that this is an essential part of his creed (*dīn*).[4]

In the introductory section of this chapter Khusrau clarifies that the praise of India was reserved in this section as the presiding planet of both, the seventh sky (to which this chapter corresponds) and India was *zuhl* (Saturn).[5] He claims that although 'Rum (Greece), Khurasan (Iran) and Khotan (China)' allege (*ta'na*) their superiority, he had knowledge of the efficacy of this country's magic and thus could prove that *Hind* is better than any other country. For

If the Creator bestows upon me the gift
(So that) my easy flowing pen (*kilk*) may be empowered to express qualities to perfection,
I aspire not to leave the greatness of this land on earth (concealed).
But raise it to the sky upto the (height) of the heaven (*khuld-i barin*).[6]

Khusrau then goes on to enumerate seven rational (*aqli*) proofs (*asbat*) of the assertion (*hujjat*) that India was the earth's Paradise. The first argument is that after being thrown out from heaven Adam found refuge in this country. According to him, "As Hind was just like heaven (*khuld nishān*), Adam could descend here and find repose".[7] Secondly, India was the land of the peacock, a heavenly bird. "Had Paradise (*firdaus*) been in

3 Amir Khusrau, *Nuh Sipihr*, ed. M.Wahid Mirza, Calcutta, 1950, p.150. For an English rendering of the third chapter of this work see, *India as seen by Amir Khusrau*, tr. R.Nath and Faiyaz Gwaliari, Jaipur, 1981. Some other works on this theme are: Sabahuddin Abdur Rahman, 'Nationalist Sentiments in Indo-Persian Literature', *Indo-Iranica*, 28, no.1,March 1965, pp.1-34; S.B.Nigam, 'Amir Khusrau and India', *Indo-Iranica*, 24, no.3-4,1971, pp.67-73; Shujaat A.Sandilvi, 'A great Indian patriot', *Amir Khusrau Memorial Volume*, Govt.of India pub., 1975, pp.21-32.

4 *Nuh Sipihr*, p.150

5 Ibid., p.147.

6 Ibid.,p.148.

7 Ibid., pp.151-52.

some other country (lit. garden, '*bāgh*'), this bird would have gone thither."[8] Thirdly, the serpent, which was a companion of the peacock in heaven, also accompanied it to this land, but as this land was known for its good and beneficial deeds while the serpent had the vice of biting, it was allotted a place below the earth and not above it.[9] Khusrau puts forward four other arguments, which include the moderate climate of India as compared with the severe climatic conditions of his Central Asian homeland[10] and the tradition of the Prophet that the faithful would receive their reward not in this world but in the heaven while the unbelievers would enjoy here itself:

Hind was a Paradise for the unbelievers since the advent of Adam till the coming of Islam,
Even in recent times, these infidels (*gabar*) have had every pleasure of heaven like wine and honey.[11]

After establishing that India was the heaven on earth, Khusrau goes on to discuss the 'reasons' of his '*preference* of Hind over Rum, Iraq, Khurasan and Qandhar' and discourses on the ideal climate of his country, its flowers, and fruits. Discussing the moderate Indian climate Khusrau remarks:

They (Khurasanians) are deafened (by the excessive cold) and do not listen to the arguments (of India being heaven)
(And) instead accuse it of possessing an extremely hot climate.
In reply (to this) I cite again what the prophet had said.
The hot weather is troublesome and that is all
But every one is killed through cold weather.[12]

Further praising the Indian climate, Khusrau says that it is so moderate that a poor peasant (*dahqan*) spends the night in the pasture-land grazing his flock with only a single worn-out cloak (*kuhn chadaraki*) wrapped around him, a Brahman can take his bath in the cold water of the river early in the morning, while a mere branch of a tree is enough to shade the poor of the country.[13] There is the spring season (*bahār*) all the year round in India and thus an abundance of greenery and beautiful fragrant flowers which do not lose their fragrance even after they wilt.[14] Among

[8] Ibid., p.152.
[9] Ibid., p.153.
[10] Ibid., pp.154-56.
[11] Ibid., p.156.
[12] Ibid., p.158-59.
[13] Ibid., p.159.
[14] Ibid., pp.159-60; *Dewal Rani Khizr Khan*, Aligarh, 1917, pp.128-33.

the juicy fruits of India, Khusrau mentions mangoes (*naghzak*), bananas (*muzi*), which are extremely soft; and *nabati bamri* (? sugarcane). Cardamom (*lāchi*), camphor (*kafur*) and cloves (*qaranfal*) are mentioned by him as the dry fruits of India.[15] Betel-leaf (*tanbul*) comes for special mention as a 'leaf which is eaten like a fruit (*meva*) and there is nothing elsewhere in the world like it.'[16] He tells us that the betel leaf, presumably an expensive commodity at the time, was something meant for the *elite*:

The ordinary people (*ahl-i shikam*) have no taste (*zauq*) for it,
Only the high (*mihtar*) and their sons relish it.
Its special (preparation) is not for every one
Except for the *Qutb-i falak* (the king).[17]

Amir Khusrau's idea of India and its geographical boundaries, comes out more clearly when he mentions the different languages which the people of this country speak:

There are different languages in every area (*'arsa*) and region (*nahiyat*) of this land. Having their own special phraseology and rules which are not transient (*'ariyati*) are *Sindhi, Lahauri* (Punjabi), *Kashmiri, Kubri, Dhur-Samandri*(Kannada),*Tilangi* (Telugu), *Gujar* (Gujarati), *Ma'abari* (Tamil), *Gauri* (dialect of Northern Bengal), *Bengali, Awad* (Awadhi), *Dehli.* All around, within the boundaries of this land, are these *Hindavi* languages since olden times, and all of them are spoken by the people for all purposes.[18]

It is interesting to note that Marathi and Malayalam are not mentioned by Khusrau. Malayalam had not perhaps separated from Tamil by this time, but the omission of Marathi is difficult to explaine unless it is represented by 'Kubri'. Dealing with the commonly spoken languages during his time (*Hindavi* and Persian) and the regional dialects, Khusrau points out:

Surely! The popularity of Turkish grew similarly.
It spread with the Turkish rule on the earth.
As it was the language of the prominent people (*khasa*).
The commoners also adopted it, and it became popular in the world.
Hind similarly got its spoken languages.
Hindavi is and has been the (spoken language) of India.

[15] *Nuh Sipihr,*, p.160. See also *Qiranus Sa'dain*, Aligarh, 1918, pp.33-34, 109; *Dewal Rani Khizr Khan*, pp.43-44.

[16] *Nuh Sipihr* ; also *Qiranus Sa'dain,* op.cit., pp.145-46; *Dewal Rani Khizr Khan*, p.43.

[17] *Nuh Sipihr.*, p.161.

[18] Ibid., p.179-80.

The Ghurids and the Turks came, and
Persian was spoken by them
The people when they came into contact with them
By and by (*beh wa beh*) acquired the knowledge of Persian.
The other languages which were there
Were constrained to be confined in their own areas.[19]

Khusrau also mentions the linguistic versatility of the Indians. He says that whereas an Indian can fluently converse in any of the foreign languages, people outside India (*aqsa-i digar*) are unable to speak 'Indian dialects' (*sukhan-i Hindi*).

The people of Khita, Mongols, Turks and Arabs
In (speaking) Indian dialects get sewn lips
But *we* can speak any language of the world
As expertly as a shepherd tends his sheep.[20]

Khusrau's patriotism was not just theoretical. He claims to have himself mastered the Indian languages:

In most of these people's languages
I have gained knowledge (i.e. learnt)
I know them, enquired about them, and can speak them
And to an extent, more or less, have been enlightened by them.[21]

Amir Khusrau also mentions Sanskrit and its rich literature but remarks that it was the language of the Brahmans. Even amongst them not all can claim mastery over this language. Like Arabic, Sanskrit has its grammar, definitions, system, techniques, rules and literature.[22] Further:

This language (Sanskrit) has the quality of a pearl amongst pearls
It is inferior to Arabic, but superior to Dari (Persian)"[23]

Khusrau with great pride mentions that scholars from all over the world come to India to gain knowledge and expertise. However a Brahman never leaves the boundaries of India to acquire knowledge as there is no need for it.[24]

Brahmans in their knowledge and intellect
Are far superior to (the knowledge of) all the books of Aristotle...
Whatever the Greek revealed in philosophical thought to the world

[19] Ibid., p.178.
[20] Ibid., p.166.
[21] Ibid., pp.172-73.
[22] Ibid., p.180.
[23] Ibid., p.181; also *Dewal Rani Khizr Khan*, 41-43.
[24] *Nuh Sipihr*, p. 167, also p.169.

The Brahmans have a greater wealth (of it)".[25]

However these Brahmans are by nature quite and do not speak much, so that most of their knowledge remains hidden from the world and tends generally to be misunderstood. Khusrau however counts himself amongst those who acknowledge their virtues and qualities:

As nobody has tried to learn from the Brahmans
They have remained unrevealed.
But I to an extent have done a bit of research in this matter
(And after) putting a stamp of confidence on their heart
Have gained some insight into their secrets (of learning).
Whatever I could grasp has not been contradicted (from any quarter) so far.[26]

Dealing with the superior knowledge and learning of the Indians, he remarks:

I may be slightly biased in my views
Yet whatever I will submit, I shall justify
Though there are men of letters (elsewhere),
Nowhere is wisdom (*danish*) and philosophy (*hikmat*) so well written."[27]

Logic (*mantiq*), astrology (*tanjim*) and scholastic theology (*kalām*), except *fiqh* (Islamic law), are found and well understood in India. All rational sciences, the natural sciences (*tabi'yi*) and Mathematics (*riyazi*) originated in India.[28] Regarding the Indian origin of the numerals (*hindsa*), Khusrau writes:

Even if Wisdom (*'aql*) makes a detour of the world
It will not find such a gift of *hikmat* (i.e. arithmetic)
Take 'zero' for instance, which is a blank mark in itself
When used along with something else, becomes meaningful
When the science of mathematics (*riyazi*) developed from it
The Book *Almagest* (of Ptolemy) and Euclid came into existence
When this science of numerals with its addition and subtraction
Is not based on this system it becomes zero.
The scholars have not been able to add to(the science of *hindsa*)
And it has remained unchanged since its origin.
The inventor of it was one Asa, a Brahman
And in this there is no doubt

[25] Ibid., p. 162.
[26] Ibid., p.163.
[27] Ibid., p.161.
[28] Ibid., p.162.

From him (this science) got its name *Hind Asa,*
Which was shortened by the intelligent to *hindsa.*
Creator of this science was a Brahman
And however strange it may appear
The Greek science came to depend on it.[29]

Apart from the invention of the numerals, especially zero, Amir Khusrau also mentions the invention of chess (*shatranj*) by the Indians which according to him was 'a unique contribution of *Hind* to the world'.[30] A similar contribution of India to world culture was the '*Kalila wa Dimna*' or the *Panchatantra*, which had such an 'excellent flight of imagination'.[31] Another singular contribution of the Indians which Khusrau mentions is Indian music and its hypnotising effect even on the animals.[32]

Apart from all this Khusrau's patriotism makes him sing paeans for the Indian female beauty,[33] Indian clothes,[34] and even its animals.[35] He singles out the Indian parrot (*tuti*), magpie (*sharak*), crow, skylark, wood-pecker, crane (*bagula*), peacock, monkey and elephant which were unique in the world due to their intelligence. As to wine, he exclaims: "Give me wine, but not of any other country. Give me wine of this country(the juice of sugarcane)."[36]

India in the eyes of Amir Khusrau was not only his *watan* but a geographic, cultural and multi-religious entity. In one of his works Khusrau mentions a Hindu who worships fire. When asked why he did so, he replied that the burning fire lights a divine yearning in him and a desire to attain annihilation (*fanā*) in order to gain eternal life (*baqā*). Khusrau lauds this feeling.[37] Although a second generation migrant to India, Khusrau appears to have fully imbibed the idea of India as a unique country, distinct in many ways from other countries. To quote:

How exhilarating is the climate of this country
Where so many birds sing melodiously.

[29] Ibid., p.168.
[30] Ibid., p.170.
[31] Ibid., p.169.
[32] Ibid., pp.170-72.
[33] *Dewal Rani Khizr Khan*, pp.133-34; see also *Shirin wa Khusrau,* Aligarh, 1925, pp.25-29; *Hasht Bihisht*, Aligarh, 1918, pp.29-30.
[34] *Qiranus Sa'dain*, p.132; *Dewal Rani Khizr Khan*, p.43.
[35] *Nuh Sipihr*, pp.181-91.
[36] Ibid., p.210.
[37] *Dewal Rani Khizr Khan*, pp.195-96.

Poets, composers and singers rise from this land
As abundantly and as naturally as the grass....
How great is this land which produces men
Who deserve to be called men!
Intelligence is the natural gift of this land,
Even the illiterate are as good as scholars
There cannot be a better teacher than the way of life of the people
It is this which enlightens the masses. It is a gift of the Almighty!
This is very rare in other countries
It is the effect of the cultural environment of this land....
If perchance any Iranian, Greek, or Arab comes by,
He will not have to ask for anything
Because they will treat him as their own.
They will play an excellent host and win his heart!
Even if they indulge in humour with him
They also know how to smile like a flower.[38]

With the glory of India, Khusrau cannot help linking his own fame!

No wizard in the art of poetry like Khusrau exists under the sun
Because *Khusrau belongs to India* and he is the admirer of *Qutb-i Alam* (the Sultan).
Even if Jupiter,who is the wisest of the Celestial beings,comes from the sky
He would also not raise any doubt (to this statement)
And will acknowledge its truth.[39]

[38] *Nuh Sipihr,* pp.442-43.
[39] Ibid., p.172.

10

The Monetary Integration of India under the Mughal Empire

NAJAF HAIDER

The establishment and expansion of Mughal rule in India resulted in the political unification of regions and a unified control over trade routes and markets. The two processes were intertwined. Territorial integration was an essential precondition for regular taxation, and the viable state was increasingly the one which had the capacity to impose and collect taxes within a well defined territory and establish a degree of uniformity of custom among tax paying subjects. A state with a strong fiscal and military base was capable of holding its territories and markets together by preventing their alienation and defining the space within which power could be shared. As a result it could also have the capacity of devising and implementing uniform economic policies throughout its domain.

In no area of political and economic organization of the empire was the role of the Mughal state so decisive and its presence so palpable as the monetary system. Imperial control of coinage was an important aspect of the economic integration and unification of markets in large parts of India. In this chapter we will be concerned with the mechanism through which this control was exercised and the process by which unification was achieved. It is hoped that this study would also help us to assess recent claims about the diminishing presence of the Mughal state beyond its core area and the absence of a unified market either in money or merchandise.

I. *Metallic Currency and Money of Account*

A remarkable achievement on the part of the Mughal authorities was the creation of a currency system which was of uniform weight and fineness. In the early sixteenth century, the monetary scene of northern India was dominated by two sets of currencies, viz. the billon and copper issues of the Delhi Sultans (1215-1526) and the silver *shahrukhis* of Babur and Humayun minted on a Central Asian standard.[1] In outlying regions, local and

[1] Najaf Haider, 'Precious Metal Flows and Currency Circulation in the Mughal

foreign coins circulated and commanded customary loyalties. Like other parts of the apparatus of the state, the Mughal monetary policy during the early years of Akbar's reign (1556-1605) was in a formative stage. However, Akbar had the advantage of inheriting from the Surs a tri-metallic currency system based on the gold *muhr*, silver *rupiya* and copper *paisa*. Of these three, the silver rupee of 179 grains, gained greater popularity in the core regions of the empire compared to the *shahrukhis*.

The first step towards monetary integration was taken when the Mughal administration introduced a money of account (*tanka-i muradi*), with a fixed value in copper so that each *tanka* was worth two standard copper coins.[2] The purpose of the introduction of the money of account was to establish a link between different currencies, both the pre-existing as well as the imperial. In the fiscal system, its function was to facilitate the collection of revenue in all types of coins tendered by the tax payer (billon, copper or silver) as long as it could be accounted in *tanka-i muradi*. Since the *tanka* was also used for the disbursement of state finances, a clear balance sheet was drawn up for matching income with expenditure.

In the last quarter of the sixteenth century, a number of developments took place on the world scale which had important consequences for India's monetary economy. The eastward migration of Spanish-American silver, together with the political unification of trade routes between the Levant and the Indian Ocean by the Ottomans and between the hinterland and coastal cities by the Mughals, now turned India into the biggest importer of foreign bullion outside Europe. Supplies of precious metals and pre-existing stocks were converted into money through the

Empire', *Journal of Economic and Social History of the Orient*, XXXIX, (1996) p. 343; Shireen Moosvi, 'The Monetary System and Price Movements in India', in *History of Civilizations of Central Asia*, V, eds. Chahryar Adle and Irfan Habib (Paris, 2003) , p. 455.

[2] Of the three essential functions of money – measure of value, means of exchange and mode of accumulation – the money of account performs only the first. For *tanka-i muradi* see Abul Fazl, *Akbarnama*, Oriental and India Office Collection (OIOC), British Library MS. Add. 27247, f. 332b; text eds. Agha Ahmad Ali and Abdur Rahim (Bib. Indica, 1887), III, p. 383; 'Todarmal's Original Memorandum on the Revenue Administration, March 1582', tr. Shireen Moosvi, *Proceedings of the Indian History Congress*, 49th Session, (Dharwad, 1988), pp. 237-48; S. H. Hodivala, 'The Muradi Tanka', *Journal of the Asiatic Society of Bengal*, New Series, XIII (1917), pp. 80-96.

operation of the twin institutions of the state and the market.[3]

II. *Fiscal and Monetary Measures*

The annexation of Gujarat to Akbar's empire in 1572 strengthened the links between the ports of the western Indian Ocean and northern India and intensified the flow of Spanish-American silver to the inland mints. Soon after, Akbar embarked upon a set of measures to reorganize the fiscal structure of the empire. When the Mughal military-bureaucracy was organized around numerical ranks (*mansab*) in 1574-75, a salary structure was introduced for the nobles and their soldiers in which half of the payment was made in silver money and the rest in gold and copper in equal proportions. Simultaneously, all *jagirs* were resumed and converted into *khalisa* or directly taxable territories subject to central financial control ('the *karori* experiment'). The dissolution of payment by land assignment required large amounts of cash to be paid out by the treasury. In order to effect such massive payments, the state required sufficient stock of silver at its disposal which could only be raised from taxes. The Mughal machinery already had a device in the *zabt* system by which the revenue demand assessed in kind could be commuted and realized in cash on the basis of pre-fixed schedules of rates (*dastur-ul amals*).[4]

(a) Reorganisation of the Mint Administration

The next logical step for the state was to galvanize the supply of money to the users as well as the state treasury. To some degree, this was accomplished by a major reorganization of silver mints and their administration which took place in two stages. In 1577-78 the mint administration was transferred from local functionaries (*chaudhuris*) to officials directly appointed by the emperor. After the central administration took over control of the finances, it found it more convenient to centralize the mint administration as well and the appointment of some leading nobles of the empire to the position of the superintendent of the mint *(darugha-i dar-uz zarb*) indicates the degree of importance attached to it.[5]

[3] Haider, 'Precious Metal Flows', pp. 300-35.

[4] Irfan Habib, *The Agrarian System of Mughal India*, 2nd rev. edn., New Delhi, 1999, pp. 201-2, 236-40.

[5] *Akbarnama*, MS Add. 27247, f. 249b.

In the second stage, from 1582, mint production was integrated into the fiscal structure through a series of guidelines issued to the revenue officials, mint superintendents and money-changers (Todarmal's recommendations). The purpose of this policy was to ensure uninterrupted supply of fresh silver money from the mint to the agrarian sector where revenue officials and *sarrafs* could exchange all types of coins tendered by the tax payers at official rates. This greatly facilitated the payment of revenue in cash by freeing the peasants from the obligation of bringing currency of a particular type or denomination. At the same time, it allowed the treasury to get hold of all those coins which were to be withdrawn from circulation and would not be brought voluntarily to the mint by the users. By disbursing its expenditure in the standard Mughal specie, the state reintroduced minted silver into the economy while all demonetized and obsolete currency was channelled out of the exchange network and into the mint for constant re-coinage. Thus by streamlining currency circulation in this manner, the state was able to achieve a degree of uniformity and standardization in the core area of the empire.[6]

(b) Currency Depreciation, Discount Rates and Demonetization

The policy towards the circulation, withdrawal and replacement of substandard currencies evolved in two stages and related to two different sets of coinage: one which was previously issued by the Mughal state and the other which belonged to the older regional rulers. In both cases, the right of the Mughal state to issue, circulate and withdraw currencies in the empire formed the basis for formulating and articulating monetary policies.

In medieval market economies the value of the metallic currency was determined mainly by its weight, purity and cost of minting (mint price). To this the money-changers added their own commission while buying and selling the specie (market price). It was at the latter price that a coin was exchanged in the market either for commodities or for coins of other denominations. If a change occurred in any of the above factors, an adjustment of the exchange rate became necessary.

On purely economic grounds, the natural wear and tear resulting in weight-loss, caused by the frequency with which coins were used in exchange, was bound to affect the market

[6] See references cited in footnote 2.

value of the coins. Both the market and the state acknowledged that a precious metal coin, which remained in active circulation, lost some weight over a period of time due to the wearing of the metal. Added to this continuous loss was the loss caused by the deliberate acts of rubbing and clipping coins (*malish wa jaz*) by ordinary users, merchants and money-changers alike.[7] As a result, an enormous number of coins lighter than the standard weight were in circulation at any given time, requiring assessment by the money-changers whenever a payment in cash was effected. On the basis of this assessment a discount (Hindi *batta*; Pers. *sarf*) was levied whenever a lighter coin was proffered for payment.[8] For this purpose a system of classification of coins was evolved in which newly struck silver coins exchanged at a premium against those minted in previous years.[9] The money-changers and merchants rigorously enforced this classification, making an assessment of money by age in addition to that of real loss. With coins of similar denominations circulating at different exchange values, any transaction involving the rupee was bound to be contentious. The problem was heightened by the common temptation to receive payments in the new coins and to get rid of the old ones.[10]

The state's intervention in deciding the fate of deficient coins was motivated as much by the intention to maintain uniformity and order in currency circulation as by the desire to secure its own fiscal interest, since much of its income and expenditure was made in coins supplied by the market. The centralization of state finances for five years (1575-80) brought the imperial administration face to face with the realities of monetary management and the need to reform the system. To this effect, an elaborate schedule of exchange rates was prepared in which the values of gold and silver coins of all types were expressed in a single money of account (*tanka*) and differential rates of discount were fixed to account for weight loss. At the same time, all coins falling below the official limit were prescribed as un-coined bullion (*zar-i namaskuk*) and ordered to be withdrawn

[7] Abul Fazl, *Ain i Akbari*, 2 vols. ed. H. Blochmann (Bib. Indica, 1872-77), I, p. 27.

[8] J. B. Tavernier, *Travels in India*, 2 vols., tr. V. Ball, 2nd edn. rev. W. Crooke (London, 1925), I, p. 25.

[9] Irfan Habib, 'The Currency System of the Mughal Empire', *Medieval India Quarterly*, IV, 1961, p. 4 and notes.

[10] George Roques, *La maniere de negotier dans Les Indes Orientalles*, Bibliotheque Nationale, MS Fonds Francais 14614, Paris, ff. 226-7.

from circulation. After addressing the problems of weight loss and exchange rates, and watching its progress for about a decade, the state also acted to prevent the use of light rice grains by the 'thievish people' (*duzd peshgan*) to enhance discount in accepting payment. If Abu'l Fazl is to be believed, the Emperor took personal interest in introducing a new set of chalcedony rice grains (*baba ghuri birinj*) and made it obligatory for the first time in weighing fine metals. These monetary regulations were based on a careful assessment of the money market, the type of currency and degree of circulation, and the objective of attaining a uniform standard.[11]

The above regulations pertained to the coins already in circulation. To curb the influence of money market on future currency users, an immobilized numismatic date was given to all coins minted from 1582 so that no arbitrary discount could be charged on full weight coins simply on the basis of their age.[12]

The widespread prevalence of the system of discount on different varieties of coins and the administrative problems it caused intensified with the eighteenth century fragmentation of political authority. The problem was present ever since precious metal coinage came into common use and was so deeply entrenched in the mercantile milieu that it was very difficult for any political authority to set it right definitively. However, the Mughal monetary authorities, backed by a strong fiscal apparatus and administrative machinery, were able to impose their control, through a series of guidelines, on the currency market and were able to hold on to it for over a century.

(c) Recoinage, Regional Currencies and the Expansion of the Imperial Monetary System

While the set of measures described above concerned the reminting of Mughal imperial issues, another type related to coins issued by previous sovereigns and regional rulers. These remained outside the purview of the official discount system, and circulated due to their traditional association with a specific region, such as the billon *tanka* and Sur coins in the north, *shahrukhis* in the north-west and *mahmudis* in Gujarat, with or without the blessings of the monetary authorities. The displacement of these

[11] *Ain i Akbari*, I, pp. 27-9; *Akbarnama*, MS Add. 27247, f. 332b; Bib. Indica, III, p. 383.

[12] Najaf Haider, 'Disappearance of Coin Minting in the 1580s? A Note on the *Alf* Coins', in Irfan Habib (ed.), *Akbar and his India*, Delhi, 1997, pp. 55-65.

currency regimes by a uniform imperial system proved to be a difficult task.

Once the Mughal monetary policy towards the introduction and circulation of its own currency in the core areas of the empire was put in place, the attention of the administration was directed towards regional currencies. In 1592, an imperial order was issued to demonetize all precious metal coins of previous kings (*padshahan-i sabiq*). The premium they enjoyed on account of seigniorage was abolished and they were sold and purchased in the market as gold and silver bullion (*ba baha-i tila wa nuqra*). In the guidelines issued to the treasurer and the police chief (*kotwal*) in the 1590s, a clause referred exclusively to the treatment of the coins of previous rulers (*bastani maskuk*). It was ordered that they should be declared un-current (*na maskuk*) and should either be melted down (*ba gudazgah dahad*) or sent to the treasury at the value of uncoined bullion (*ba irj-i na maskuk*). Penalties were devised for offenders, and the money changers (*sarrafs*) were particularly targeted for their role in giving currency to regional coins as discounters of bills of exchange and buyers of foreign bullion.[13]

TABLE 1

Years	*Ahmadabad*	*Lahore*	*Thatta*
1572-1576	53.50	12.00	00.00
1577-1581	35.50	46.00	00.00
1582-1586	46.00	00.00	00.00
1587-1591	44.00	22.75	00.00
1592-1596	181.00	152.00	61.00
1597-1601	145.50	163.50	126.00
1602-1605	115.75	125.75	77.00
Total	621.25	522.00	270.00

Source: Unpublished Collections of Coins and Medals, British Museum, London; Department des Monnaies Medailles et Antiques, Bibliotheque Nationale, Paris; Heberden Coin Room, Ashmolean Museum, Oxford; *Catalogue of Coins in the Cabinet of the Chittagong University Museum*, Abdul Karim (Chittagong, 1979); *Catalogue of Coins in the Central Museum Nagpur*, part I, *Coins of the Mughal Emperors*, V. P. Rode (Bombay, 1969); *Catalogue of the*

[13] Abdu'l Qadir Badauni, *Muntakhab u't Tawarikh*, 3 vols., eds. William Lees and Ahmad Ali, Bib. Indica, 1864-9, III, 1869, p. 380; *A'in i Akbari*, I, pp. 284, 289.

Coins in the Indian Museum, Calcutta, vol. III, *Mughal Emperors of India*, H. Nelson Wright (Oxford, 1908); *Catalogue of Coins in the Panjab Museum, Lahore*, vol. II, *Coins of the Mughal Emperors*, R. B. Whitehead (Oxford, 1914); *Catalogue of Coins in the Provincial Museum, Lucknow*, *Coins of the Mughal Emperors*, 2 vols., C. J. Brown (Oxford, 1920); *Catalogue of the Collection of Coins illustrative of the History of the Rulers of Delhi up to 1858 AD in the Delhi Museum of Archaeology*, R. B. Whitehead (Calcutta, 1910); *A Supplement to Volume III of the Catalogue of Coins in the Indian Museum, Calcutta (The Mughal Emperors of India)*, Shamsuddin Ahmad (Delhi, 1939); *Supplementary Catalogue of Mughal Coins in the State Museum, Lucknow*, C.R. Singhal (Lucknow, 1965).

The purpose of passing laws against the circulation of regional coins was to allow the Mughal imperial issues to take their place. The corelation between re-coinage and regional expansion in rupee circulation becomes stronger if we relate our textual information to the numismatic material. Figures assembled in Table 1, from museum specimens serialized at five year intervals, depict the order of magnitude of rupee production at Ahmadabad, Lahore and Thatta, the three most prolific silver mints in the last quarter of the sixteenth century. The data for the entire period can be divided into two distinct segments: the pre-re-coinage period (1572-1591) and the period of re-coinage (1592-1605). The total for the first five years of re-coinage (1592-96) shows a four-fold increase from the previous quinquennium in the case of Ahmadabad and a jump of almost seven times in the case of Lahore. The trend continues up to the end of Akbar's reign. The data clearly indicate massive conversions of *mahmudis* of Gujarat and *shahrukhis* of the north-western territories into rupees following the new monetary policy.[14]

The regional mint of the lower Sind opened when the laws regarding the reminting of regional currencies were about to be formulated. Unlike the Mughals, the rulers of Lower Sind, both the Jams and the Tarkhans, never issued coins in gold and silver and allowed *laris* of Hurmuz and Basra and *reales* of Spain and Mexico to circulate freely in the market as legal tender.[15] In

[14] Najaf Haider, 'Mughals and Mahmudis: The Incorporation of Gujarat into the Mughal Monetary System', *Negotiating India's Past. Essays in Memory of Partha Sarthi Gupta*, eds. B. Pati, B.P. Sahu and T.K. Venkatasubramanian (New Delhi, 2003), pp.134-52.

[15] Tahir Muhammad 'Nisyani', *Tarikh-i Tahiri*, ed. Nabi Bakhsh Khan Baloch, (Hyderabad, Sind, 1964), p. 170. For the Jams see Simon Digby, 'The Coinage and Genealogy of the Later Jams', *Journal of the Royal Asiatic Society of Great Britain and Ireland*, 2 (1972), pp. 125-6.

1591, the Thatta mint became operational and began to strike rupees at an increasing rate till 1605. Between 1591 and 1605, the output of this mint was the largest for any comparable phase in the seventeenth century, and next only to Ahmadabad and Lahore in the whole of the Mughal Empire. This suggests that not only incoming bullion and specie were minted into rupees but also much of the existing stock was recoined. In the early seventeenth century, all transactions in lower Sind were quoted in rupees including the prices of commodities and the rates for bills of exchange.[16]

III. *Strong Currency and Stable Money*

After three decades of intense administrative, fiscal and economic developments, a monetary structure was evolved that prevailed in the seventeenth century, setting a benchmark in the history of the Mughal Empire. This meant a uniform currency system of standard weight and fineness (Tables 2 and 3) put in the place of the old regimes of billon-copper and of variegated regional currencies, and geared to a constant flow of silver through foreign trade. By the time we reach the seventeenth century, the silver rupee becomes the principal medium of exchange by relegating copper coins to the domain of small transactions.[17]

TABLE 2

The Weight of Mughal Silver Coins

Year	*Name of the Coin*	*Theoretical Weight (Contemporary Standard)*	*Theoretical Weight (troy grains)*	*Average Weight of Museum Specimens (troy grains)*
1526-1540	Shahrukhi	1 misqal	78.00	74.00
1545-1556	Rupiya	–	–	175.00
1556-1605	Rupiya	11.50 *masha*	177.94	173.00
1605-1611	Jahangiri	12.00 *masha*	213.52	206.00
*c.*1609-1611	Sawai	12.50 *masha*	222.42	215.00

[16] *Original Correspondence 1549*, OIOC, series E/3, ff. 135-6; *English Factories in India (1618-1669)*, 13 vols. (each volume titled by the year/s it covers), ed. William Foster (Oxford, 1906-27), *1634-36*, p. 131.

[17] Irfan Habib, 'A System of Trimetallism in the Age of 'Price Revolution', Effects of the Silver Influx on the Mughal Monetary System', *The Imperial Monetary System of Mughal India*, ed. J. F. Richards, (Delhi, 1987), pp. 137-70

1611-c.1657	Rupiya	10.00 *masha*	177.94	174.00
c.1657-1659	Rupiya	11.50 *masha*	177.94	175.00
1659-c.1671	Rupiya	11.50 *masha*	179.44	175.00
c.1671-1707	Rupiya	10.25 *masha*	179.37	175.00

Source: Najaf Haider, *The Monetary System of the Mughal Empire*, OUP, 2004 (forthcoming)

TABLE 3

The Fineness of Mughal Silver Coins (Rupees)

Ruler	*Mint*	*Date* (AH)	*Date* (AD)	*Silver* (%)	*Copper* (%)	*Gold* (%)	*Lead* (%)
Akbar	Agra	977	1569-70	**99.10**	0.30	0.54	0.06
Akbar	Lahore	989	1581	**99.20**	0.20	0.53	0.11
Akbar	Ahmadabad	1001	1592-93	**98.70**	0.80	0.08	0.08
Jahangir	Agra	1026	1617	**98.70**	0.90	0.46	0.21
Jahangir	Agra	1033	1623-24	**97.90**	1.00	0.07	0.93
Jahangir	Surat	1035	1625-26	**98.90**	0.50	0.73	0.24
Shahjahan	Agra	1038	1628-29	**99.20**	0.30	0.41	0.18
Shahjahan	Surat	1067	1656-57	**98.60**	1.10	0.20	0.20
Aurangzeb	Surat	1071	1660-61	**98.60**	0.80	0.10	0.47
Aurangzeb	Agra	1071	1660-61	**98.80**	0.80	0.20	0.11

Source: M. R. Cowell, *MS. Report of Energy Dispersive X-ray (EDX) and Energy Dispersive X-ray Fluorescence (XRF) Analyses of Mughal Silver Specimens*, Department of Coins and Medals, British Museum, 1996.

A strong currency has a greater degree of acceptance and mobility. The reputation commanded by the Mughal rupee on account of its unvarying weight and fineness expanded its area of circulation beyond localized points of production. The figures assembled in Table 4 are illustrative of the inter-regional mobility of the silver coin. It can be seen that out of 1967 specimens of Akbar's rupee recovered from the hoards discovered in the United Provinces (Uttar Pradesh), 81 percent came from mints situated outside the map area of UP (exclusive of Delhi which lay at the western border). One reason for this was the gravitational pull of the area which housed the imperial capital (Agra) and the central exchequer. But the other, and perhaps more important, factor was the presence of markets which supplied goods for long-distance trade. The rupee by moving across regions and localities ensured that networks of exchange operated without frontiers throughout the empire.

TABLE 4
Silver Coins (Rupees) of Akbar in UP Hoards

Name of the Mint (outside UP)	*Number of Coins*	*Percentage*	*Name of the Mint (within UP)*	*Number of Coins*	*Percentage*
Ahmadabad	1149.0	58.4	Agra	134.0	6.8
Bangala	8.0	0.4	Allahabad	42.0	2.1
Burhanpur	57.0	2.9	Bairata	27.0	1.4
Lahore	172.0	8.8	Delhi	90.5	4.6
Narnaul	12.0	0.6	Fatehpur	26.0	1.3
Patna	33.5	1.7	Jaunpur	41.0	2.1
Thatta	116.0	5.9			
Ujjain	59.0	3.0			
Total	1606.5	81.7		360.5	18.3

Source: *Treasure Trove Reports*, MS. Lucknow Museum (Courtesy Professor Shireen Moosvi).

The economics of minting in the Mughal Empire also ensured the stability of money. The imperial control of currency was accompanied by a system of open coinage in which the freedom to receive money was granted to every one on payment of brassage and seigniorage. This meant that the state decided the weight, fineness and fabric of currencies while the market determined their volume and prices. The level of mint output became a function of the supply of metals and the demand for money in the economy. This factor was decisive in shaping the geographical distribution of mints in the regions of the empire. Mints were located in market towns, in provincial capitals and in close proximity of the sources of monetary metals.[18]

The strength and stability of the Mughal silver currency, linked also to the rhythm of international exchange, was indeed tested time and again during fiscal and monetary crises, following declines in silver imports in the seventeenth century. In order to restore monetary equilibrium, the state responded with measures ranging from a rise in the mint price of bullion, to the implementation of revised and more manageable weight standards of coins, the re-introduction of copper coinage and the

[18] Haider, *Monetary System of the Mughal Empire* (forthcoming).

establishment of new mints. These changes were at once symptomatic of a rising demand for money at the current level of supplies and effective in bringing stability to the monetary circulation before the continuity in silver imports was restored.[19]

In most European states, the Ottoman Empire and Safavid Iran, debasement accompanying increasing flows of precious metals was a direct outcome of the rising expenditure of the state which led to currency mutations. In contrast, sound money remained the order of the day in the Mughal Empire and debasement was introduced once to meet the disparity between the demand and supply of money and at another time to gain profit. On both occasions it was abandoned within a short space of time. In ordinary circumstances, the state managed the fisc by spending reserve funds rather than by incurring debts or resorting to currency manipulations to lighten any debt burden.[20]

The trust and mobility enjoyed by the Mughal money suffered as a result of the declining power of the state and economic dislocation in the eighteenth century. A downturn in the hinterland, rising transaction costs due to fear, uncertainty and lack of safety for goods and money in transit, and Maratha expeditionary raids which began in 1703 and reached their highpoint in the second quarter of the eighteenth century, boded ill not only for the vigorous conduct of business but also for the efficient functioning of the state apparatus.[21] A report of 1732 in a local history of Ahmadabad mentions the removal of imperial officials (*mutasaddiān-i bādshāhī*) from the mint and the production of debased gold and silver coins (*tila wa nuqra mis amez*) for profit. As a result, 'the *ashrafi* and rupee of Ahmadabad which were always struck without alloy and to full fineness (*be ghash wa tamām 'aiyār*), lost currency outside the limits of the city'. The author informs us that for their ill-repute, the coins were no more acceptable in his own time (1761) even after the alloy was removed.[22]

IV. *Money-Changers and Monetary Unification*

The medieval Indian money market was dominated by the *sarrafs*

[19] Haider, 'Precious Metal Flows and Currency Circulation', pp. 335, 351-55.

[20] Ibid., p. 354.

[21] Roques, *La maniere de negotier*, ff. 239-40; Ashin Das Gupta, 'Trade and Politics in Eighteenth Century', in *Islam and the Trade of Asia*, ed. D.S. Richards (Oxford, 1970), p. 189; Ali Muhammad Khan, *Mirat-i Ahmadi*, 2 vols. and *Supplement*, ed. Syed Nawab Ali (Baroda, 1927-30), I, pp. 356, 359-69, 377-79.

[22] *Mirat-i Ahmadi*, II, p. 141.

who used their presence and expertise to determine the supply of currency and the rates of exchange. The fiscal interests of the local and provincial officials required the services of the *sarrafs*, a fact which underlined the symbiotic nature of their relationship with the state. The two often worked together in harmony to allow a smooth transition from one form of currency to another or to resolve the problems arising out of metallic circulation. At other times, as we saw, a conflict of interests seemed evident when the imperial bureaucracy attempted to regulate the market either for fiscal reasons or for perceived considerations of public welfare.

The monopolistic influence of the money-changers on the treatment of imperial coinage and determination of exchange rates was strengthened also by resilient regional customs which dictated the behaviour of currency users in resisting any drive for standardization. The state too visualized the activities of the money-changers and bankers as an essential aspect of the process of monetization. Currency circulation was an area in which the possibilities of conflict and cooperation arose in tandem between the state and the money market. Money was a symbol of the sovereignty of the state and crucial for its fiscal organization. The interest of the state lay in streamlining the exchange rates of the circulating medium, while the *sarrafs* thrived on exchange rate differences. However, regulations restricting mono-metallic arbitrage on the imperial as well as the regional issues were high on the state agenda and continued to be implemented with varying degrees of success (the success was greater in the case of the regional issues) through ordinances and exaction of bonds (*muchalka*), the monitoring of money-changing and, in one case, introducing the year-less *alf* coins.

V. *The State and the Market*

The Mughal state also contributed to the creation of a viable environment for conducting business in all parts of the empire. Although political interference was present (such as the exaction of forced labour), it did not materially affect the free-trade character of the Mughal state. There were no legal restrictions on accumulation (the law of escheat worked only for indebted nobles), business methods (including usury), and the movement of artisans and professionals. Indeed, the state made efforts to break the monopolies of skill-based professions engendered by the caste system to boost the supply of labour in individual sectors. Aurangzeb's declaration that the monopoly held by the gold wire drawers of the Srimal caste was illegal is a case in point.[23] We have the testimony of the Dutch factor, Geleyenssen, that the Mughals followed their predecessors in allowing and encouraging artisans and workers to settle in newly founded cities.[24] The territorial unification and political stability under Mughal rule appear to have facilitated the short and long distance migration of skilled and unskilled workers and artisans to areas of employment.

Conclusion

The fiscal and monetary policies of the Mughal state, such as the introduction of a cash-nexus in tax payments and wage disbursements (triggering a cycle of monetary circulation), the establishment of an open coinage system through imperial mints, and the implementation of a series of measures to create a standardized currency system in the empire (through recurring recoinage of demonetized specie and the introduction of freshly minted money into the exchange circuit), resulted in the creation of a uniform currency market in India.

Monetary circulation also found a common identity by the integration of markets in which mercantile groups played an important part. Despite their role in preserving the diversity of exchange rates and of commodity prices, money-changers and merchants were responsible to a large extent in offering a certain uniformity and cohesion to the areas covered by the network of monetized exchange by negotiating the movement of cash and goods across customs barriers.[25]

There is no reason to believe that Mughal India was a fully homogeneous economic unit despite being a unified political entity. The experiences of the different regions of the empire were varied. Not all were in a position to maintain a uniform level of commercialization or monetization. But the principles which governed the acquisition of money and the institutions which regulated its circulation could be seen to be working with more or less similar effect in all areas of the empire. To this extent, the role of the Mughal state remained extremely

[23] *Mirat-i Ahmadi*, I, pp. 292-93.

[24] W. H. Moreland, 'A Dutch Account of Mogul Administrative Methods', *Journal of Indian History*, IV, April 1925, p. 75.

[25] Najaf Haider, 'The Monetary Basis of Credit and Banking Instruments in the Mughal Empire', *Money and Credit in Indian History*, ed. Amiya Bagchi, (Delhi, 2002), pp. 58-79.

important. The standardized currency system, the organization of the mint, the taxation system, and the maintenance of law and order were integrative elements of state policy which worked together to provide a formal unity to the diverse market and monetary structures within the country.

11

Seventeenth-Century India as Seen by the Dutch

OM PRAKASH

The European perception of India as a distinct geographic and political entity probably does not go back to a time earlier than the late eighteenth, if indeed not the nineteenth century. This is certainly true of people of countries such as Netherlands whose historical association with India was entirely commerce-based and who regarded different regions of India essentially as constituent elements of a larger geographical area they described as the East Indies. This area embraced not only South Asia and Southeast Asia but also parts of the Middle East, and in a loose sense even the Far East. The relevant area of operation for the Dutch East India Company was what I have elsewhere described as the Great Arc of Asian Trade, extending from the Persian Gulf in the north-west to Japan in the north-east.

India had traditionally occupied a position of central importance in this trading network. In part, this was a function of the midway location of the subcontinent between West Asia on the one hand and Southeast and East Asia on the other. But perhaps even more important was the subcontinent's capacity to put on the market a wide range of tradable goods at highly competitive prices. These included agricultural goods, both food items such as rice, sugar and oil and raw materials such as cotton and indigo. While the bulk of the trade in these goods was coastal, the high seas trade component was by no means insignificant. The real strength of the subcontinent, however, lay in the provision of large quantities of manufactured goods, the most important amongst which were textiles of various kinds. While these included high value varieties such as the legendary Dhaka muslins and the Gujarat silk embroideries, the really important component for the Asian market was the coarse cotton varieties manufactured primarily on the Coromandel coast and in Gujarat. There was a large-scale demand for these varieties in the eastern markets of Indonesia, Malaya, Thailand and Burma as well as in the markets of the Red Sea, the Persian Gulf and East Africa. While it is impossible to determine precisely what proportion of total domestic demand for mass-consumption textiles in these societies was met by imports from India, the available evidence would seem to indicate that it was not insignificant. India's capacity to manufacture these textiles in large quantities and to put them on the market at highly competitive terms made it in some sense the 'industrial' hub of the region surrounded by west Asia on one side and southeast Asia on the other.

This circumstance also determined to a large extent the nature of India's demand for imports from the rest of Asia. This demand consisted essentially either of consumption goods which were not produced domestically for climatic or other reasons, or of minerals and metals of various kinds whose domestic supply was either nil or substantially below the total demand. In the first category were items such as fine spices like cloves, nutmeg and mace from Indonesia, and horses and rosewater from west Asia. The second category included rubies and other precious stones from Burma, as well as metals — both precious and non-precious. By far the most important non-precious metal imported was tin from Malaya. Precious metals, mainly silver, were imported overwhelmingly from West Asia. It was for this reason that, from the sixteenth century onward, the port of Mocha was repeatedly referred to as the 'treasure-chest' of the Mughal empire. It is really immaterial for our purpose whether the imported precious metals are treated as a commodity import or as a means of settling the adverse balance of trade that the concerned trading partner of the subcontinent had with it. The important point to emphasize is that by virtue of her relatively more advanced structure of manufacturing production and her capacity to provide large quantities of basic manufactured consumption goods such as inexpensive cotton textiles, India significantly enhanced the scale of trade in the Asian continent. She not only provided textiles and foodgrains and other provisions in demand in the neighbouring countries but also provided an important outlet for their specialized agricultural, mineral and other products. Trade satisfied different kinds of consumption needs for India as compared with her numerous trading partners in the Indian Ocean region. This by itself provided an excellent basis for a significant and growing level of trade. It is really in this sense that the critically important role of India in the structure of early modern Asian trade needs to be assessed.

The key position of India in the structure of Asian trade was also reflected in the important role of the Gujarati and other Indian trading groups in the conduct of this trade. This role, if anything, was strengthened in the course of the fifteenth century which witnessed the fragmentation of Asian trade into well-defined segments. Increasingly, the participation of the Arab merchants became confined to the trade between West Asia and the west coast of India. This left the trade between west and the east coasts of India, on the one hand, and the eastern Indian Ocean region, on the other, almost exclusively in the hands of Indians — the Gujaratis more than anyone else, but also the Chettis, the Chulias and other groups from the Coromandel coast, besides the Oriyas and the Bengalis. The participation of the Chinese merchants was now restricted by and large to the trade between China and Malacca, while the Indonesian and the Malay merchants hardly seem to have ventured beyond the inter-island and the port-to-port trade in the Malay-Indonesian region. In sum, Indian merchants from different regions of the country constituted an important trading group operating in the Indian Ocean.

It is critically important to realize that among the European corporate enterprises engaged in Euro-Asian trade between the sixteenth and the eighteenth centuries, which included the Portuguese Estado da India and the English, the Dutch, the French and the Danish East India Companies, it was the Dutch East India Company more than anyone else which truly realized the potential of exploiting the opportunities of trading within Asia with India as a key area of operation, in addition to trading between Asia and Europe. To a certain extent, the richness of this potential had also been recognized by the Portuguese in the sixteenth century, but in their case the bulk of the participation in intra-Asian trade was at the level of private Portuguese traders under the patronage of the Estado da India rather than by the Estado itself.

Over centuries, and indeed millennia, the principal commercial interest of the Europeans in Asia had been the procurement of spices such as pepper, cloves, nutmeg, mace and cinnamon and other luxury goods such as Chinese silk and Indian textiles. For the simple reason that Europe had traditionally been unable to supply western products with a potential market in Asia at prices that would generate a large enough demand for them to provide the necessary revenue for the purchase of the Asian goods, these goods had always been paid for overwhelmingly in precious metals. Considering that wealth had traditionally been associated exclusively with precious metals, this particular pattern of trade had persuaded authors such as

Gibbon to complain that in return for trivialities, Europe was allowing itself to be bled by Asia. This perception lasted for a long time and indeed assumed a great deal of respectability under the vulgar bullionist version of Mercantilism in the early modern period.

By far the most important item traditionally figuring in the Euro-Asian spice trade was pepper whose major centres of production in Asia were the island of Sumatra in the Malay-Indonesian archipelago and the south-west coast of India comprising the Malabar and Kanara coasts. The Portuguese landed at Calicut in 1498 and through the sixteenth and the early part of the seventeenth century, the Malabar and Kanara coasts remained nearly the sole providers of pepper to the Estado da India. In order to avoid conflict with the Portuguese as also to be able to procure at source other spices such as cloves, nutmeg and mace, grown exclusively in the Moluccas at the eastern extremity of the archipelago, both the English and the Dutch East India Companies in the early years of the seventeenth century reached out to Java in the archipelago rather than to India. As it turned out, the larger resource base of the Dutch East India Company together with other factors combined to give it a distinct edge in the archipelago over its English rival. Regional authorities in the Spice Islands were successfully coerced into granting to the Dutch exclusive monopsony rights in all the three spices grown in the area — cloves, nutmeg and mace. In this context, a situation of armed conflict between the English and the Dutch was becoming inevitable. The hostilities erupted in 1618, and the English emerged distinctly the worst of the two. The London agreement of 1619 provided for an English share of one-third in the trade of the Spice Islands, and of one half in the pepper trade subject to the English contributing one-third of the cost of maintaining the Dutch garrisons in the area. But due to both to Dutch hostility and the shortage of resources with the English, the arrangement did not quite work. The 1623 incident at Amboyna led to a recall of English factors from the shared centres in the archipelago to Batavia and hastened the process of the English withdrawal from the Spice Islands. This made them turn to India where they had first appeared at Surat in 1608 (though it was not until 1612 that formal trading rights were obtained there, followed by the establishment of a factory in 1613) on an almost full-time basis.

The position of the Dutch East India Company was very different. Having obtained the exclusive monopsonistic rights in the Spice Islands, they wanted to make the best of the situation. This was done by the creation over a period of time of an extensive network of participation in intra-Asian trade on a large scale. This eventually became by far the single most distinguishing element of the Dutch East India Company's trading strategy among all the European corporate enterprises as also the principal factor explaining their domination of intra-Asian as well as Euro-Asian trade throughout the seventeenth century. The control exercised by the Company on the Spice Islands enabled it to procure spices other than pepper at incredibly low prices. This ensured a very high rate of gross profit on these spices, often exceeding 1,000 per cent. Before the arrival of the Dutch, the spice growers had been used to exchanging their wares for Indian cloth, rice and other necessities brought to them by Indian and other Asian merchants. The Company could have obtained the Indian textiles — by far the most important medium of exchange in the Spice Islands — at Acheh and other places in Indonesia, but its acute business instinct drove it to their source, the Coromandel coast, where four factories were established between 1606 and 1610, covering both the northern and the southern stretches of the coast. Gujarat, the other major Indian region supplying textiles to the Indonesian archipelago, was reached in 1618 with the establishment of a factory at Surat. Within a few years subordinate factories were opened at Cambay and Broach, and at Agra in northern India. Since the textiles bought on the Coromandel coast had to be paid for mainly in gold, and those in Gujarat mainly in silver, the next stage in the expansion of the Company's participation in intra-Asian trade was to reach out to areas providing gold and silver. By far the most important Asian producer of precious metals at this time was Japan. A factory was established at Hirado in southwestern Japan in 1609. Since Chinese silk was the principal commodity in demand in Japan, trade relations were established with Taiwan in 1624. From the early 1640s Bengal emerged as a major supplier of raw silk for Japan. The last of the major Indian regions figuring in the Company's intra-Asian trade was Malabar, where it established itself in 1647. However, it was only in 1663 when the Dutch, collaborating with the Raja of Cochin, managed to throw the Portuguese out that the Dutch trade in Malabar began on a regular and substantive basis. Efforts to reach the other major Asian source of precious metals, namely the Red Sea and the Persian Gulf at the other extremity of the great arc of Asian trade, had also been initiated quite early, using the Company's establishment at Surat as the base. Indeed, from 1643 onward Persia emerged as an important supplier of silver *abassies* and gold *ducats*, which were smuggled out on a regular basis, often by concealing them in cavities made into bales of raw silk. By about the middle of the seventeenth century, then, the Dutch East India Company had become a major participant in intra-Asian trade with trading links all along the great arc of Asian trade. The two key factors that enabled the Dutch to achieve this enviable position were the spice monopoly and the exclusive right to trade with Japan in the 'closed country' era of its history, extending from 1639 to 1854.

While extensive participation in intra-Asian trade was the principal feature that distinguished it most from its fellow European corporate enterprises throughout its trading history, the Euro-Asian trade was by no means neglected at any point in time. As we saw above, the principal constituent of the cargo procured in Asia for Europe in the initial stages consisted of pepper and other spices. The proportion of spices in the total invoice value was thus as high as 74 per cent in 1619-21 and 68 in 1648-50. By 1698-1700 this figure had come down to a mere 23 percent. This was essentially an outcome of the fashion revolution in Europe which resulted in a dramatic increase in the demand for Asian finished textiles and raw silk. From 16 percent of the total exports in 1619-21, the share of this group went up to as much as 55 percent by the end of the seventeenth century. The fact that India was by far the most important supplier of this commodity group put her at the very centre of the Euro-Asian trade of the Company. At the end of the seventeenth century, goods procured in Bengal alone — the principal Asian supplier of textiles and raw silk sent to Europe — accounted for as much as 40 percent of the total Dutch exports to Europe valuewise. If goods procured in the three other principal Indian regions — Gujarat, the Coromandel coast and the Malabar coast — are added to the Bengal cargo, this proportion goes up to as much as around 70 percent.

This extended discussion of the trading strategy of the Dutch East India Company, while not entirely germane to the theme of this chapter which is a discussion of the Dutch perception of seventeenth-century India, must nevertheless be regarded as crucial in order to place the rest of our discussion in perspective. More than any other major European corporate enterprise at work in India between the sixteenth and the middle of the eighteenth century, the Dutch East India Company was the largest in terms of the volume and value of trade carried on in and from the subcontinent. This would include the Portuguese in the sixteenth and the English and the French in the seventeenth and the first half of the eighteenth century. But even more importantly, the nature of the Dutch Company's relationship with the subcontinent was qualitatively very different from that of any of its fellow enterprises. The Company's connection with India started in 1606, i.e. within four years of its establishment in 1602 and lasted all the way until its liquidation in the 1790s. The Dutch connection with India formally came to an end in 1825 when the remaining Indian establishments were handed over to the English East India Company in exchange for the latter's establishments in Southeast Asia. Throughout this long period, the sole interest of the Company in the subcontinent was commerce with no involvement whatever in political processes. The only exception to this was Cochin on the Malabar coast where the Company did, indeed, enjoy a certain amount of political power and patronage in alliance with the Raja of Cochin. But the role of Cochin in the Company's overall profile in the subcontinent was of no particular significance at any point in time.

This unidimensional involvement of the Company with India throughout its history ensured that for all purposes India was to be looked upon simply as a provider of goods for other parts of Asia as well as for Europe and, on a more limited basis, as an absorber of goods from other parts of Asia and, on a negligible scale, from Europe. The country had no other attraction or significance for the Company, which was only interested in interacting with groups and institutions that were inseparably linked with the successful conduct of its trade. An example would be the Mughal Indian as well as South Indian coinage and minting and monetary systems in general. Neither the Mughals nor the South Indian rulers allowed the circulation of foreign coins in their dominions. Since the principal import of the Company into the subcontinent consisted of gold and silver bullion and coins of foreign origin, it was critically important that the conversion of these into Indian coins was done quickly, knowledgeably and as cost-effectively as possible. So one finds a great deal of commentary on and analysis of Mughal Indian as well as South Indian coinage systems in the Company's documentation. Another example would be the commercial activities of the Indian mercantile classes engaged in coastal and overseas trade. Given the enormous interest of the Company in intra-Asian trade, Indian merchants engaged in this trade were regarded as important rivals whose activities needed to be constantly watched and monitored. This attempt at monitoring resulted in the compilation of by far the largest and the most detailed body of both quantitative and qualitative information regarding Indian merchants' coastal and overseas trade from different regions of India available in any primary source — Asian or European — that is available today.

So this was the India that the Dutch were interested in and which they commented upon and recorded extensively. By the same token, they were not interested in reaching out to other spheres of activity involving access to power or authority which were regarded essentially as projects involving avoidable expenditure and shifting the focus away from the central concerns of trade. An example of this was the passing over of an opportunity to fortify the factory at Hugli in the 1690s. The context was the revolt by the Zamindar, Sobha Singh of Chatwa-Barda in Midnapore district in Bengal, which kept the province in a state of serious disorder for nearly two and a half years between the middle of 1695 and the close of 1697. Initially, the Dutch factors turned down the request by the provincial administration for assistance in crushing the revolt. But in August 1696 the rebels succeeded in capturing the fort at Hugli, exposing the local Dutch factory to grave danger. It was then decided to disregard the standing instructions by Batavia to maintain strict neutrality in situations of this sort, and steps were taken to restore the control of the fort to the Mughal authorities. A contingent of Dutch soldiers was deployed to sorround the fort, and the *Berkensteyn* was stationed in the Hugli river at a point from which its guns could cover the fort. The known superiority of European weaponry persuaded the rebels not to put up a fight. The fort was promptly vacated and the Dutch restored it to the Bakhshi, Mirza Hasan Ali's control. Needless to emphasize, the Dutch action was in response to compelling local circumstances and did not represent a shift from the basic policy of neutrality. This is borne out by the Company's reluctance to take advantage of the permission given by the Subahdar Ibrahim Khan to all the European Companies to strengthen their defences and even fortify their settlements. In fact, once the revolt had been crushed, the temporary measures taken to strengthen the defences of the Hugli factory were rescinded.

If its naval superiority enabled the Dutch Company to oblige the Mughal authorities in times of need (another example was the naval assistance provided in the Mughal campaign against

Chatgaon in 1665-66), it was also its strongest weapon to fight the authorities when its central concerns were threatened. A case in point was the demand the Mughal authorities made on the Dutch, the English and the French in the 1690s to provide protection to Indian shipping against the depredations of European pirates operating mainly from their bases in Madagascar. The plunder of the *Ganj-i-Sawai* in 1695 was instrumental in the introduction of the system of Dutch and English convoys to the Red Sea. A large ship of 1,000 khandies paid a fee of Rs.20,000 for a round trip while a smaller vessel qualified for Rs.15,000. Half the sum was found by the *mutasaddi* of Surat from the customs duties, while the rest was jointly subscribed by the merchants whose ships were to make the trip. The Company was allowed to carry its own cargo or freight goods on the escort vessels it made available. This arrangement worked well until 1698, when a Surat merchant Hasan Hamadani lost a richly laden ship. The ship had not formed part of the convoy, but each of the three Companies was nevertheless obliged in February 1699 to give a bond (*muchalka*) accepting responsibility for any losses that vessels from Surat might in future sustain at the hands of the pirates. The English were made responsible for the vessels going to the southwest coast of India, the Malay peninsula and the Indonesian archipelago, the French for those going to the Persian Gulf, and the Dutch for vessels going to the Red Sea. Abdul Ghafur and other merchants interpreted the *muchalkas* as implying the Companies' responsibility for losses whether or not a particular ship that might be captured formed part of the convoy, an interpretation that the Europeans contested.

An occasion for testing the enforceability of the *muchalkas* arose in September 1701, when news reached Surat that one of Abdul Ghafur's ships from the Red Sea, the *Husaini*, had been plundered. The Dutch refused to pay compensation, claiming that this was one of the ships that had broken convoy. Ghafur organized his fellow merchants, who decided that until the Dutch paid the compensation, no one would fit out a ship. They also demanded suspension of the Company's trade until a settlement was reached. The imperial court decreed in favour of the merchants, and ordered the Dutch to pay the compensation claimed. Pending this, their trade was banned throughout the Mughal empire. As was usual in such situations, however, the ban was only partially enforced. The demand for compensation was met, but it was only in November 1702 that the ban on trade was withdrawn.

In August 1703, yet another of Abdul Ghafur's ships was attacked and captured while it was anchored at the Surat bar. The Dutch refused to pay compensation, as the piracy had not occurred on the high seas. They also decided to use their naval muscle power to find a long-term solution to this problem. A strong Dutch naval force arrived from Batavia off Surat in September 1703 and blockaded the port, cutting off the port's life line. This was repeated a year later. The Company, of course, recognized that from the perspective of the Indian maritime merchant, Surat at this time was by far the premier port of the subcontinent linking the west coast of India to the Red Sea and the Persian Gulf. It was also perhaps the most cosmopolitan of the Indian ports attracting a large number of merchants who were the subjects of the Persian or the Turkish monarchs. Being mindful of not jeopardising the Company's relations with these countries, the commander of the blockading fleet decided to exempt these merchants from the blockade. But that led to the problem of defining precisely as to who was an Indian merchant and which was an Indian ship. To take advantage of the exemption, many of the Muslim merchants of Surat claimed foreign connections. Using his discretion, the commander released a ship saying that it was an Arab rather than a Mughal vessel. It belonged to Haji Muhammad Ali of Kung in the Persian Gulf and the *nakhuda* (captain), the sailors and the soldiers on board were mostly Arabs. The factors at Surat disagreed and pointed out that it was without any doubt a Gujarati ship and that it was a common practice to employ Arab sailors and even claim Arab ownership. At any rate, the Dutch strategy of putting the Mughal authorities under severe pressure by blockading the port worked in its entirety. At the suggestion of the new governor of Surat, Najabat Khan, the Emperor agreed to relieve the Dutch of the 1699 *muchalka*, thereby restoring the *status quo ante* of 1696 stipulating only the provision of convoy to the Surat ships. This was in January 1705, but the Dutch blockade of Surat was lifted only in 1707.

It need hardly be stressed that the relationship between the Dutch and the other European Companies on the one hand and the Mughal Indian authorities on the other was a delicately fine tuned one based on a perception of mutual benefit. An increase in the volume and value of foreign trade brought about by the functioning of the Companies in the Empire was highly welcome. In particular this was related to (a) the accretion to the customs revenues at the Empire's ports which accrued directly to the imperial exchequer and (b) the fact that the Companies' imports consisted overwhelmingly of precious metals which were not produced domestically but were nevertheless needed in large quantities to run the empire's monetary system as well as to cater to other needs. On their part, the Companies fully realized the critical significance and value of their Indian operations and would always be wary of using their naval superiority except under the most pressing circumstances.

II

On the specific question of the Dutch perception of seventeenth-century India, the bulk of the massive documentation of the Dutch East India Company is understandably devoted to issues related to trade and commerce. On the more general questions of polity and society, unfortunately, there is not very much available. I would, however, like to deal in some detail with one specific set of documents available for the Mughal empire for the 1620s. Indian historians working on the seventeenth century have for long been familiar with *Jahangir's India* translated and edited by W.H. Moreland and Pieter Geyl, and published by Cambridge University Press way back in 1925. This is a small part of the set of documents that I will analyse in the rest of this paper. In this endeavour, I will draw heavily on D.H.A. Kolff and H.W. van Santen (ed.), *De geschriften van Francisco Pelsaert over Mughal Indie, 1627: Kroniek en Remonstrantie*.

Jahangir's India was one part of Francisco Pelsaert's two-part account of Mughal India written at Agra in the 1620s. Several other accounts of a similar nature have been published over the years in the Linschoten Society series, the Dutch counterpart of the English Hakluyt Society. These include the two-volume W.Ph. Coolhaas (ed.), *Pieter van den Broecke in Azie*, W. Caland (ed.), *De Remonstrantie van W. Geleynssen de Jongh*, W. Caland (ed.), *De Open-deure tot het Verborgen Heydendom door Abraham Rogerius*, A.J. Bernet Kempers (ed.), *Journaal van Dircq van Adrichem's Hofreis naar den Groot-Mogol Aurangzeb, 1662* and J.Ph. Vogel (ed.), *Journaal van J.J. Ketelaar's Hofreis naar den Groot Mogol te Lahore 1711-1713*. The two last mentioned are accounts of the embassies to the Mughal emperor's court in 1662 and 1711-13 respectively. The account of Abraham Rogerius is almost a theological work regarding the Hindus of South India. Of the two part journal of Van den Broecke, the second part deals with the Surat factory of the Dutch East India Company between 1620 and 1629. The account of Geleynssen de Jongh basically analyses the commercial possibilities in Gujarat around 1630, but it also contains a good deal of information on the various Hindu sects and castes to which the Gujarati merchants belonged.

As far as the writings of Francisco Pelsaert, a Dutch factor at Agra in the 1620s, himself are concerned, the two parts, viz. the chronicle and the *Remonstrantie* (Report or Relation), indeed together comprise a single unified account. The first part of the *Remonstrantie* which deals with trade has a good deal in common with Geleynssen's *Remonstrantie* except that while Geleynssen confines himself to Gujarat, Pelsaert claims to write about the Mughal empire as a whole. The latter part of the Pelsaert's *Remonstrantie* where he talks about the customs of the land follows logically from his chronicle. In addition to Moreland and Geyl, Pelsaert's writings have in the past found other editors. In 1631, Ioannes de Laet included portions of the *Remonstrantie* and nearly the whole of the chronicle in his Latin work *De Imperio Magni Mogolis sive India Vera Commentarius, etc.*, dealing with the Mughal empire. An English version appeared in Bombay in 1928 as J.S. Hoyland (translator) and S.N. Banerjee (annotator), *The Empire of the Great Mogol: A Translation of De Laet's "Description of India and Fragment of Indian History"*. Parts of the *Remonstrantie* appeared in French in 1664 in Melchisedech de Thevenot, *Relations de Divers Voyages Curieux*. The Chronicle, translated and edited by Brij Narain and Sri Ram Sharma, appeared in book form as *A Contemporary Dutch Chronicle of Mughal India* in 1957, after having been published in parts in *The Journal of the Bihar and Orissa Research Society* (1942 and 1943) and *The Journal of the Bihar Research Society* (1946). The translation unfortunately was rather defective and the annotation did not do justice to the text. As a result, the Chronicle has not really received the attention of the historians of India to the extent that it deserves.

The Chronicle basically deals with the political and military history of the Mughal empire between 1537 and 1627. After a short introduction, Pelsaert begins his account with Humayun's campaign of 1537. In 11 folios, Pelsaert describes Humayun's defeat by Sher Shah Sur in 1540, his subsequent wanderings in Western India, his trip to Persia, the campaign that led to his return to the throne of Delhi in 1555 and finally his demise in 1556. Akbar's reign is then taken up in great detail in 42 folios. A very lively account of the 1606 rebellion by Khusro follows.

All this takes up about 40 percent of the chronicle. The years between Khusro's rebellion and 1621 when Pelsaert arrived in Agra are then commented upon in great detail, though the chronology is not always faultless. It is unlikely that this section was based on a proper evaluation of the existing chronicles with the help of knowledgeable experts. The last part of the chronicle — again occupying nearly 40 percent of the total — covers the last seven years of Jahangir's reign when Pelsaert was himself present in the empire. Personal observations come through very richly in this part of the account. The campaign of Shahjahan against the Centre receives much attention. The part dealing with the conflict that reached out to Gujarat is particularly rich in detail and perhaps deserves to be regarded as an important historical document.

In order to convey an idea of the richness of the contents of the Chronicle, let me in conclusion draw attention to three quantitative accounts that the Chronicle provides. The first of these details the treasure left behind by Akbar at his death in 1605. The second is a list of the empire's umara and mansabdars while the third catalogues the various animals probably belonging to the emperor. It is for the specialists of Akbar's reign to determine the reliability of these accounts.

List 1

The value of the treasure left behind by Akbar is stated to be 34 crores, 82 lakhs and 26386 3/4 rupees as follows:

Coins	*Rs.*
6,970,000 gold muhrs reckoned at Rs. 14 per piece	97,580,000 3/4
Silver rupees	100,000,000
230,000,000 copper paisas	766,666
Total	198,346,666 3/4

Precious stones etc.	
Diamonds, rubies, emeralds, pearls and other precious stones	60,520,521
Silverware such as jars, plates, cups, vessels, candleholders, pedestals, beds, etc.	2,225,838
Clothing using gold	19,006,745
Golden pots, plates, spoons and figures of elephants, camels, horses, etc.	9,507,992
Copper plates, pots, pans, cups, etc.	51,225

Fine porcelain consisting of large plates, cups, bottles etc. of extraordinary curiosity	2,507,747
Total	93,820,068

Fine Persian carpets, etc.	
Gold and silver sheets from Persia, Turkey, Gujarat and Christendom together with silk textiles, etc., from Bengal and other places	15,509,979
Woollen stuffs from Christendom, Persia and Kashmir, etc.	503,252
Tents etc. for the palaces	9,925,545
Books written by great masters of which 24,000 volumes are bound in costly material	6,463,731
Guns, firelocks, lead for ammunition, etc.	8,575,971
Harnesses, shields, swords, daggers and other weapons	7,555,525
Gold and silver saddles, bridles for horses etc.	2,525,646
Carriages for use in war etc.	5,000,000
Total	56,059,649
Grand Total	348,226,383 3/4

List II

The second quantitative account deals with the Mughal *umara* and *mansabdars* who were inherited by Jahangir from Akbar and were listed in the king's register.

	Rank	*Number of horses (these are seldom maintained in full)*
8 umara	5,000	40,000
9 gentlemen	4,500	40,500
25 umara	4,000	100,000
30 "	3,500	105,000
36 "	3,000	108,000
42 "	2,500	105,000
45 "	2,000	90,000
51 "	1,500	76,500
55 "	1,000	55,000
58 "	700	40,600

80 mansabdars	500	40,000
73 "	400	29,200
58 "	350	20,300
72 "	300	21,600
85 "	250	21,250
150 "	200	30,000
242 "	150	36,300
300 "	100	30,000
245 "	80	19,600
397 "	60	23,820
298 "	40	11,920
240 "	30	7,200
232 "	20	4,640
110 "	10	1,100
741 ahadis	4	2,946
1,332 "	3	3,966
1,428 "	2	2,856
950 "	1	950
7,281 umara, mansabdars and ahadis		1,068,248

List III

Then follows a list of elephants, horses, camels, mules, oxen, etc. (probably belonging to the emperor)

		Number
a.	Elephants, big and small, male and female, of whom 100 are particularly large and handsome	6,751
b.	Horses	
	Persian of particularly good breed and beauty	3,200
Turkish		5,970
From Kutch		2,500
From the mountains of Gond		210
	Mares from all over	120
	Total of horses	12,000
c.	Camels	6,223
d.	Mules	260
e.	Oxen	7,000
	Total	32,234

12

Francois Bernier's Idea of India

ANIRUDDHA RAY

I

Francois Bernier was born on 25 or 26 of September 1620 at Joue near Chemilly in Anjou, of Pierre Bernier and Andree Grimmault. His father was a holder of a farm at St. Marie at Angers.[1] Francois was baptised on 26 September by the Cure of Changeaux.[2] At the age of four, Francois Bernier lost his parents and went to live with his paternal uncle with his two sisters, whose later whereabouts cannot be traced. His uncle, a Cure, wanted Francois to join the Church, but Francois refused and got protection from two Magistrates for his studies. One of them was a high official, Bernard de Champigny, *Intendent* of the province and allied to Lhuillier, Councillor of *Parlement* in Metz as well as a high judicial officer. They introduced Francois to the philosopher Pierre Gassendi, the *Prevot* of the Cathedral of Digne. Gassendi was against the doctrine of Aristotle and wanted to revive the materialism of Epicurus.[3]

In 1642, Gassendi came to Paris and began teaching philosophy to Chapelle, son of Lhuillier, in whose house he was staying. There Gassendi began to teach a young group of students including Moliere and Cyrano de Bergerac. Bernier followed Gassendi to Paris in 1645 and began to attend his public lectures on Astronomy at the Royal College.[4]

Through the courtesy of M. de Merveille, an old student of Gassendi and then in charge of diplomatic missions abroad, Bernier went to Poland with one of his friends and returned via Germany and Italy after visiting Rome and Venice.[5] It is thought that this trip fired the imagination of the young Bernier and he now wanted to see the world. Others however alleged other

[1] Louis de Lens, 'Notice Sommaire sur Francois Bernier', in *Dictionnaire Historique d'Angers de M.C.Port*, November 1872, 1.

[2] See Act of Baptism of Francois Bernier in H. Castonnet des Fosses, *Francois Bernier: Ses Voyages dans l'Inde*, Angers, 1888, 1, notes (hereinafter *Voyages*).

[3] Lens, op. cit., 1.

[4] Ibid.

[5] Ibid.

reasons for Bernier's tour abroad that followed. In any case, Bernier delayed his trip since Gassendi had fallen ill at Provence. On 26 August 1652, Bernier received the Doctorate of Medicine from the University of Montpellier,[6] after studies in medicine which, as recounted by Bernier himself, saved him from perils to his health in India.

While Gassendi was emphasizing the explanations of phenomenon by scientific observation, such a view was gradually pushing him to a position of conflict with the orthodox Church. In a strict sense this was not an anti-Church position as the Jansenist movement, entirely ignored by Bernier, had already spread by the 1650's within the fold of the Catholic Church.[7] But the view of Gassendi was still being resisted by those who were allied to the orthodox viewpoint of the Church. Morin, a mathematician and a teacher of Mazarin, wrote against Gassendi. Bernier, without taking permission from Gassendi, wrote a spirited defence (*Apologie Contre Morin*), dedicating it to Chapelle, containing also an attack on Morin. This brought on a war of words between Bernier and Morin.[8] In a broader sense, this involved a conflict between Cartesian mathematics and the observations of the school of Gassendi. The conflict did not degenerate into a vulgar level as Henry Louis Hebert de Montmor tried to hold a balance between the two views. Gassendi, known to him, secured his protection for Bernier, who on the order of the pacifist Gassendi stopped the pamphlet war.[9]

Meanwhile, Morin, who had credit at the Vatican, denounced Bernier as an atheist, and Bernier allegedly even received a letter of excommunication, although no such document has come to light so far. It has been stated also that Bernier wanted to dispute it but was prevented by Gassendi. Morin was said to have asked from Mazarin for an order to arrest Bernier as an atheist.[10] Gassendi, then very ill in Provence, was brought to Paris by Bernier in 1653 to the house of a friend.[11] It is stated that Bernier fled to Palestine and Syria in 1654 and returned to find Gassendi

[6] See Robert Mandrou, *From Humanism to Science, 1480-1700,* (tr. by B. Pearce), Harmondsworth, 1978 (first published in French 1973), chapter V, 228 ff.

[7] Lens, op. cit., 2. Also see Marie-Louise Dufrendy, *Francois Bernier et l'Idee de Progres*, Paris, 1960, 1-2.

[8] Dufrendy, op. cit., 2.

[9] Lens, op. cit., 2-3.

[10] Ibid.

[11] Dufrendy, op. cit., 2.

on his deathbed. Gassendi died on 24 October 1655.[12]

Whether it was the fear of arrest and excommunication that forced Bernier to flee to a distant land or whether it was to see the "other world" that took Bernier to the route to the East is difficult to determine. But by 1656, he had gone to Egypt and stayed one year at Cairo despite the plague raging near Rosetta,[13] and this lends substance to thesis of his precipitous flight. Bernier actually wanted to go further into Africa via Ethiopia, but on the way got information about the persecution of the Christian priests there. He went to Mocha, from where he took passage on an Indian ship to land at Surat,[14] He proceeded to Delhi, meeting the fugitive Dara Shukoh on the way.

Bernier returned to Surat in 1667 at a time when Francois Caron and De Fay were establishing the French East India Company's factory at Surat.[15] At the request of Caron, Bernier wrote a *Memoire* on 10 March 1668 on the eve of his departure from Surat for Persia. This was duly sent to Colbert, who wrote notes in the margin in his own hand.[16] We would see later that this document contradicts some of the assertions made by Bernier in his letters. By 4 June 1668, Bernier arrived at Taduan near Shiraz, from where he addressed a letter to Chappelain, which was received at Paris on 15 February 1669. Bernier was still at Shiraz in early October 1668 and then embarked for Marseilles,

[12] Ibid.

[13] Ibid.

[14] Bernier himself narrates this part (see Francois Bernier, *Travels in the Mogul Empire, 1656-1668,* tr. by A. Constable based on Irving Brock's translation, Indian edn., New Delhi, 1972, 1-2, hereinafter to be referred to as *Bernier*). This one-volume work includes the translations of two books of Bernier first published in French in 1670 and 1671.

[15] See Paul Kaeppelin, *La Compagnie des Indes Orientales et Francois Martin,* Paris, 1908, 54-55. Francois Caron left Fort Dauphin for Surat in February 1668, but two French envoys had already secured the *farman* of the Emperor Aurangzeb in 1666.

[16] The late Sylvia Murr, in an excellent article on Bernier, wrote inaccurately that this Memoir was addressed to Colbert in 1670 and that it was not published so far ('La Politique 'au Mogol' selon Bernier: Appareil conceptuel, Rhetorique Strategique, Philophie Moral' in *Collection Purusartha*, Paris (EPHE), 1991, no. 13, 249). The Memoir was written from Surat on 10 March 1668 and was addressed to Caron and De Fay, two directors of the French Company. The date and the address had been inscribed at the bottom of the last page. This was later sent to Colbert and was first published by Castonnet des Fosses, *Documents inedit sur son sejour en Inde*, Paris, 1885. It was first translated into English by Theodore Morison, *JRAS,* NS, 1933, pp.1-21; and also translated and published by Aniruddha Ray in *Francois Martin: Memoires*, Calcutta, 1990, Appendix D, 541-566. Fosses has quoted the comments of Colbert (op. cit., 37-38).

which he must have reached by April/May 1669. Shortly after September 1669, he left for Paris.[17]

At Paris Bernier began to make arrangements for the publication of his books. The licence of Louis XIV for printing and publication was issued on 25 April 1670.[18] The two volumes of Bernier containing the history of the Civil War and its aftermath in the next volume appeared in 1670 and 1671, followed by many editions with slight differences in each edition.

From 1672 onwards, Bernier wrote exclusively on liberal arts, science and philosophy. He did not write on India again. One reason could be that the old friends of Gassendi had disappeared, such as La Mothe, Le Veyer, de la Chambre, Guy Putin, etc. Only Chapelle, his friend of the younger days, was still around. As to the younger generation of poets and writers like Boileau, Racine and La Fontaine, their disorderly conduct was not liked by Bernier. He renewed his contact with Moliere, to whom he gave some tips for his work *Malade Imagninaire.* Similarly he gave some suggestions to La Fontaine. It was stated that he had contact with Racine as well as with chemists like Renault and Regis.[19] At the same time Bernier was much sought after in various salons at Paris for telling the anecdotes of his travels, all of which evidently were not included in his books.[20]

It is perhaps in one of these salons that Bernier met Madam de la Sabliere, who received him with marks of attention. He wrote several letter to her, some of which have been published. One letter written in 1685 deals with the division of land on the basis of races of men living there. His theory of races propounded here was substantially different from the one he had written about in the letters published in his book.[21]

From 1674 the principal occupation of Bernier was to acquaint the public with the philosophy of Gassendi. However in 1678, he expressed his doubts on several aspects of Gassendi's philosophy. Bernier was then living as a bachelor in the house of Madam de la Sabliere, who later threw him out of her house. Yet his admiration of her persisted and he continued to inform her of the opinions of Gassendi and Descartes.[22]

[17] See the chronology in *Bernier*, xvi-xvii.
[18] Ibid.
[19] Lens, op. cit., 2-3.
[20] Fosses, *Voyages*, 54.
[21] Ibid., 56.
[22] Ibid., 55.

Bernier did not forget Montpellier either. He used to spend several months there, where he met Abbe Picard, known all over Europe for his publications on Astronomy. Some time later Bernier went to England, invited by St. Everemond. The Duchess of Mazarin was also there. Bernier was already known in the English circle since his books had been immediately translated into English and had become quite popular. Dryden wrote a play on Aurangzeb based on the writings of Bernier, and this had already been staged. Bernier came back via Holland after arranging there the publication of his books, which came out in 1699 from Amsterdam with illustrations. It is not clear who supplied these illustrations on India.[23]

If Bernier had hoped for a position in the Academy in France particularly when some of Gassendi's men had got such positions, the hope was belied for reasons which we would attempt to explain later. In 1684, an Academy was established at Angers. In 1686, Bernier was nominated on a thirty-member committee. In 1688, Bernier went to Provence from where he wrote two long letters to Madam de la Sabliere. One was on the wind pressure in the atmosphere and the other on the junction of the two seas by a projected canal in Languedoc.

Bernier now wanted to write on the "Orient" and perhaps on his voyage again. In 1688, he published a long letter on China dealing in detail with the history, philosophy and customs of the Chinese people. This emphasis on China is certainly a departure for Bernier as in the earlier letter of 1685, on the racial division of the world, he did not recognize the yellow race.[24] Bernier wrote a letter to his nephew, Philippe Bourigault, who was practising medicine at Angers, that he would come there and make plans for his future projects. But he died suddenly at his house in Place Dauphine at Paris on 22nd September 1688. It is alleged that this was caused by a fit of apoplexy in the office of the Procurer General, de Harlay. He was interred in the Church of St. Barthelemy the next day (within the Parish of St. Sulpice). His old friend, the Orientalist d'Herblot, and his nephew participated in the ceremony. In the Register of the Church, the age of Bernier was shown as seventy-three while in reality, it

23 Lens, op. cit., 2-3. John Dryden wrote his tragedy on 29 November 1675. It was acted in the Royal Theatre of London.

24 Fosses, *Voyages,* 65-66; Dufrendy, op. cit., 11-12. Some of these letters were published in *Journal des Savants* in the 1680's. See an excellent bibliography by Sylvia Murr, op. cit., 303-10.

was sixty-eight only.[25]

Bernier's books on his travels in India did not cause as much enthusiasm in France as he expected. Racine wrote flatteringly two limes in his *Memoires*. Sixty years later, Voltaire called him "the Great Mogul" in his *Encyclopaedia*. It was only from the middle of the nineteenth century that the French woke up to the significance of the writings of Bernier, although Bernier had remained steadfast to the forgotten principles of Gassendi, of "atom" and "nothingness".[26] Perhaps the situation in France in his own time was not such as could receive his criticisms of despotism with open arms.

II

Bernier's writings on India were influenced by two elements – the rapidly changing situation in France and the controversy on the philosophy and scientific assertions of Gassendi, challenging some of the customs and superstitions in France. These elements often coloured the perception of Bernier and made him unique among European travellers to India. There was a great difference between him and other contemporary French travellers like Jean-Baptiste Tavernier, whom Bernier knew well, or Jean Chardin, who accompanied Bernier to witness a *sati* near Surat on the eve of Bernier's departure from India. The difference is not in the details of the narrative of the voyage, which Bernier usually failed to provide in the manner of some of his contemporaries, but in the systematic consolidation and organization of data that Bernier accomplished. He sought to explain the system of the Mughal government in the background of his perception of the "Asiatic tyranny" in contrast to the rule of law he saw prevailing in European States, a kind of interpretation that was not lacking in the writings of other travellers but not presented with such sophistication and consistency. Bernier was highly interpretative and organized his history of events in a schema instead of making a simple narrative of his voyage, as was the case with other European travellers. It is in search for such a schema that his subjective appreciation of events, largely influenced by French history, helped him to look at those in India so differently from

[25] Ibid., 77-78. For the Act of Exhumation from the Church Register, see *Bernier*, xvii-xviii.

[26] *Lens*, op. cit., 3. In 1658, a Society was created which made arrangement in 1859 to name a street in Angers after Bernier.

others. Two factors particularly formed the context for Bernier's opinions. The first was the attempted centralization of the French State leading ultimately to the "Grande Siecle" of Louis XIV, a process taking place in Bernier's own time. It would perhaps be worthwhile to look at the same time the social formation in France during the time of Mazarin and Colbert, to the latter of whom Bernier wrote perhaps the most important letter giving his interpretation of "Asiatic tyranny". The concept of the "Oriental tyranny" of Bernier (he mentioned the term "despotism" only twice in the case of the Orient) was consciously held forth as a contrast to the system of Europe. At the same time, as would be seen, there was a veiled warning against the increasingly absolutist tendencies in the State of France, where conditions might degenerate to the level of the Asiatic States. Therefore one could perhaps read into Bernier the double meaning that has been overlooked so far in his writing, in even such an influential work as that of Edward J. Said.[27]

The other element that influenced Bernier was the philosophical assumption of Gassendi that emphasized the de-mystification of the phenomena of the universe by scientific observations. In a way this challenged the concept of the universe that was the pillar of the Church. It is on this question, as seen above, that a conflict developed between Bernier and Morin. We will see presently how far the observations of Bernier in India were influenced by the methodology of Gassendi.

III

We shall begin now by first looking at what France was like when Bernier wrote about India. The Sun King (Louis XIV) assumed control of the State in 1661. The royal absolutism became supreme with the silencing of the *Parlements* while other courts were reduced to obedience. Estates could no longer bargain over taxes and the deployment of the garrisons in the Municipal areas checked the independence of the military authorities. Governors were appointed for three years and they were forced to reside at the court. The nobility resented these measures but their economic interests were now linked with those of the State. Only 2% of the nobility appropriated nearly 30% of the national income. The sovereign power was now

[27] Edward J. Said, *Orientalism*, Harmondsworth, 1995 (first published in 1978).

concentrated and rationalized.[28]

The French society rested mainly on the production of the peasantry. With regional variations, the French peasants owned less than half of land, but under the control of the lords. Only with explicit permission and payment of certain taxes, could they sell and purchase land, which belies the thesis of royalist historians that the French peasants were free. The land was not equally divided. The majority of the peasantry possessed some small parcels of land, which forced them to find other occupations as well. The rich peasants were *farmiers* of large areas of land and the lords could be deemed as intermediaries.[29] Despite their scale and frequency of occurrence, the seventeenth century peasant revolts in rural France were marked by their alliance with the local lords against the King.[30] Apart from the village community, which raised taxes for various purposes, the Church also got a part of the revenue from the peasants. To pay all these, the peasantry often became indebted to both rural and urban bankers. It has been estimated that the small French peasantry could keep very rarely even half of their gross produce.

The condition of the urban workers in France, twenty times less in number than those of the peasants, was deplorable. Without owing any land or any house, all living in rented quarters almost without any provision for family and furniture, they resembled the archetype of the proletariat. A system of advances by the employers made these workers permanently indebted and so thrown entirely into the clutches of creditors. The Church often came to their defence and gave some assistance however slight. Most often they worked at home or came every day to the houses of their employers. The factories formed an exception. The profit generally went to the big merchant rather than to the small master. But compared to the peasants, the urban workers paid less tax and enjoyed some of the advantages of the cities, like access to a hospital. Only in times of violent crisis or epidemic, were they left in the hands of some priests and physicians to die in herds. Their revolts, which often erupted in cities, due to the imposition of a new tax or circulation of rumour,

[28] Perry Anderson, *Lineages of the Absolutist State*, London, 1984 (first published in 1974), 98-101.

[29] Pierre Goubert, *Louis XIV et Vingt Million de Francais*, Paris, 1966, 62-63.

[30] Pierre Goubert, *The French Peasantry in the Seventeenth Century*, Cambridge University Press, 1981(tr. Ian Patterson, first published in French in 1982), 205-19.

were badly organized and easily suppressed by royal soldiers.[31] The middle class, small in number, was composed of shopkeepers, small patrons and master artisans, who worked with their hands for their living. The rentier class enjoying high social status included all the nobility, the higher clergy and the bourgeoisie. The revenue of land came to them in different channels and by different forms, principally through indirect exploitation by *farmiers* and *Intendents*: a recent study has shown particularly the rapacity of the nobility living in the west of France. They not only held hundreds of families under their control, but also acted as lords and *fermiers* in different places, collecting taxes, which the Revolution was later to designate "feudal".[32]

The bourgeoisie, in the process of rising to the level of the nobility, were engaged in manufacture and in commerce. They purchased lands around the cities and turned into aristocrats. They became *Intendents* of the nobles and the clergy in their domains and often imposed new taxes on the peasants. One could say that some sort of capitalism in rent was the key to the social structure of the kingdom. The richest families of the kingdom were the nobility of the sword, the members of *Parlements* who owned lands and the lords getting most of their income from rent.[33]

There was not one French code of law for rendering justice. It was pronounced often that the King was the fountain of justice. In reality, different customs in different areas continued, and different ordinances since the sixteenth century multiplied the number of laws. In the countryside and in certain cities, the tribunals were under the influence of the lords. Only cases concerning merchants were done quickly.

Much before the seventeenth century, the King had begun to sell offices of state to lords who had private properties with the right to judge and collect revenue. These privileges became hereditary and it was sufficient to pay annually a certain sum of money to the King, who gained financially but lost the rights. When the King sent his *Commissaires* these hereditary officers resisted, which was one of the factors behind the Fronde. By 1670, however, all these rebels, including the officers,

[31] Goubert, *Louis XIV*, 67-70.
[32] Ibid., 70-71.
[33] Ibid., 72-74.

Parlements and the big lords had submitted to the will of the King.[34]

It is in this background – the growth of an absolutist State and the fading away of the rights and privileges of the small and middle nobility – that we should look at Bernier's statements on India and his comparison between the French system and the Indian system of government as well as of the society and civilization of the two countries. It should be borne in mind that Bernier's father was a *farmier* or rich peasant and so a beneficiary of the system before the coming of the absolutist State under Mazarin and Colbert. Bernier was brought up by his paternal uncle, who was a clergyman and who had also benefited from the system. It is not clear how Bernier had met the two Magistrates, who were obviously supporters of the "liberty" of the *Parlement* and against the centralization of the State, in a corner of France, which was proverbially a "rebel" area. It was therefore perhaps natural that they introduced Bernier to the philosopher Gassendi, who was preaching the materialism of Epicurus against the rather rigid views of Aristotle that led Bernier to his controversy with Morin. To understand Bernier's interpretation of the Indian system, it is thus necessary to look into the contemporary situation in France as well as the ideas current there.

As stated above, the man who influenced Bernier most was the philosopher Pierre Gassendi, whose influence in France during the second half of the seventeenth century was considerable, perhaps far more than that of Descartes. But Gassendi was not a great philosopher and did not invent any new law. He could not be compared to Descartes or Pascal.[35] However for our understanding of the thought process of Bernier, it is perhaps necessary to look at the thoughts of Gassendi and what he preached.

Gassendi propagated the thesis of "nothingness" and "atom", while Descartes, following Aristotle, was for "filling up" or "fullness". This attack of Gassendi on Aristotelian thesis thus opened up the question of the basis of traditional science. The final conflict was between science inspired by mathematics and science supported by observations. In his book published in 1642, Gassendi showed the inequality of man in the same social

[34] Ibid., 80-81.
[35] Dufrendy, op. cit., 10.

environment, which was adopted by Bernier and developed later into the theory of races by him.[36] In Kashmir, Bernier shows that different zones of climate exist side by side.[37] Thus he differs from the thesis of Jean Bodin that differences in climate were accidental.[38]

Gassendi and Bernier refused to accept that the world has been created by Divine Will. They ignored all mysticism and metaphysics.[39] Gassendi, reposing faith on human nature, was a proponent of human diversity, a theory that was later developed by Bernier in his theory of races. The description of Bernier of different races in the Mughal court and the preference given by the Mughal Emperor to the "well-made white and foreign-born" was only the beginning of Bernier's theory of race.[40]

Gassendi propounded the theory of the speed of the body in movement. His system was of dynamic vitality, which appears in the writing of Bernier as well. To them the "world is far more living in the way like an animal or plant," — everything here is animated. The world is something more than a mere mechanism. This was the fundamental point of difference between Gassendi and Descartes. Locke, Fontaine and Rousseau followed the view of Gassendi that social law was subordinate to natural law.[41]

IV

After looking at the history of the Civil War in the Mughal Empire in which Bernier was unwittingly involved for a time, Bernier gave an interpretation of the system of the Mughal government, which naturally interests us most. He also made comments on the Indian religious groups and the Indian social customs for which he has utilized different sources. These sources are of his

[36] Ibid., 8.

[37] *Bernier*, 405-406, for two zones of climate. For his observations on the mysterious formation, see 413-416.

[38] Dufrendy, op. cit., 8. Jean Bodin published his *Theory of Climate* in 1556.

[39] Ibid., 11.

[40] "...he (i.e. the Omrah) may obtain the advancement of his children by royal favour, particularly if the persons be well-formed and their complexion sufficiently fair to enable them to pass for genuine Mogol.." (Bernier, 213). Bernier developed his idea of race by publishing a long letter in *Journal des Savants* (1685) entitled "Division de la Terre par les differentes especes due races d'hommes qui l'habitent et la beaute des femmes" (Fosses, *Voyages*, op. cit., 56-62). Bernier divides the races on the basis of their physical characteristics. He puts the Mughals as part of the Asiatic race in the third division, after the Europeans and the Africans.

[41] Dufrendy, op. cit., 12.

own choosing and therefore his knowledge remained fairly subjective. It is certain that Bernier could speak and write Persian. It has been shown by recent research that one of his friends wanted him to learn Persian (this means that he had learnt some of it in India) well so as to fill the post of Orientalist in the court of the King of France.[42] In a letter written in June 1668 from Shiraz on his way back to France from India, Bernier points out that he had translated into Persian the writings of Gassendi and Descartes.[43] for Danishmand Khan in whose house he was staying at Delhi. During his long stay at the Mughal court and in the house of his Agha (Master) Danishmand Khan, he conversed in Persian without the help of an interpreter, thus picking up information from Mughal officials. He did identify some of these sources. He could also get hold of official Mughal documents, such as the correspondence between Shah Jahan then in confinement and Aurangzeb, bȳ then the Emperor. He admitted however that he could get only half portion of the letter, which suggests that his access to the State documents was not a smooth one. His tabulation of the Mughal revenues, obviously taken from a document, seems also either to be incomplete or a draft before finalization.[44]

However Bernier picked up other sources of information as well, although he does not reveal how he got access to them. One such source was a half-caste Christian maid who had worked for long time in the *harem.* She told Bernier of the escapades of Roshanara (Raushanrai) Begum and the consequences that followed.[45] The question remains as to why Bernier picked up such stories, which could not be verified. His own method of verification in order to de-mystify a phenomenon is to set aside the stories of the *harem.* Another such spicy story of the *harem* is given by Bernier in the hint that Shah Jahan was sleeping with his daughter Jahanara Begum. Bernier asserted quite falsely that the Mullas had approved of it. It may be pointed out that such a story concerning Shah Jahan and Jahanara had been related in

[42] Friends of Bernier tried to get him an interview with Louis XIV and Colbert obviously for getting a post for him (Murr, op. cit., 249-50). The author suggests that Bernier had brought some diamonds and some money saved from the salary given to him by Danishmand Khan.

[43] Dufrendy, op. cit., 3-4.

[44] *Bernier*, 167-68 for the letter. For the Mughal revenue figures, see ibid., 455-58. The editor did not believe it reliable due to various reasons.

[45] Ibid., 131-33. For a long discourse on the evil effects of the *harem*, see ibid., 144-45.

great detail by an anonymous Italian traveller nearly thirty years earlier.[46] Since no other traveller contemporary to Bernier has referred to it, Bernier must have picked it up obviously from same bazar gossip. Bernier was looking at India, as part of Asia and therefore to him the Orient (he did not mention the term Occident), was a place of gold, luxury items and suppressed sex, where women were not given any liberty, even the liberty to live after the death of their husbands, some examples of which he has narrated in great detail.

Apart from some Mughal nobles and Danishmand Khan, whom Bernier termed "the most learned man of the East",[47] Bernier's other principal sources were the European merchants, travellers and the priests, some of whom he names. It is clear that Bernier was quite well known to Niccolai Manucci, J.B. Tavernier and Jean Chardin, the last narrating the incident of *sati* seen at Surat in company of Bernier, which made Bernier furious.[48] From Dutch merchants, Bernier got the information of the alleged oppression committed by Mughal officials on European merchants in Indian ports (the French established their factory at Surat only in 1666). Needless to say, he believes their version of the oppression once again without verification, which he could have obtained easily from Danishmand Khan fòr a long time in charge of the foreigners in Mughal India. Bernier did not bother to verify them since such tales of oppression would fit easily into his schema of the system of Mughal government.

Bernier has often referred to rumours, particularly in connection with his narrative of the Civil War. Obviously he was not present in the battlefields and does not specify his sources.[49]

[46] Ibid., 11. For the account of the Italian traveller see the article of Aniruddha Ray, 'An anonymous contemporary Italian Document on the March of Shah Jahan from Agra to Lahore in September 1638' in *Proceedings of the Indian History Congress*, 1995, Calcutta, 55th Session, 220-26. The Italian has mentioned the approval of the Mullas for the act in the same vein as Bernier.

[47] *Bernier*, 4. He was a Persian merchant (according to Constable, his original name was Muhammad Shafi, who came to Surat in 1646, ibid., 4, note 2).

[48] Fosses, *Voyage*, 51.

[49] For example, in giving an account of the battle of Samugarh of 29 May 1658 between Dara and Aurangzeb, Bernier refers to the treachery of Khalilullah Khan, in revenge for a past insult to him by Dara, by asking Dara to come down from his elephant by which Dara lost the battle (Bernier, 53-54). Jadunath Sarkar, basing himself on contemporary Persian sources, gave a different version, although he admitted that Khalilullah Khan did not take much part in the battle (*History of Aurangzib*, Calcutta, 1973, reprint of the first edition of 1912, vols.I & II, 249-50).

Sometime he discounts such rumours. He has narrated the final fate of Sultan Shuja at Arakan, which he got not only from the servants of Shuja with whom he was travelling, but also from the contemporary letters of the Dutch merchants, whom for reasons not known he does not name. This he did after recounting various rumours current in India and even at the court of Delhi that had created a mystery around the death of Shuja. Once again Bernier turns to clear up the mystery from his personal knowledge culled from sources of his own, thus making the methodology of verification of the event seemingly as far scientific as possible. It may be stated that the account of the last days of Shuja at Arakan and the manner of his death has been confirmed from the account of a Dutch merchant,[50] perhaps the same person who gave information to Bernier. Despite the use of such a method to demystify a current event, Bernier is used to mentioning rumours. The use of such rumours, including their mention even when discounted, would suggest that Bernier was hinting at the circulation of news and formation of opinion of the Indian people without verification, obviously different from what could have been judged necessary in Europe. The current public opinion in India, as asserted by Bernier, was based on credulous acceptance of unverified information.

In a significant article, Sylvia Murr refers to the fact that Bernier used drama to illustrate the history of the Civil War.[51] While this could be accepted, Murr does not explain how this "drama" was enacted. Not only in narrating the history of the Civil War, but throughout in his writings, Bernier emphasizes again and again the contrasts, both among the personalities or in the situation chosen. Through this method, Bernier draws the scenario of long-term tragedy of Corneille, as suggested by Sylvia Murr,[52] rather than of a Greek tragedy, which was of a temporal nature. The reason for Bernier's adopting such a strategy was two-fold – predicting the tragic fall of the Mughal government (as a matter of fact of all Asiatic States) and of giving a veiled

[50] For the rumour of Shuja's death, see Bernier, 112-14. For the authentic version, Bernier, 113. For a contemporary Dutch account of the last days of Sultan Shuja, see Aniruddha Ray 'A Contemporary Dutch Account of Shah Shuja at Arakan' in *The Proceedings of the Indian History Congress*, 1974, Jadavpur, 35th Session, 112-18.

[51] Murr, op. cit., 254.

[52] Ibid.

warning to the French rulers of such a future if certain conditions were not changed or if they insisted on playing the same game.

The contrasts in personalities depicted by Bernier could be seen very clearly in the one between Aurangzeb and Dara, between cool calculation and spontaneous outburst, between the orthodox and the liberal. The means by which Aurangzeb managed to turn the seemingly adverse situation in his favour would show also the superiority of natural selection against social law (Shah Jahan had nominated Dara as his successor). Perhaps far more important to Bernier was the vindication of the thesis of inequality of men coming from the same environment. This same kind of contrast is seen among the nobles as well — between Jai Singh and Jaswant Singh, the former more calculating than the latter. Such contrast could also be seen in Bernier's assessment of the loyalty and treachery of the Mughal nobles, and in the contrast between Murad and Shuja. In depicting the treachery of some of the Mughal nobles, Bernier did not apparently make any attempt to verify the sources, although he had access to contemporary Mughal nobles, who had recently taken part in the Civil War on both sides. The basic feature of the history of the Civil War, from Bernier's point of view, is one of constant movement, of dynamic vitality, of different bodies moving over space and time, both acting and reacting on each other, sometimes becoming almost impersonal by the natural law of selection. One could perhaps detect, if one wishes, a faint trace of the past history of the resistance and conspiracy of the French nobility in times of crisis, particularly the execution of the treacherous nobles, from the point of view of the French State and the silence that followed. The details of the execution of the brothers of Aurangzeb, seemingly denounced by Bernier, was of course the "Asiatic type", resulting from the absence of a proper law of succession in Islam, neatly serves as a pointer to the future of France.

Such use of contrasts can be seen in the writing of Bernier in other places as well. Apart from the general contrast between France and India, between Europe and Asia, between cities of Europe and those of India, there are contrasts within the structure of social formation in India. Bernier makes a contrast between the Mughal Emperor ruling by force and the Hindu Rajas, who rule by the consent of their subjects following the rules set by their tradition. He does refer to the disunity among the Hindu Rajas, allegedly fanned by the crafty Aurangzeb, that prevents them from uniting against the Emperor.[53] But within the Mughal court nobility, Bernier differentiates between the "well-made" white Mughals, who got the top positions compared to others i.e. Indian Muslims, who were rather black or of "brownish complexion", Persians, who were regarded with suspicion for their loyalty to the Persian Emperor, and the Afghans. There is therefore not only a conflict among the races, albeit subdued at the time, but also a conflict of ideology not necessarily limited to Muslim religious groups. To Bernier, the basic ideological difference lies in the rule by force and oppression, obviously the rule of the "tyrant" of Aristotle, and the other legally constituted Rajas, hereditary Zamindars ruling in their lands with the consent at grass root-level, although doubt remains about Bernier having had any direct experience of the rule of any of the Rajas. As would be seen, one of the main pillars on which Bernier has laid his schema was the possession of hereditary private property, and he may be assuming that Hindu rajas, as against the Mughals, could claim ancient rights of property, and being free from the fear of transfer of their assignments, treated their peasants better.

The same kind of contrast could be seen in the assessment of Bernier on two major religious groups in India. Bernier narrates the subdued protest of the Brahmans to the Emperor Aurangzeb asking for the ban on cow slaughter since a large number of cattle had been decimated during the last few years. The Emperor accepted the request in lieu of payment by the Brahmans. But that was the only evidence of protest of the Brahmins given by Bernier, who does not refer to any conflict between the two communities on religious grounds. Yet Bernier finds contrasting situations within these two religious communities.

Here the method of Bernier is again different from that of his contemporary European travellers. He divides the two religious groups internally at different levels, almost as parallel forces, thus avoiding any conflict within the given structures. At the higher level were the religious scholars in both the Hindu and the Muslim communities, while at the lower levels, there were priests and *Ulema* (he calls the latter priests also), who dupe the common people of both their communities. In case of the Hindus,

[53] *Bernier*, 208-09. For migration to the territories of the Rajas, ibid., 231-32. For the strength of the Rajputs, ibid., 208-10. For less oppression in the territories of the Rajas, ibid., 205. Bernier considers the Rajas as legitimate sovereigns in contrast to the Mughals (discussion in Murr, op. cit., 269-70).

he finds many examples of the priests forcing the observance of *sati* (he narrates the story of his saving one).[54] In a different example, he narrates the ceremony of bathing during the solar eclipse and the common philosophy behind it as given by the priests. This was done to show how the priests dupe the people by making mysteries out of rationally explicable events. Incidentally, he mentions the same kind of credulity of the common people in France during the solar eclipse. The difference between the Indian and the French situations lay in the fact, as Bernier records it, that in France a number of philosophers and astronomers, including Gassendi, tried to tell the people that such a phenomenon was quite natural and would occur again and again, which is quite absent in India.[55] However, he finds the upper-level Hindu Pundits, at Delhi and at Banaras, disliking the lower level of the Hindu priests. He was pleasantly surprised that these Hindu Pundits (his term) as well as the Muslim philosophers, meaning probably Sufis, knew about "nothingness" and "atom", so far regarded by him as the contribution of Gassendi. Yet Bernier reassured himself that these Indian scholars did not know anything about the origin of the Universe while trying to explain unverifiable theories. Bernier finds the same kind of deficiency in the case of Muslims.[56] In Kashmir, he could verify by his personal observations that the Muslim clergymen were duping the people by showing the miraculous power of a saint,[57] while he himself could expose the pious fraud by scientific observation and rational thinking.

In the case of Christianity in India, Bernier was in some difficulty since he could not create two different levels among Christians by their knowledge of the scripture. He therefore follows a different method of approach and suggests an alternative Christianity (he did not use this term) for the propagation of the faith, which he supports. Instead of two parallel levels, Bernier brings out two kinds of Christian missionaries in India. The worst kind, as he sees it, has been spoiling the chances of making conversions by their debauchery and wayward living. Significantly Bernier did not name the group

[54] "The Brames encourage and promote these gross errors and superstitions to which they are indebted for their wealth..." (Bernier, 305).

[55] Ibid., 300-03.

[56] For religion, see the chapter 'The Gentiles of Hindoustan', particularly 316-49.

[57] Ibid., 413-16.

guilty of such behaviour.[58] Actually in the Mughal Empire, there were Portuguese Augustines, French Capucins and the Jesuits. Out of these, the Augustines had a few centres and fewer priests. The French Capucins also had their limitations and were operating generally in the European enclaves. The Jesuits, most favoured at the French court were rapidly expanding within India as well as in the neighbouring countries. Some of the French merchants later became very bitter towards the Jesuits due to their alleged greed and aggressive behaviour against the Indians in general.[59] It is possible that Bernier was referring to their scandalous mode of living but could not name them for their excellent position in the eyes of the French court. Yet, Bernier wholeheartedly supported the attempt of conversion to Christianity and has given some examples of the courageous work of the Christian priests, even at the Mughal court, with great risk to themselves. Bernier however did not mention the sources of information of such incidents narrated by him and it is not clear whether he had verified the information from other sources since these related to the period before his arrival in India. Bernier also suggested that the Hindus were easier targets — a hint at the supposed fanaticism of the Muslims. To be accurate, unlike other contemporary European travellers, Bernier found that the Muslims respected Christ, even believing in his miraculous birth.[60] He also records the gradual shifting of the policy of the Mughal Emperors, from the liberalism of Akbar and Jahangir, obviously on the basis of the reports of the Christian priests, to the anti-Christian policy of Shah Jahan.[61]

Bernier believes that conversion to Christianity would make the Indians, both Hindus and Muslims, see the correct path.[62] But he gives far greater importance to education as the means of getting rid of the superstition of both communities. To illustrate his point, he quotes the speech of Emperor Aurangzeb to his teacher Mulla Sale (Salih?) in which he admonishes his teacher for not teaching him subjects like Geography or the art of war, necessary for kingship.[63] Bernier rues the fact that there was no

[58] Ibid., 289-90.

[59] For an incident of conflict with the Jesuits, see Paul Olagnier, *Les Jesuits a Pondichery et L'Affaire Naniappa, 1705-1720*, Paris, 1932.

[60] Bernier, 290.

[61] Ibid., 286-88.

[62] For sending missionaries to every part of India, ibid., 290.

[63] For the speech of Aurangzeb to Mulla Sale (Salih), see ibid., 154-61. For the lack of education and absence of any University or College, see ibid., 229.

University or college of the European type in India to teach secular subjects instead of teaching merely religious precepts.[64] Once again, he brings out the credulity and superstition of the Indians in their extreme dependence on astrology. His own observations in this regard for both the upper and lower classes, including women, are narrated in great detail with examples and anecdotes while recalling the throngs of people crowding in the Chowk in front of the Delhi fort.[65] That the medical education in India had not progressed to the standard of Europe has been ascribed by him to the fact that the Indians would not dissect the human body. He himself brought the theory of Harvey on the circulation of blood to the notice of Danishmand Khan and demonstrated it by dissecting a lamb. He however concedes that the Muslims were less superstitious in this regard since they practised the letting of blood by following the teachings of Avarroez and Avicenna.[66] To Bernier, there was one fundamental cause for all aspects of this backwardness and superstition, and this lay in the specific structure of the polity of the Orient.

V

Bernier emphasizes the absolutism of the Oriental Kings, namely those of Turkey, Persia and India, which were deemed to be under a tyranny in being administered by the will of the sovereign and not by a multi-polar authority.[67] Bernier lumped these three great powers in one category, although he found some difference in the case of Turkey on the question of the assignment of land. By so doing Bernier brought out a new concept of Asia in contradistinction to that of Europe.

Bernier illustrates his concept of oriental tyranny, by taking a cue from Aristotle as been shown by Sylvia Murr.[68] He dwells on the absence of the judiciary as an effective force in India. He quotes the views of the European travellers that justice in India was quick, and so better than a delayed one. He also concedes that there are laws in India by which justice is supposed to be rendered. But in reality, he says, no justice could be achieved

[64] Ibid., 244-45.
[65] Ibid., 338-39.
[66] Ibid., 338
[67] Ibid., 206-38, for his letter to Colbert.
[68] Sylvia Murr, op. cit., particularly 238 ff. She states that Bernier did not use the word "despotism" (257). But Bernier has used the word twice (see for example, 227).

without giving bribes and presenting false witnesses, although he gives an example of the rendering of proper justice in the King's court.[69] Since there was no possibility of redress, the provincial Governors and other officials extorted money — the tyranny then percolating to the lowest levels of the officialdom. There was very little liberty from the oppression of the lords, since there were no *Parlements* or Magistrates championing the cause of liberty of common subjects.[70]

In reality in France, the lords manipulated the judiciary to a great extent, while by the end of the 1660's, the *Parlements* had been silenced with a consequent increase of the power of the nobility. It seems, although Bernier did not clearly specify it, that one of the objects of Bernier's writing on Mughal tyranny was to criticise the absolutism of the Sun King by referring to the traditional local institutions fading away under the centralizing tendencies in France.[71]

According to Bernier, the fundamental cause of the prevalence of tyranny in India and in other Asiatic States was the absence of private property: the King was the owner of all land and he distributed it to his nobles in exchange of sums of money as rent.[72] The King, in exceptional cases, did allow some of his subjects to purchase and sell land.[73] Colonial historians accepted this postulate of Bernier and added that the right to private property in India was the contribution of British rule,[74] the issue having been discussed in detail during the formulation of the Permanent Settlement in Bengal at the end of the eighteenth century. But recent research of Irfan Habib belies the fundamental axiom of Bernier on which he has built up the thesis of "Oriental Despotism" (he used the word only twice in his writings). Habib has postulated that that the land belonged to both the King and the peasant on certain conditions. He has further shown that since man-land ratio was favourable to man, there was a natural

[69] Bernier, 236-37.

[70] Ibid., 237-38.

[71] See the last paragraph of his letter to Colbert (238). See also an article by S. J. Tambia, 'What did Bernier actually say? Profiling the Mughal Empire' in V. Das, D. Gupta & P. Uberoi (ed.), *Tradition, Plurality and Identity*, New Delhi, 1999, 220-44. There are some factual inaccuracies in this article. I am indebted to Mr Ishrat Alam for bringing this article to my notice.

[72] Ibid., 211-12.

[73] Ibid., 204.

[74] See for example W. H. Moreland, *From Akbar to Aurangzeb*, New Delhi, 1972 (reprint of 1923 ed.).

limitation to the oppression on the peasants who could migrate elsewhere to settle on vacant land.[75] It should be remembered that Bernier did not dwell much on the peasantry, his travels being limited to the cities. Also, it is possible that being descended from a family of *farmier* (rich peasantry), Bernier did not pay much attention to the ordinary peasants, whose condition in France, was deplorable at that time.

Another assertion of Bernier was that the crown lands (*Khalisa*) in India were given to *jagirdars*, who tried to extort as much revenue as possible in the shortest time.[76] Whether such a system of unrestrained and oppressive tax collection was prevalent on a large scale in the crown lands is a point that is not yet free of doubt. Obviously this fits in with the schema drawn by Bernier of Asiatic tyranny, but it is quite clear that he was anticipating the events of the early eighteenth century. In a way, Bernier was recording the past experience of such an experiment in France with the concommitant warning of the disasters that would follow.

Apart from the existence of the *jagirdars* and tax-farmers in India, Bernier found other officials, from the provincial Governor to the lowest level, who were bent on extorting money to recover the amount they had spent in getting their posts. He found that the nobles and the officials had to give rich presents not only for getting their offices, but also to offer presents on all important festivals for staying in their posts. Bernier makes such presents equivalent to the sale of offices in France,[77] where annual payments to the king were given. Bernier however points out that the situation in Europe was different compared to that of India, thus deliberately laying his finger on a much deeper conflict in France — the regional liberties enjoyed by the local *Parlements* to elect their own officers and the suppression of that right by the claim to appointment of the State officials in the same localities by the King.

Concluding from the absence of private property and the unrestrained exercise of the power of the nobility, Bernier asserts that such a situation in India prevented the development of the

[75] Irfan Habib, *The Agrarian System of Mughal India, 1556-1707*, Oxford University Press, 2nd revised ed., 1999, particularly 123 ff (1st ed. 1963).

[76] Bernier, 224-25. He called them *Timariots*, after Turkish *timar,* a soldiers' pay-assignment.

[77] Ibid., 231.

arts. The nobles hung the whip (Bernier uses the word *kora*) on their door and whipped the artisans to force them to work for them, often without or with very little remuneration.[78] The artisans, obviously among Hindus, had no internal mobility and never aspired to go higher up in the social ladder since they were bound by a rigid caste system in which the son followed the occupation of his father.[79] This would suggest, if one follows Bernier's statement, that production was only for the nobility. Here he states that some people getting the patronage of the court were in a good position in comparison to others. We would see that Bernier contradicts himself later when he spelled out the possibility of the newly established French Company of the East Indies to make unlimited purchases of commercial goods produced by independent artisans in India for the open market. In highlighting the luxurious and extravagant living style of the high nobility in Mughal India, Bernier could also have been trying to draw attention to the French situation, but with one exception.

The statement of Bernier that there was no middle state (meaning middle class) in India has been contested in recent research.[80] Bernier would have liked to see not only the existence of such a class in India, because he himself came from such a class that had resisted the centralization of state power in France, but he also thought that this class could be the harbinger of civilized norms in Indian society. Bernier includes the bourgeoisie in that class and compares the freedom given to women in France with that given to women in India. He exclaims how in contrast to India, in Pont Neuf at Paris, one could enjoy the sight of men and women walking in the afternoon glow of the setting sun.[81] Here the bourgeoisie and the lesser nobles created a situation where there was equality, at least apparently, for women in France. The beautiful scene in the evening lights at Pont Neuf at Paris emanating from the houses far and near, which again was sadly lacking in India, because not only the urban morphology in India was different from that of France, but because the "spirit" (should be *elan* in French although Bernier did not use the word)

[78] For the general oppression of the nobles, ibid., 225; for the use of the whip, ibid., 228.

[79] For the lack of social mobility among the artisans, ibid., 259.

[80] Ibid., 252. Also, see Iqtidar Alam Khan, 'The Middle Class in the Mughal Empire' in *Proceedings of the Indian History Congress*, 1975, Aligarh, 36th Session, 113-41.

[81] *Bernier*, 285-86.

of urban life was missing here. After being a superior Christian who does not bind women in shackles, Bernier is a superior European, a cultured urban Frenchman, looking at the outside world at the dawn of French enlightenment.[82] In a larger sense it was his plea, meant for France as well, to let the middle class thrive for ushering in a better quality of life.

VI

At Delhi, Bernier found the quality of life to be badly inferior in comparison with those of the European cities. However he disputes the claims of other European travellers that the buildings in Delhi and Agra were inferior in style to those of the European cities. To Bernier, the buildings in urban India suited the warm climate, being much more airy and with terraces where one could sleep at night during the intolerable heats of summer.[83] He therefore looks from the "other" point of view as well. But Bernier felt that the services in urban India were very poor, even at Delhi, there being no good shops for bread and meat. He confesses that he could not have sustained himself at Delhi had he not managed to buy meat from the shop within the fort that supplied meat to the royal kitchen.[84] However like other European travellers, he finds that most of the streets of Delhi were tortuous excepting two streets, which were straight – the European concept of urban planning was always looking for "regular" streets in India. Apart from the shops in the buildings lined on both sides of these two streets, these on the rest, as Bernier found were practically inaccessible due to shanty shops and crowds of people. Most of the houses were constructed of mud and straw, thus vulnerable to frequent fires.[85] He found the cities to be over-grown villages, maintained by the presence of the army and the court, a perception which Max Weber so elaborately formulated later.[86] There was not much planning in Indian cities unlike those of Europe. In India, the cities were

[82] See his comparison between Constantinople, Delhi and Agra and his comment: "Paris is the finest, the richest and altogether the first city in the world" (286).

[83] Ibid., 240-41. For the description of Delhi and Agra, see his letter to Monsieur de la Moth Le Vayer, written from Delhi on 1 July 1663, 239 ff.

[84] Ibid., 251.

[85] Ibid.

[86] Ibid., 246-47. "...Delhi is a collection of many villages, or as a military encampment..." This was the basis of the classification of medieval Indian cities by Max Weber (*The City*, Glenco, 1958).

dominated by the fort and the mosque, surrounded obviously by the buildings of the top nobility and the rich merchants, while the shopkeepers could stay either on the back of the shop or on the first floor. Bernier did not suggest any particular dwelling places for the artisans, which meant that they lived in those shanty cottages dispersed all over the city without any proper segregation of areas on a class basis. Interestingly, Bernier mentions that the artisans working for the royal *karkhanas* at Delhi within the fort would come from outside in the morning and go away at sunset.[87] Apparently these artisans were better off than other working people although Bernier does not give us any details.

The high standard of living of the top nobility resulted, according to Bernier, to their indebtedness. Bernier himself stayed in the house of a top noble, Danishmand Khan and described the lavish breakfast at his house. It seems that Bernier used to have his own cook and servant who used to buy bread and meat for him from the market. Bernier tells us that since there was no hereditary property in India, the nobles used to live extravagantly. They also hoarded much wealth under the ground and make ornaments thus preventing the gold and silver coins from circulating.[88] This resulted in the fact that after the confiscation of the property of the dead noble, his son would have to start from the bottom. Therefore there was no ancient family in India or hereditary Dukedoms like those of France.[89] This was the major element in the Oriental polity that made it different from that of Europe, particularly France. We have seen earlier that there was a major attempt by the French royalty to resume the hereditary properties and Bernier was evidently pointing out the evil consequences of such a policy, with the hint that absolutism was based on such a mistaken concept. He

87 While describing the square, Bernier mentions that the artisans work during the day (Bernier, 245), implying that they go back to their homes in the evening. In case of the merchants selling goods in the shops, Bernier mentions where they live. Inside the fort, in the royal Karkhanas, the same system was followed (Ibid., 259).

88 Ibid., 204-05. For the indebtedness of the nobility, ibid., 213; for lack of circulation of precious metals in India, ibid., 223-24.

89 Ibid., 211. "The King being proprietor of all the lands of the empire, there can exist neither Dukedoms nor Marquisats; nor can any family be found possessed of wealth..." The superiority of the French system is very clear in his praise for the existence of hereditary nobility based on the landed estates. As seen earlier, these French nobles resisted the centralization of State power in Bernier's own time.

had in mind the law of escheat used by the Mughals, which was however not applied without discrimination. After the death of Mir Jumla, his son Muhammad Amin Khan was elevated to a high rank and the property was not confiscated, perhaps due to the fact that Muhammad Amin Khan was by then an official. But to Bernier, this was done for political reasons.[90] Incidentally after the death of Muhammad Amin Khan in Gujarat in 1684, his property was confiscated after an inventory.[91] The inventory clearly shows that not all the Mughal nobles became indebted despite their high standard of living. But Bernier insists on such indebtedness as it fits in with his schema and serves as a warning to the French aristocracy as well.

Bernier makes an exception in creating the prototype of an Oriental King in the personality and character of Aurangzeb. It has already been seen that the speech of Aurangzeb to his teacher Mulla Sale has brought out the element of rationality in Aurangzeb, who was termed by Bernier a Machiavelli.[92] In contrast to the imagined irrational and emotional Oriental King in general. At the same time Bernier marked him as a fanatic Muslim,[93] who had to rule by force in the midst of the majority of the population who were Hindus. Bernier equates him with Machiavelli since Aurangzeb suppresses his personal inclination for reasons of the State. In other words, Bernier was making a case that the management of the State system in Asia was irrational compared to that in Europe. Yet Bernier finds that there are differences in the natural selection, as there are differences in the leaves of a tree. He therefore feels, but does not point it out clearly enough, that there was a conflict within the polity of Aurangzeb – between the rationality and calculation which brought him to the throne and the fanaticism of faith, which hung like a shadow, but is concealed by the cover of rationality. Till Bernier was in India (that is, at least March 1668), the rationality dominated, which, to Bernier, was a cloak for political expediency and therefore not real. This certainly sets Aurangzeb far closer to Machiavelli. Incidentally recent

[90] Ibid., 173-74.

[91] Saqi Musta'd Khan, *Maasir-i Alamgiri* (tr. Jadunath Sarkar), Asiatic Society, Calcutta, 1947, 140.

[92] For discussion, Sylvia Murr, op. cit., 258-59.

[93] Again and again Bernier brings out the "zealous" attitude of Aurangzeb. But in the beginning, Bernier suggests that such "devotion" was a true one (Bernier, 10).

research[94] has shown that after the political and military failures in the first decade of his reign, Aurangzeb leaned more towards the faith, but by that time Bernier must have reached France. Significantly Bernier did not mention the conflict between the State power and the religious community, excepting in the case of Sarmad (whose execution that he applauded was considered by him to be due to moral reasons, which can be doubted); neither did he dwell on any conflict between Hindus and Muslims. Could it be that he was so close to the sensitive issue of the Huguenots and the deliberate choice made by Henry IV for Catholicism, that he did not want to remind the French readers of such sensitive issues? Could it be that Bernier was pleading for a rational policy of toleration towards other religious communities in France through his comments on the changed Mughal policy towards the Christians from Shah Jahan onwards?

VII

Bernier's assessment of the inferiority of the Mughal system of government as well as their culture and civilization rests on two arguments. One is that the land belongs to the King and he has absolute power to dispose of it. This has brought various results including oppression that percolated right down to the lowest level. The King being a foreigner had to rule by force of arms for which a huge expense had to be incurred for the maintenance of the army. This was in contrast to the system under the Hindu Rajas, who were ruling in accord with the will of their subjects having come from the same population. This irrationality in the State management, Bernier predicts, would result in the collapse of the Mughal State.[95] Although it did not come by the route envisaged by him. The vast gulf, in income and style of living, that separated the miniscule minority from the vast impoverished majority with no middle class in between, strongly propelled the State to use brute force to extort money and in the process made it vulnerable to internal devastation and decay.

The other element was the influence of superstitious beliefs held by both the major religious communities, which prevented the growth of scientific education. The absence of such education

94 See M. Athar Ali, *Mughal Nobility Under Aurangzeb*, Bombay, 1966.

95 This has been emphasized in several places. See, for example, Bernier, 227. Also, while concluding the letter to Colbert, Bernier states "...take away the right of private property in land and you introduce...tyranny, injustice, beggary and barbarism: the ground will cease to be cultivated and become a dreary wilderness...the road will be opened to the ruin of Kings and the destruction of nations..." (ibid., 238).

encouraged the growth of dependence on the priestly class, who deceived the common people for their own ends. This resulted in the growth of social evils including *sati* and the bondage of women, obviously of the higher classes since the lower class women always worked outside their homes. With no middle class, with the women in bondage, with the artisans bound by caste rules and whipped by the lords, Bernier saw no prospect of the development of art and culture in India, although as seen above, he contradicted himself in a *Memoire* written from Surat in March 1668 for the French Company in which he highly praised the workmanship of the Indian artisans and their abundant production for the open market.

Bernier's idea of India was therefore partly made up of his experience of the historical evolution of France and the thought of Gassendi in contrast to that of Aristotle, although Bernier has made use of the concept of tyranny as defined by Aristotle in case of the Asiatic States. Bernier chose India to propound his theory but took care to include Persia and Turkey in his broad picture. This was done much before the advent of the nineteenth century English colonial historians. One would therefore like to modify the view of Edward J. Said, who has viewed "Orientalism" as a product of both the enlightenment and colonialism. Bernier remains unique among the general run of contemporary European travellers, unlike whom he was able to develop a notion of an "Oriental" system of government as a kind of warning post for the absolutism of the Sun King. Bernier remained true to his class of rich peasant and small nobility, who had resisted the centralization of the State power. It is not surprising that the late eighteenth century French traveller, Count of Modave, quoted a phrase from Warren Hastings to call Bernier "the Prince of Travellers". It is also not surprising that in the wake of the decline of the Mughal Empire in the eighteenth century, Count of Modave, narrating the superiority of the English power in India against that of the French, referred to the writings of Bernier again and again to show how the prophecy made nearly a hundred years back was coming true.[96] But Modave was wrong on one count. Bernier prophesized the decline of the Mughal Empire, but he had no idea that the English would oust the "richest nation" of the earth (France) from one of the richest parts of the globe.

[96] Jean Deloche (ed.), *Voyage en Inde du Comte de Modave, 1773-1776*, Paris, 1971.

13

The Vision of a Free India in the Bengal Renaissance

GAUTAM CHATTOPADHYAY

The roots of the idea of India as a nation in the modern period of history first appeared nearly two centuries back, in the twenties and thirties of the nineteenth century. It appeared first in the writings of Henry Louis Vivian Derozio. Born in 1809, he was at the age of 17 in 1826 already a teacher at the Hindu College when he composed a poem called "To India; my native land". Before this date, no poem had been composed in English by anyone calling India his native land. It runs thus:

My Country! In thy days of glory past
A beauteous halo circled round thy brow
And worshipped as a deity thou wast!
Where is that glory, where that reverence now?
Thy eagle pinion is chained down at last.
And grovelling in the lowly dust art thou.
Thy minstrel hath no wreath to weave for thee
Save the sad story of thy misery!
Well let me dive into the depths of time
And bring from out the ages that have rolled
A few small fragments of those wrecks sublime
Which human eyes may never more behold;
And let the garden of my labour be
My fallen country!
One kind wish from thee.

Derozio not only passionately loved India, but also humanity in the whole wide world. In February 1827, he composed a poem called "Freedom to the Slave", in which he wrote,

How felt he when he was first told
A slave he ceased to be;
How proudly beat his heart when first
He knew that he was free!

Derozio and his disciples had quite a few differences with Rammohan Roy and his friends, because while the latter worshipped one universal God, Derozio and his disciples were mostly atheists. Yet Derozio never hesitated to support every progressive move by Rammohan and his friends. Derozio strongly supported the campaign for the abolition of Suttee. When the Governor-General of India, Lord William Bentinck prohibited Suttee in 1829, Derozio at once wrote a poem greeting this step:

Hark! hark! Have you not heard
The suttee's wails are heard no more.

In the sonnet written by Derozio for his pupils of the Hindu College, now Presidency College, Calcutta, he wrote;

Expanding like the petals of young flowers
I watch the gentle opening of your minds,
And the sweet loosening of the spell that binds
Your intellectual energies and powers.
That stretch (like young birds in soft summer hours)
Their wings, to try their strength.
O how the winds of circumstances and freshening April showers
Of early Knowledge, and unnumbered kinds of new
perceptions shed their influence;
What joyance rains upon me, when I see
Fame in the mirror of futurity?
Weaving the Chaplets you have yet to gain
Ah then I feel I have not lived invain

In 1828 Derozio set up in his residence an organisation, in the nature of a club, called Academic Association, which was attended by his most enthusiastic pupils. Commenting on the nature of this Association, Reverend Lal Behari De wrote in his book "Reflections of Alexander Duff" in 1879: "Week after week, the cream of Calcutta's youth, discussed and debated in the meetings of Academic Association the main social, moral and religious issues of the day. The main tone of their discussions was to sound the tocsin of rebellion against prevalent blind religious superstitions and conservatism". The eminent historian Professor Susobhan Chandra Sarkar has observed that in a sense the Academic Association was the first student organisation of India, which followed Derozio's dictum that his twin gods were reason and liberty.

In 1829, Derozio's students printed a journal *Parthenon*. No scholar, to my knowledge, has seen this copy of *Parthenon*, but the contents of that issue were reprinted in another journal of the period named *Jnananvesan*. From that reprint, we find that articles written in the *Parthenon* discussed the necessity of spreading education to women, support for freedom of the Press and introduction of the jury system in India. The orthodox authorities of Hindu College and most of the students' guardians were deeply disturbed by this event. The second issue of *Parthenon* was being printed, when the Hindu College authorities stopped its printing and confiscated the journal. The Hindu conservative weekly *Samachar Chandrika* and the reactionary weekly *John Bull* strongly supported this move by the Hindu College authorities.

Two years later, the Hindu College authorities forced Derozio to resign from his post in Hindu College. Towards the end of the same year Derozio passed away at the young age of 22. He thus taught in Hindu College for a brief span of 5 years from 1826 to 1831. Yet in this short period he lit a flame of quest for truth in the minds of his young students and friends. This led to an awakening of mind, which can truly be called the origin of the Bengal Renaissance. His admirers came to be known as "Young Bengal".

Derozio himself edited several papers, one of which was *Kaleidoscope*. In that journal, in an article written on 2 September, 1829, Derozio wrote: " Even those who are superficial analysts, they too certainly realize that India has been kept subjugated by means of military power. Withdraw the troops, and one will find that instead of loyalty to British rule Indians were getting ready to drive out the British." On 23 April 1831, Ramkamal Sen and others placed a resolution in the governing body of Hindu College declaring that Derozio was the root of all mischief and a matter of anxiety for the people, and so he should be sacked. In the resolution it was also stated that if any student goes to any public meeting, he should also be driven out of Hindu College. Does it not remind us of the Carlyle Circular during the anti-partition Swadeshi movement of 1905, nearly eighty years later? On 25 April, Derozio sent in his resignation letter. In that letter he courageously wrote that the authorities had sacked him, without even giving him the right of defence. This was a mockery of justice!

For our purpose, we have now to examine how far "Young Bengal" was conscious about colonial rule in their concept of India. Let us give some instance. In a letter to *Calcutta Monthly Journal* in February 1831, a supporter of "Young Bengal" wrote: "In order to remove the misery of India, it is necessary to end British rule. It is only, then, that people of this country would be able to live in a more dignified manner. The case of America shows the difference of what it was when it was under the British and what it has become after America won its independence".

On 5 January 1835, a public meeting was held in the Calcutta Town Hall to criticize the Charter Act of 1833. In that meeting a leading member of Young Bengal and editor of the Bengali weekly *Jnananvesan*, Rasikkrishna Mullick said "This Act has been passed not for the good of India, but for the benefit of the bosses of the East India Company. It has been passed for the prosperity of the people of England, not for the welfare of India's millions" (*Bengal Harkaru*, 6 January 1835).

In 1835, 16-year old Kylash Chandra Dutt, a student of Hindu College, won the first prize in an essay competition whose subject was "India of my dream - 110 years later". In that essay Kylash Chandra writes about an imaginary mass rebellion in India in 1945 which overthrew the rule of Lord Fell Butcher, the Governar-General of India and established for some time an Independent republic with the most patriotic men of the land. The rebellion was ultimately crushed and its leader, on the eve of being executed, told his countrymen to carry on the struggle for freedom. (*Calcutta Literary Gazette*, 6 June 1835).

In 1838, some ex-students of Derozio like Ramtanu Lahiri, Ramgopal Ghosh and others formed an organisation called the Society for the Acquisition of General Knowledge (SAGK). Every third Wednesday of each month, they held a meeting of the society in the Sanskrit College, Calcutta, and one or the other member of SAGK presented a paper. The first paper was presented by Reverend Krishna Mohan Bannerji, who was not a pupil but an ardent friend of Derozio and also editor of a paper called *The Enquirer*. In 1832 Krishna Mohan had written a play called "The Persecuted", which supported the cause of women's emancipation. Another member of SAGK Uday Chand Addhya, presented a paper in Bengali in which he wrote that "if the people of the country can become masters of their own language, then they can end their slavery and be free".

In early October 1841, several hundred youths of Calcutta held a meeting and formed a patriotic organisation called Deshahitaishanee Sabha. Sarada Prasad Ghosh, a student of Derozio and now a school-teacher, delivered the main speech in the meeting. He said; "From the very beginning of British rule in India, the British have taken away all political rights from the Indians. This lack of political rights is at the root of all our misery and degradation" (*Bengal Harkaru*, 6 Octobr 1841). In the concluding part of his speech, Sarada Prasad appealed to all Indians, irrespective of religion, caste or creed, to unite in the struggle to win political rights. This is a truly remarkable speech, when we remember that it was given in 1841.

In 1841 the SAGK held a meeting in the Sanskrit College where Tarachand Chakraborty presided. The speaker Dakshina Ranjan Mukherjee was sharply criticising British rule in India and D.L. Richardson, Principal, Hindu College, who was present there protested and asked Dakshinaranjan to stop his speech. Tarachand told Richardson that he was presiding over the meeting and it was his prerogative to decide what the speaker would say or not say. If Richardson did not like his speech, he could leave the meeting, but not interrupt the proceeding. Richardson left the meeting in a huff. Next day Tarachand, who was a teacher of Hindu College, went to teach there. Richardson sent him a note through a bearer asking for his apology for his behaviour to him in the previous day's meeting. Tarachand at once wrote a note of resignation from the Hindu College and throwing the letter on Richardson's table left the College, never to come back.

In 1843, members of the SAGK transformed their Society into Bengal British India Society. They brought out a bi-lingual weekly, *Bengal Spectator*. In September 1843, *Bengal Spectator*, printed in its columns a long questionnaire whose aim was to know the social and economic condition of the peasants. One of the leading lights of Young Bengal, Pearychand Mitra wrote an article criticising the Permanent Settlement and in defence of the rights of the peasants.

His friend Radhanath Sikdar worked in the Survey of India. There, the British officers very often physically assaulted local labourers. Radhanath once strongly protested against it and slapped a British officer. He had to pay a heavy fine for this act, but he never apologised and he was applauded by the youth of Bengal.

However, all this do not mean that 'Young Bengal' had no limitations. When they said 'India' or 'Our Country' they meant India of people of their status — the well-to-do middle class. The common people, the toiling masses had little or no place in their consciousness. By the second and the third decade of the twentieth century, the idea of India certainly meant the India of all classes fighting to a lesser or greater degree for liberation from British colonial yoke. After the emergence of Gandhiji and the non-cooperation movement, millions and millions of Indian peasants certainly played a very big role in our freedom struggle and no concept of India could be accepted then without the role of the peasantry.

We have rushed ahead, but I think it is necessary for us to go back to the nineteenth century again for some time. Rammohan Roy was totally non-communal and in the declaration of the Brahmo Sabha that he set up in 1828, it was written that the Sabha would be open to all those who believe in one God and the Brotherhood of man. This can truly be called the origins of secularism and internationalism in Indian politics. Rammohan went to England to defend the Regulation abolishing Suttee before the Privy Council, where the conservative forces of India had prefered an appeal, demanding cancellation of the abolition of Suttee. In England, agitation was going on for Parliamentary Reform and Rammohan became an outspoken supporter of Parliamentary Reform.

The idea of India gained new dimension in the Great Indian Revolt of 1857. The Indian Sepoys who led the revolt had Hindus, Muslims and Sikhs among them. As Karl Marx wrote in 1857, it was truly a "national revolt and not a military mutiny" ('Message of Freedom'). The Indian rebels brought out an Urdu weekly from Delhi called 'Payam-e-Azadi'. In two of its issues, in August and September 1857 (quoted in British Parliamentary records) the paper gave a call to all Indians, irrespective of religion, creed or caste to unite and revolt to drive out the British from India. Thus, certainly a new dimension was given to the concept of India during 1857-58.

The Indian educated middle classes, who had not supported the Revolt in 1857-58, gradually changed their opinion. The racist arrogance of the victorious British and the savage brutalities committed by them in 1857-58 turned the opinion of Indian educated middle classes against British rule in India. They started with protests and joint petitions, and gradually went over to agitations. In 1859, the Government of India issued an odious notice, known as the 'Salam Circular'. In this it was stated that when an Indian, howsoever respectable he might be, came to meet a British official, he must take off his shoes, his head gear and then bow low and salute the British official. The progressive weekly *Somprokash* edited by Dwarkanath Bidyabhusan and enjoying the backing of Ishwarchandra Vidyasagar, published a bantering reply to the 'Salam Circular'. It wrote that "in Indian mythology, once lord Vishnu took the shape of a boar. Is that any reason why the entire human race shall lie down and touch the feet of all the pigs of the world?" Thus the idea of India changed with passing years, though the idea of an Independent India was as yet the dream of only a very few people.

In 1876, an Indian Association or Bharat Sabha was formed in Calcutta with the effort of the nationalists headed by Surendranath Bannerjea, Anandamohan Bose, Sivnath Shastri, Dwakanath Ganguly and others. Contact was established by the leaders of the Indian Association with nationalists of Bombay and Poona. Surendranath travelled by train to Patna, Allahabad, Delhi and Lahore to set up branches of Indian Association there. Then in 1878 the Indian Association organised the first ever all-India protest day against Lytton's Vernacular Press Act. In almost all major cities of India protest meetings were held on the protest day declared by the Indian Association. Thus the idea of India reached a higher dimension with this event.

Lytton did not repeal the Vernacular Press Act despite the all-India protest. Hence the Indian Association decided to collect one lakh signature demanding the repeal of the notorious Act and send a representative of the Indian Association with the mass of signatures to England to present their case before the English Parliament. Lalmohan Ghosh, an organiser of the Indian Association and also a brilliant orator, was chosen as the Association's representative to go to U.K. and present their case. A Tory government headed by Disraeli was in power then with the Liberals led by Gladstone in opposition. Lalmohan presented India's case before the Liberals and Gladstone promised that if in the next general elections the Liberals won, then they would repeal the Vernacular Press Act.

This was 1879-80. A few years later in 1885 the Indian National Congress was born and with it in an embryonic form the idea of Indian Independence. However, the early leaders of the Congress had faith in the Liberal Party and had the idea that with their help India might be able, step by step, to march towards self-government. A radical strain was injected by the Bombay leader Bal Gangadhar Tilak, who towards the close of the century uttered the famous slogan "Swaraj (Self-Government) is my birthright, and I shall have it". Not petitions but struggle — this was the new idea that electrified the youth of India.

After the Partition of Bengal in 1905, the Indian nationalists headed by the radicals launched the anti-partition struggle, with Swaraj as their goal. Their twin weapons were Boycott of all British goods and Swadeshi or self-help. The result was a powerful movement throughout India, especially in Bengal,

Bombay and the Punjab led by Aurobindo Ghosh, Bipin Chandra Pal, B.G. Tilak and Lajpat Rai. Unfortunately, there was a serious weakness in the movement. No efforts were made to draw the Muslims into the movement. British Imperialists took advantage of this to drive a wedge into the movement. None the less, some radical Muslims notably in Bengal joined the Boycott movement, though the majority of Muslims kept away. In 1906, in Dacca, at the house of the Nawab of Dacca, with the connivance of a high ranking British official, the All India Muslim League was born as a counter to the Indian National Congress.

We should mention here two notable exceptions. One was the overwhelmingly Muslim-populated east Bengal district of Barisal. Here the anti-partition movement was led by Aswini Kumar Dutt. He had a volunteer organisation of students and youth called the Bandhab Samity, who rendered self less service to the poorer masses, irrespective of religion caste or, during flood or epidemics. This created a mass base for Dutt among the entire populace of Barisal — the Muslim peasants and dock workers, the lower caste Hindus (Namashudras) and the educated Hindus. This resulted in the boycott movement being a total success in Barisal.

The other instance to which I refer happened in Bombay when in July 1908 Tilak was tried and convicted for six years by the High Court for writing powerful articles in his daily *Kesari* condemning British atrocities in Bengal. The day after his conviction, several lakh textile workers of Bombay went on a general strike with the slogan of immediate and unconditional release of Tilak. The British shot down scores of workers but the strike went on for over a week. Among those killed were both Marathas and Gujratis — it was a stike by Indians. This was the first political general strike in India and in far — off Geneva, Lenin commented on this strike as the beginning of the awakening of the working class in Asia.

A relatively small section of the radicalised nationalist youth all over India but notably in Bengal, Bombay and the Punjab took to the path of revolutionary armed struggle. Their goal was complete Independence for India. During the First World War in Bengal alone, nearly ten thousand young men were detained without trial under Regulation III of 1818. A daring Bengal revolutionary called Jatindranath Mukherjee contacted Indian revolutionaries who had fled to Berlin and formed an Indian Independence League there. With their help Jatindranath

Mukherjee obtained promise from Germany to send them a shipload of arms. Unfortunately the British came to know of this and intercepted Jatindranath and four of his comrades at a point near the sea-coast in Balasore in Orissa. A big contingent of British soldiers attacked this valiant band of youth, killing Jatindranath and Chittapriyo, while three others were arrested, tried and executed. They were all considered martyrs to the cause of Indian Independence.

Jatindranath had sent out earlier his trusted assistant Narendranath Bhattacharya to China, Japan and Indonesia in search of arms. After Jatindranath was killed Narendranath went to USA under the pseudonym of Manabendranath Roy. There, after diligent study of the works of Karl Marx in New York library, he accepted Marxism as his new ideology. After USA entered World War I on the side of Britain in 1917, M.N.Roy went to Mexico where he soon became secretary of the Mexican Socialist Party. After the victory of the Russian Revolution in November 1917, Lenin contacted Roy through his organizer Borodin. Roy was converted to communism by Borodin and he was persuaded to go to Moscow to attend the second congress of the Communist International in 1920. Roy now took the message of the Communist International to the Indian freedom fighters with a new concept of India: Complete Independence as the immediate but Socialism as the ultimate goal of the Indian national liberation movement.

Thus the idea of India went through various stages from the twenties of the nineteenth century to the middle of the twentieth century. Now at the beginning of the twenty-first century the present day rulers of India are trying to distort the concept of India, according to their communal fundamentalist outlook. But we have to remember that the concept of India right from the time of Young Bengal in the thirties of the nineteenth century, had been progressive and secular and not sectarian and communal. This is shown above all in the writings of the most finished product of the Bengal Renaissance — Rabindranath Tagore. In numerous essays Tagore spelt out his idea of India or Bharatbarsha which is unity in the midst of diversity and which is a united homeland of all Hindus, Muslims, Christians, Brahmins as well as Untouchables. He would have utterly rejected the kind of parochial India that is being projected today in the guise of Savarkar's "Cultural Nationalism".

14

Swami Dayanand's Aryavarta

INDU BANGA

Literally, the 'land of Aryas', Aryavarta for Swami Dayanand (1824-1883) is the 'best of lands', the 'golden land', and the 'veritable philosopher's stone'.[1] In his major doctrinal statement, the *Satyarth Prakash* (first published 1875),[2] he refers to Aryavarta both as a country (*desh*) and motherland (*swadesh*). It figures as a geographical as well as cultural entity, comprehending religion and language along with territory. This conception of Aryavarta is given by him essentially to deal with colonial rule, identify its problems, and prescribe remedies for its regeneration through the agency of the Arya Samaj.[3] Founded at Bombay in 1875, the Arya Samaj as a movement spread to different parts of India and abroad by the 1940s.[4] The particular conception of Aryavarta, its past, present, and future, offered by Swami Dayanand has continued to influence the attitudes of a large number of educated Indians, both Arya and non-Arya.[5]

In a geographical sense, denoting a specific territory, the term Aryavarta occurs only twice in the *Satyarth Prakash*, once in the main body of the text, and then at the end in the summing up of the author's own position. Bounded by the Himalayas, the Vindhya mountains, the Attock (Indus) and the Brahmaputra

[1] Dayanand Sarasvati, *Satyarth Prakash* (cited hereafter as *SP*), 36th imp, Delhi: Arsh Sahitya Prachar Trust, 1988, p.187.

[2] Written in Hindi prose, the *Satyarth Prakash* was revised by Swami Dayanand in 1882, but was published after his death in 1884. This second edition, regarded as the full and final statement of his ideology and doctrinal position, became the 'principal text book of the Aryas' (J.T.F. Jordens, *Dayananda Sarasvati : His Life and Ideas*, Delhi, 1979, p. 269.)

[3] Indu Banga, 'The Ideology of Swami Dayanand', *Cultural Reorientation in Modern India*, ed. Indu Banga and Jaidev, Shimla, 1996, pp. 24-35.

[4] Kenneth W. Jones, 'The Arya Samaj in British India', *Religion in Modern India*, ed. Robert R. Baird, 2nd edn, Delhi, 1989, pp. 36-52. The *Arya Directory* of 1941 lists over 2000 Samaj units affiliated to the Arya provincial organizations, but Jones thinks that the actual number of the Arya Samaj chapters and other institutions may have been larger: ibid., pp. 39 & 53 n 36.

[5] For the influence of the Arya ideology on the crystallization of a Hindu consciousness, see Indu Banga, 'The Emergence of Hindu Consciousness in Colonial Punjab', *Self-Images, Identity and Nationality*, ed. P.C. Chatterjee, Shimla, 1989, pp. 201-17.

river, this 'great land mass' is stated to be the original home of the Aryas.[6] Peninsular India (Deccan and South India) does not figure in any significant way in the *Satyarth Prakash*; Rameshwaram and Shringeri occur once each, vaguely or with reference to Shankaracharya.[7] Thus, the term Aryavarta is generally used notionally for the Indian subcontinent, a large part of which was recognized as being subordinate (*paradhin*) to foreigners. Only 'a few' areas under the princely rulers are said to be independent (*swadhin, swatantra*) by Swami Dayanand.[8] This understanding of the geo-political situation under the British may account for his increasing reliance on the princely states of Rajputana for testing his ideas for the regeneration of Aryavarta.[9]

The first inhabitants of Aryavarta, according to Swami Dayanand, were the noble (*shreshtha*) people who had originated in Tibet and not in Iran and who came to this great land on account of the disturbances caused by ignorant scoundrels. Gradually, and on the basis of their relative qualities and learning, they got divided into four classes. The first three of these — Brahmans, Kshatriyas, and Vaishyas — came to be called 'Arya', while the ignorant fools called Shudras constituted the fourth class.[10] The Aryas are stated to be distinct from the other peoples who are variously described as the Dasyus, Mlechhas, Rakshasas, Asurs, Huns, Habshis and Negroes and who have black or red faces, the latter with light eyes like those of monkeys. They are believed to have been racially, culturally and politically inferior to the Aryas. The specific regions or countries figuring in the *Satyartha Prakash* as distinct from Aryavarta are America (Patal) and Europe (Harivarsh), with an occasional mention of France, Greece, Rome, Egypt, Iran, Kandahar, and China.[11]

The history of Aryavarta is traced in terms of three broad phases. First, the age of imperial glory up to the reign of King

[6] *SP*, pp. 151-52 & 407.

[7] *SP*, pp. 152 & 196. The Swami's correspondence of 1883 indicates, however, that he was contemplating a visit to Madras. (Jordens, *Dayananda Sarasvati*, p. 226.)

[8] *SP*, p. 153.

[9] Cf. Jordens, *Dyananda Sarasvati*, pp.226-28.

[10] *SP*, pp. 151-53. In one of his pamphlets Swami Dayanand explains why he prefers the label 'Arya' over 'Hindu' : this was because of the latter's foreign origin and supposed association with the 'slavery to Muslims'. 'Bhranti Nivaran', *Dayanandiya Laghu-grantha Sangraha*, ed. Yudhishthar Mimansak, Bahalgarh, Sonepat, 1975, p. 198.

[11] Ibid., pp. 152-53, 179 & 187-89.

Yudhishthar when the Aryas ruled over the entire world and all peoples subscribed to the Vedic religion. Second, the age of political disunity, religious decline, and social degeneration, beginning after the great Mahabharata war and continuing till the reign of King Yashpal (*sic*). Third, the fall of Aryavarta, marked by a period of slavery or foreign rule, from the conquests of Shihabuddin Ghuri to the present.[12]

A diversity of causes operating at different levels are said to have led to the decline and fall of the Aryavarta. On the whole, indifference to the true religion (*satya-dharma*) of the Vedas emerges as the root cause of all evil in Swami Dayanand's writings. The ignorant and grasping priests diverted people from self-study and self-effort to a life of passivity, characterized by belief in astrology, charities, pilgrimages, fasts and rituals. Above all, the priests had a vested interest in perpetuating idol-worship (believed to have been started by the Jains) for material gain and misuse of temple precincts for immoral purposes. The Swami disparagingly uses the terms *'pop-lila'* and *'pop-maya'* for the various ways in which the priestly classes, including the self-styled *gurus*, misled and exploited innocent devotees, most of whom happened to be women. He is equally critical of the ignorant and selfish self-styled *sannyasis*.[13]

The decline of Vedic religion and education went together. Its social fall-out was the growing disregard of the four stages of life (*ashramas*), particularly *brahmacharya*. Acquiring education should be the sole concern of man, and to an extent also of woman. According to Swami Dayanand, the early and incompatible marriages became the rule, which affected the health of the woman and the quality of her offspring. The disrespect for women, multiplicity of wives, and exploitation of widows were a corollary of this situation. The Swami seems to suggest that ignorance, religious diversity, and social disequilibrium ate into the vitals of this land and never allowed it to recover. It was but logical that Aryavarta should fall prey, first, to the mutual feuds and political disunity of its rulers, and then to the foreigners. Its misfortunes have got compounded 'ever since the meat-eating, kine-killing and spirit-drinking foreigners' became its rulers.[14]

[12] *SP*, pp. 271-74.
[13] *SP*, pp. 189-269.
[14] *SP*, pp. 181-82.

Swami Dayanand's prescription for an 'all-round progress' of Aryavarta consists of a combination of right belief, right ritual, right knowledge, and right action, essentially amounting to reinstatement of Vedism through reform and education. The foremost obligation of the Aryas is belief in the Vedas, that is the four *Samhitas* as the revealed word of God, and so the repository of all knowledge and, therefore, infallible and universal.[15] This was intended to provide a scriptural basis of unity to the Aryas and a source of confidence to deal with the progress made by the West. The Swami enjoins the study of the Vedas upon the *dwijas,* or the three upper *varnas*, as a duty and permits the rest as well to study the Vedas.[16] Vedic study should be accompanied by the Vedic form of worship. He revived and systematized the Vedic fire-sacrifice (*homa*) and accorded it a central place in the prescribed daily and weekly rituals of the Aryas, and also in the purificatory sacraments (*samskars*).[17] To enable the ordinary (*sadharan*) householders of the *dwija* castes to perform the *homa* properly, he explains the method as well as the rationale in his *Panch Mahayajnavidhi* (1875) and *Samskar Vidhi* (1877).

The Swami enumerates sixteen obligatory *samskars* in the *Samskar Vidhi* but dwells at length only upon four: the pre-natal rite (*garbhadhan*), beginning the Vedic study (*vedarambha*), marriage (*vivaha*), and renunciation (*sannyas*). More like the 'rites of passage', these *samskars* appear to be of crucial importance in his scheme of social reconstruction. In the first, his primary concern is with eugenics, or the necessary preconditions and preparations for the birth of a male (or even female) child of superior physique and intellect. A higher age of marriage is also considered essential for the health of the child. The chapter on *vedarambha* too dwells at considerable length

[15] *SP*, pp. 134-35 & 405. Swami Dayanand's exclusive stress on the four Vedas proper as 'an original revelation with an authority that took precedence over the whole tradition' was not a part of the Hindu tradition. However, his strong affirmation of this idea through platform and press gradually made its general acceptance possible. (J.T.F. Jordens, *Dayananda Sarasvati: Essays on His Life and Ideas* (cited hereafter as *Essays*), New Delhi, 1998, pp. 46-47 & 71-75.)

[16] *SP*, pp. 49-50. See also, another of the Swami's books, *Samskar Vidhi* (cited hereafter as *SV*), 25th imp., Ajmer, 1968, p. 155.

[17] Indu Banga, 'The Place of Ritual in the Arya Samaj Movement', *Organizational and Institutional Aspects of Indian Religious Movements*, ed. Joseph T. O'Connell, Shimla, 1999, p.274.

on the observance of *brahmacharya* till the age of twenty-four for the man and sixteen for the girl. A disciplined married state is regarded as the mainstay of social organization. At the same time, the Swami thinks that a Brahman *sannyasi* (probably in his own image) who takes the vows straight after completing education, and dedicates his life to public affairs and propagation of true religion, can make the greatest contribution to the cause of regeneration of Aryavarta.[18]

The *varna* system remains basic to the social order in the Aryavarta, albeit with a difference. A man's place in the *varna* order rested on his qualities (*guna*) and actions (*karma*) rather than on birth. Thus, the Swami maintains that a born Shudra could change his position in the social hierarchy by acquiring education and studying the Vedas, and a *dwija* could sink into the Shudra's position by neglecting these. On the whole, however, his preference is for the people born in a particular *varna* performing its duty (*dharma*) well.[19] It seems that his prescriptions by and large exclude those who are outside the pale of the *varna* order. He generically refers to them as the *ati-shudra*, or specifically as '*chandal, neech, bhangi, chamar*, etc.', and disapproves of the *dwijas* having any physical contact or commensality with them.[20]

The progress of Aryavarta is contingent upon education without which a proper study of the Vedas is not possible. Education thus constitutes the 'eyes of man', and a person without education is 'human only in name'.[21] Therefore, all human beings, including the Shudras and women (even the *ati-shudras*, the Swami happens to say at one place), have a right to receive education.[22] He visualizes a society in which children of all *varnas*, both boys and girls, are obliged to receive suitable education in separate institutions. The duration and content of this education would vary, first, according to gender, that is eight years for women and around twenty years for men, and, then, according to their *varna* or social background. What is prescribed by and large is a somewhat broad-based Sanskritic education intended to equip the *dwijas*, particularly Brahmanas and

[18] Ibid., pp. 275-84.
[19] *SP*, pp. 49-61; *SV*, p. 155.
[20] *SP*, pp. 183-4.
[21] Ibid., pp. 178, 269 & 271.
[22] Ibid., pp. 24, 31, 37 & 49-50.

Kshatriyas, for different kinds of roles.[23] The educated man (especially the Vaishya) is advised to learn new languages, travel to other countries, and use this knowledge to his material advantage.[24] Beyond a certain core consisting of subjects of practical use in the household, the curriculum prescribed for women also varies according to the *varna*.[25] The values that education is expected to impart are self-discipline and dignity, fearlessness and prudence, kindness and generosity, and self-effort and selfless service. The Swami expects a certain degree of social commitment from the educated man and exhorts him to work for the progress of Aryavarta by leading a life of active involvement on the side of truth, justice and fairplay.[26]

The new man visualized by Swami Dayanand is not possible without the new woman. Not only should she be educated, she should also be respected. Mutual respect and compatibility in a monogamous marriage contracted at a higher age alone would ensure the birth of superior offspring, so essential to his scheme of regeneration (perhaps under the influence of eugenics). The education prescribed for her is geared to 'domestic bliss' which would equip her to bring up children till the age of five, discharge her household duties, and perform her role in the daily rituals.[27] The Swami also visualizes the possibility of the educated woman becoming a teacher in a girls' school and even entering public life.[28]

A substantial number of the *dwija* women in Swami Dayanand's day consisted of hapless widows whose exploitation was increasingly becoming the concern of social reformers. The Swami's prescription for the plight of widows is twofold: remarriage for virgins and *niyog* (a legally acceptable, but temporary marriage to obtain male offspring) for the women of child-bearing age.[29] Here, the concern appears to be mainly with the 'regulation of sexuality', because 'illicit and unbridled indulgence' in his view 'led to social degeneration'.[30] The Aryas,

23 *SP*, pp. 24, 26-27, 36-37, 44-47 & 51.

24 Ibid., pp. 21, 73 & 179-80.

25 Ibid., p. 51.

26 Ibid., 237, 261-63, 266 & 269.

27 Ibid., pp. 24, 31, 37 & 49-51. See also, Indu Banga, 'Socio-Religious Reform and Patriarchy', *Women in Indian History*, ed. Kiran Pawar, Patiala, 1996, pp.247-50.

28 *SP*, pp. 24, 51 & 71.

29 Ibid., pp. 73-79.

30 Indu Banga, 'Socio-Religious Reform', p. 249.

however, were not comfortable with the idea of *niyog*.[31]

The Swami appears to regard the role of the state as of crucial importance in effecting regeneration of Aryavarta. He visualizes an eventual correspondence between religion, language and polity in India when the state would ensure a revival of the Sanskrit language and Vedic studies, the spread of compulsory education, a higher age of marriage and monogamy, proper functioning of the *varna* system, propagation of right beliefs, and 'reconversion' to the 'true' religion.[32] He insists that there cannot be any 'progress' of Aryavarta till all its inhabitants subscribe to the same religion, have the same idea of loss and gain, and share the same sense of joy and sorrow.[33]

This sense of unity rested on an equally strong sense of the 'other', without which the Swami's comprehensive definition of the 'Arya' and Aryavarta would be incomplete. Thus, more than half of the *Satyarth Prakash* (214 pages out of 404) is given to the negation (*khandan*) of unacceptable beliefs and practices, collectively labelled *'purani, jaini, kirani* and *kurani'*.[34] The Swami is vehement in denouncing them all, though the degree of vehemence varies with the degree of disapproval in the light of his own conception of the 'true religion'. There is a qualitative difference, however, in his emphases and tone in the 'exposition' of Christianity and Islam in the last two chapters of the *Satyarth Prakash*.[35]

The Swami's objections to Christianity and Islam – the two Religions of the Book – appear to stem from several sources. To establish the scriptural supremacy of the Vedas it was essential to denigrate the Bible and the Quran on grounds of irrationality and untenability. He attempts to do so by a literal and particularistic interpretation of the two scriptures, and by belittling their prophets, basic beliefs and essential practices. He contrasts the glory of Aryavarta in the ancient past with the then 'barbaric' (*jangli*) state of the Christians and Muslims.[36] On a more immediate plane, he objects to the drinking of spirits and eating of meat, especially beef by them; disapproves of their

[31] Jordens, *Dayananda Sarasvati*, pp. 117-18.
[32] *SP*, pp. 27, 61, 114-15, 153 *et passim*.
[33] Ibid., p. 181.
[34] Ibid., p. 186.
[35] These chapters were added to the second edition of 1884.
[36] *SP*, pp. 333-39 & 373.

'unclean' habits; disallows inter-dining with them; and condemns their avariciousness and greed for the wealth of others.[37]

Swami Dayanand denounces Christians for misleading and entrapping innocent people, and separating young boys from their parents, presumably by converting them.[38] He became particularly conscious of the impact of the missionaries during his stay in 1877-78 in the Punjab which at that time was 'a hub of missionary activity'.[39] He is critical of the Brahmo Samaj and Prarthana Samaj for praising Christianity, attributing this to a lack of patriotism. While obliquely critical of the economic exploitation, racialism and discriminatory justice of the British, and extolling the virtues of *swadeshiya rajya*, he equates patriotism (*swadesh-bhakti*) with an anti-Christian stance.[40] Only at one place does he make a distinction between Christianity and the British, here he expresses his admiration for the rational attitudes and disciplined conduct, of the British and their concern for the progress of their own country, its products and people.[41] However, the Swami has nothing positive to say about Islam which is supposed to inculcate treachery, cruelty and lack of respect for women, and sanctify war, plunder, slaughter and demolition of idols and temples.[42]

Swami Dayanand deals with the 'other' mainly in three ways. Since winning over the adherents of the 'false' religions is basic to his conception of Aryavarta, he advocates their inclusion in the fold of 'true' religion which he demonstrated by 'reconverting' some Christians in the Punjab, and a Muslim in the United Provinces.[43] To neutralize the growing political importance of Muslims in the United Provinces, and to show

37 *SP*, pp. 181, 184-85 & 335-36.

38 Ibid., p. 341.

39 Jordens, *Essays*, p. 42. The Punjab was looked upon by the missionaries as a relatively easy conquest for Christianity which accounted for their aggressive denunciations of Hinduism. For their activities in the Punjab, see J.S. Grewal, 'Christian Presence and Cultural Reorientation : The Case of the Colonial Punjab', *Proceedings Indian History Congress*, Calcutta, 1990, pp. 534-42.

40 *SP*, pp. 153, 180, 259-60, 345 & 354.

41 Ibid., pp. 261-2.

42 Ibid., pp. 204, 217, 220, 261, 370, 378-81, 391-92, 395-99 & 402. Cf. Jordens, *Dayananda Sarasvati*, p. 269

43 *SP*, p. 269. See also, Jordens, *Essays*, pp. 43-44 & 164-65. At this stage, there is no evidence that the Swami prescribed any particular rite for 'reconversion' or *shuddhi*, but he clearly proclaimed its desirability. It was the Punjabi Aryas who evolved a procedure for 'reconversion' and 'purification' after his death : ibid., pp. 165-76.

how religion could be united with language and politics, Swami Dayanand appropriated three ongoing agitations in the province during 1880-82: those against cow-killing and Urdu, and for reversal of the indictment of Munshi Indramani for his inflammatory writings against Islam. In all the three cases, the supposed beneficiaries of official decisions were Muslims. By exhorting his Aryas to send money and memorials in support of Indramani, Hindi and cow-protection, the Swami clearly indicated who the 'other' was, and what the new symbols of political unity were. In a pamphlet entitled, 'Gokarunanidhi' published by him in Hindi in 1881, cow-protection is presented as an act of *dharma*, and Hindi (now called Arya-Bhasha) as the appropriate medium of communication in Aryavarta.[44] The Swami was thus contributing towards the shaping up of a political attitude which was directed more against the Muslims than the British.

By the time of the publication of Swami Dayanand's final statement in the revised edition of the *Satyarth Prakash* (1884), his idea of Aryavarta had crystallized into a multi-faceted construct, with a scripture, ethic, and history of its own, and a set of new symbols and new priorities for a new future identity. Its modernizing and nationalizing tendencies notwithstanding, the idea of Aryavarta is embedded in an hierarchical, patriarchal and exclusivist view of Indian society in which the state is visualized as acting in support of the Aryas to the disadvantage of 'others'. The democratic and secular constitution of India, has thus little that conforms to Swami Dayanand's concept of 'Aryavarta'.

[44] *SP*, pp. 182-83 & 361. See also, Indu Banga, 'The Ideology of Swami Dayanand', pp.31-33; Jordens, *Dayananda Sarasvati*, pp. 220-25. One of the underlying considerations, probably, was to also place the Arya Samaj at the vanguard of the 'Hindu' revival, because till then it had been looked upon as a sectarian movement within Hinduism.

15

A Juster India for Women — The Thought and Work of Pandita Ramabai and Rameshwari Nehru

KAMLESH MOHAN

With respect to India one may fairly raise a number of questions: Where and what is the real India? How is it experienced and discovered? From what perspective is the real India to be represented so that its portrayal is diverse and rich but not homogeneous, inclusive and total? Whose narrative is it going to be? Certainly, it should be the 'people's'; but the term 'people' covers a wide spectrum of positions, identities and social backgrounds. How should these many sub-identities be unified or integrated in the idea of India and its vision in future so that it continues to be of significance to all sections of Indians?

It is in this spirit that the discovery of India (a different one from that of men leaders and reformers) was undertaken by Pandita Ramabai and Rameshwari Nehru. Before going further, it may be noted that a certain kind of India (read Indian society) already existed. However, it was waiting to be touched, known and narrativized at a particular historical juncture by a select band of discerning and articulate men and women who possessed a heightened sensitivity regarding caste and gender inequalities as well as the courage to contest patriarchal representations and social norms in the religious scriptures and classical literature.

I wish to underline one important point before discussing the perception of traditional India and the alternative social vision(s), offered by the militant feminist Pandita Ramabai and the moderate Rameshwari Nehru. As nationalism underwent transmutation through the late nineteenth century into the first decades of the twentieth century, it faced a 'politico-epistemological predicament'.[1] As Indian society was (and is) composed of a large segment of oppressed members, specifically women and low castes, mere political dichotomization resulting in freedom and birth of a new nation-state might be a pre-requisite

[1] Cf. Partha Chatterjee, *Nationalist Thought and the Colonial World*, Delhi, 1986, pp. 38-39.

but would not be sufficient. Elaborating this point, Partha Chatterjee has argued that the nationalist politic was required to grow out of its commitment to Euro-centric Enlightenment and carve a new space wherein it could fashion its own epistemological, cognitive and representational modalities.

By locating the real India in its villages, Gandhi made space for a different epistemology and vision, which countered the urban-elitist versions of India. After his return from South Africa, he travelled throughout the country and realized that it is in its villages that India was to be experienced and discovered. It was through his contact with the masses that he gathered his knowledge about the real India. His plan of socio - political transformation based on these insights and knowledge was geared to involve peasants, Harijans and women. Its ultimate goal was to empower the people in a way that would enable them to lead themselves. Rameshwari Nehru, who became his disciple from 1919 onwards, was inspired to broaden the scope of her agenda of empowering middle-class women by enabling the contributors to her *Stree Darpan* to understand the linkages between social and political oppression. Pandita Ramabai, whose sole mission of life and activities was the recovery of social space for high-caste widows and low-caste destitute women, remained an uncompromising critic of Indian (Hindu) society throughout her life.

II

It is pertinent to glance briefly at the social background and career of Pandita Ramabai and Rameshwari Nehru in order to understand their perceptions of India, their response to male iconography and their activities for refashioning women's mind, self-image and world-view.

Let us first turn to Pandita Ramabai whose intellectual roots go back to the twilight of the (Brahmin) Peshwa regime just before Baji Rao II lost political power to the East India Company in 1818. Despite this political upheaval, Brahmin supremacy based on religious, economic and social status survived. Thus, there was no loosening of patriarchal control over high-caste Hindu women.

Born in April 1858, Ramabai was the daughter of Anant Shastri Dongre, a Chitpavan Brahmin.[2] Ramabai had an unusual

[2] For a first-hand account of her life and career see 'An Autobiographical Account'

childhood as her father refused to conform to the norms of the conventional Maharashtrian society and traversed the length and breadth of India while earning a precarious living by reciting the *Puranas*. His life-style was marked by unorthodox elements. For one, Anant Shastri insisted on giving his daughters a Sanskrit education. In Ramabai's case, her mother Lakshmibai educated her as the father was too old for the exertion. Then, he refused to arrange the customary early marriage for Ramabai as a result of his elder daughter Krishnabai's unhappy child marriage.

A significant implication of her unconventional upbringing was that Ramabai escaped a rigid gender-specific role unlike her peers who were trapped into wifehood and motherhood at an early age, being thereupon confined to the domestic space, subjected to the pressures of the extended family and denied even access to literacy. Educated and trained in public speaking like her brother, Ramabai found it easy to collaborate with or challenge the men social reformers on concerns and issues relating to women. Acutely sensitive to the voice of her conscience coupled with a persistent intellectual curiosity, Ramabai became intensely individualistic, despite a life of poverty and physical hardship. Later, it was to lead to her conversion to Christainity and a life-long contest against patriarchy and its biased representation of women in the *shastras* and classical literature especially the epics.

As a member of an impecunious but close-knit family, Ramabai had some enjoyable moments, spoiled by the traumatic experience of losing her parents during the severe famine in 1874. So extreme was the poverty of the Dongre family that no Brahmins could be persuaded to carry her mother's bier to the cremation ground. Finally, two Brahmins took pity and offered help. Ramabai had to carry the bier on her head owing to her small stature. Just a year later, her elder sister Krishnabai died. Hereafter, Ramabai, along with her brother, continued her travels over a distance of 2000 miles, often on foot. The travels gave them a good opportunity of "seeing the sufferings of Hindu women."

(September 1833), and 'A Testimony of Our Inexhaustible Treasure', in Meera Kosambi, compiled and edited with translations, *Pandita Ramabai Through Her Own Words*, New Delhi, 2000, pp. 115-18 and 295-314. See also Pandita Ramabai Sarasvati, *The High Caste Hindu Women* (first published, 1888; reprinted, New Delhi, 1984, and Uma Chakravarti, *Rewriting History: Life and Times of Pandita Ramabai*, Delhi, 1998.

In 1878, the two young persons reached Calcutta where Ramabai's mastery of Sanskrit created a sensation. For ahead of many women in her times for her learning and bold views, she was honoured with the titles of 'Pandita' and 'Sarasvati' by Sanskrit scholars in Calcutta. These years of personal triumph were marred by her brother's death. Her consequent loneliness and the persistent wooing by Bipin Behari Das Medhavi (a Brahmo and a non-Brahmin Bengali) obliged Ramabai to marry the radical-minded young man in 1880. After less than two years of happy married life in Kochhar (Assam), Medhavi died in 1882 of cholera. A twenty-four year old widow without any money, she was now left with an infant daughter.

Ramabai decided to return to western India where she was eagerly acclaimed as a 'native' daughter owing to her fame as a Sanskrit scholar and for her statement in favour of female education before the Hunter Commission (1883). With her arrival in Bombay Presidency, the reformers conceded that "the cause of women's education had gained in her a supreme treasure". Soon after the public recognition of her mastery of Sanskrit, Justice Ranade and his young wife and Mrs. Gargabai helped Pandita Ramabai to establish the Arya Mahila Samaj dedicated to the uplift and enlightenment of women.[3] It was hoped that the Samaj would become the nucleus of a movement for the emancipation of women.

It was, however, frustrating work. Ramabai acknowledged the difficulty of urging women to act independently in a social melieu where distrust and suspicion about women was so deeply rooted. In her view, it had been incorporated into Hindu custom, law and behaviour. Nevertheless, she was determined to bring about a change in the system. In order to fulfil her aim, Ramabai argued that women must gain support of the colonial government and this could only be done through proficiency in English. Extremely annoyed with her own inability to communicate in English with the Hunter Commission (she submitted her evidence in Sanskrit), she travelled to England, where she had been appointed Professor of Sanskrit at Cheltenham College and utilized this opportunity to learn English.[4] Her association with

[3] 'Arya Mahila Samaj', in K.J. Chitalia ed, *Directory of Women's Institutions*, Bombay Presidency, vol. I, Bombay 1936, p. 6.

[4] Rajas Krishnarao Dongre and Joseph F. Patterson, *Pandita Ramabai: A Life of Faith and Prayer*, Madras, 1969, pp.10-11.

the Sisters of Community of St. Mary the Virgin at Wantage and later her conversion to Christianity in September 1883 under conditions of unusual emotional stress was to make her public career fairly controversial.

After almost three years in England Ramabai went to the U.S.A. where she was lionized as an internationally known advocate of the cause of Indian women. While reproducing her speech at a special gathering the day after Anandibai's graduation, *The Mahrata* of Pune (2 May, 1886) tried to simultaneously denigrade Ramabai and glorify Anandibai Joshi by projecting the latter as the icon of the educated Maharashtrain womanhood owing to her well-publicized conformity to the conventional code of conduct.

Ramabai's two and half years' stay (from March 1886 to October 1888) in the U.S.A. for studying its educational system in Philadelphia and later her extensive travels for raising funds for a high-caste Hindu widows' home filled her with admiration for its environment of freedom and democratic functioning. During this phase, her major achievement was the formation of The Ramabai Association of Boston in 1887 that pledged its financial support for ten years to a secular widows' home.

Soon after her return to India in February 1889, Ramabai opened a widows' home, called Sharda Sadan (Home of Learning) at Chowpatty, Bombay, later shifted to Pune in November for reasons of economy and direct access to the orthodox Brahmin community. Despite initial support from leading social reformers of the Bombay Presidency namely Ranade, Bhandarkar and Telang, Ramabai's efforts for mobilizing financial and moral support of upper-caste society for widows and deserted women failed owing to her focus upon lower caste famine victims. Alienated from Hindu society, she opened the Mukti Sadan (House of Salvation) in 1896 in collaboration with her Christian friends to house the victims of famine from the Central Provinces and Gujarat. She also established Kripa Sadan (Home of Mercy) for sexually victimized women. It had a separate section for blind women who were given instruction in Braille and taught useful crafts; and also a section for the care of old women. Her earlier empathy with Hinduism was now gradually replaced by total alienation from it and identification with Christianity. Henceforth, her feminist reading of social problems, ideology and daily experiences were filtered through a Christian sensibility. However, scars of emotional and cultural uprooting remain visible in her writings, which document her religious transition.

The preceding account of her early life-experiences and activities show that her intellectual growth had been deeply influenced by her sensitivity to gender discrimination in Hindu society. In the course of her evolution as a feminist, Pandita Ramabai formulated her concept of a patriarchal society, particularly Indian, which lacked compassion and sensitivity towards the problems of high-caste widows, deserted wives and sexually exploited women. It was sharpened by her triadic encounters with reformist groups in the East and West, orthodox or liberal Hindu leaders, Christian missionaries and colonial officials. It is within the international context that Ramabai raised a number of issues in her narrative of oppressed Indian womanhood. Unlike many of her contemporaries, she questioned the validity of the concept and existence of a 'golden age' for Hindu women in ancient India. On the basis of her Sanskrit knowledge, she discarded the myth of the glorious Aryan woman. In fact, she used the term 'golden age' pejoratively in which a man "takes a woman (from) where she may be found and drag her to his house".[5] But she argued that the Christian British rule was no better. The only difference was that now a man was required to file a suit against a woman to claim her as his 'marital' property as in the case of her elder sister Krishnabai.

It must be pointed out that Ramabai's perception of Hindu society and of the status of high-caste women had undergone radical changes in response to her own experiences from 1881 to 1887 as is evident from her writings. One of her significant early writings 'Stri Dharma Niti' (1882), which facilitated her entry into the male-reform discourse, is literally an endorsement of the Sita-Savitri model of femininity. Castigating the average woman as 'lazy, stupid and obstinate', Ramabai held her responsible not only for her own but also for the entire country's subjection and stagnation.[6] At this juncture, Ramabai spoke like

[5] Pandita Ramabai Sarasvati, *The High Caste Hindu Women*, p. 62.

[6] 'Stri Dharma Niti' in Meera Kosambi, op. cit., pp. 42, 45, 51. Explicating the link between woman's nature and her miserable plight, Ramabai remarked, "The root-cause of unhappiness is that women are too slothful and don't help men as much as they should. Then why would men not subject women, who can't serve their self - interest, to harsh and shameful rebukes.... We don't possess important virtues such as knowledge, industry, etc., which is why we have no standing among men."

a female patriarch[7] believing that the Indian nation's strength and identity specifically of its culture lay in Indian womanhood. Based on this negative perception of woman, 'Stri Dharma Niti' was written as a guide to morality and deportment for women who were in urgent need of being reformed. Quite logically, it glorified mythological models of Indian womanhood and historical heroes like Shivaji and Napoleon.

In this early phase of her life, Pandita Ramabai sought to reinforce the traditional social perceptions of gender-roles as the following extract shows:

> Domestic duties are the work of women. They should never neglect them. A home in which women do not perform household work themselves is not a happy home. A woman does not attain the rank of a housewife merely by virtue of being born into the female sex or by becoming a housewife.[8]

Like the male reformers she favoured 'competent domesticity' as the ideal for women on the Victorian model and prescribed a code of conduct for brides and for mothers for the care and nurturing of children in order to produce a healthy progeny. She made a little departure when she attributed the "dispirited, weak and dependent condition" of men in her times to the lack-lustre constitution of the women, who had been reduced to a state of animal-like ignorance and undeserved slavery by the wrong deeds of the selfish, short-sighted men.[9] Ramabai believed that the real reason for depriving women of knowledge through scriptural injunctions was the men's fear of losing their superiority and their freedom for licentious behaviour. It led to the low status of women and their lack of social and economic power. Linking political and economic slavery of India with the long- term social devaluation of women, she urged men "to give up their misguided selfishness" and to enable women to acquire knowledge and "energetic as well as vigorous disposition". In their turn, they would nurture the future generations as "trustworthy, courageous and dutiful" individuals. Clinching her argument, she remarked:

> Then, their (women's) efforts will deliver the country from its wretched state and revive its fortunes. Nothing will be achieved by thousands

[7] This is evident from *Kesari's* comment in its issue dated August, 1882, after the publication of 'Stri Dharma Niti': "... the task of championing the women's cause and of speaking or writing on their behalf, which hitherto fell to the lot of men, has now been undertaken by one belonging to the female sex herself."

[8] 'Stri Dharma Niti', p. 77.

[9] Ibid., p. 90.

of declamations, assemblies, etc., until this happens.[10]

Despite her patronising homilies to women in 'Stri Dharma Niti', Ramabai made radical departures from reformist positions on two counts: her advocacy of relatively late marriages by mutual choice and her exposure of the misogynist bias of the *Dharmashastras*. However, her view of Indian society lacks clarity as she described women as guilty of their own subjection and as victims conditioned to internalize their own subjection in the same breath. The contradictions of this approach are made manifest in 'The Cry of Indian Women' (June 1883), which focussed upon the oppression of women through early marriage, marital harassment, desertion by husbands and the humiliations of widowhood.[11]

The transition from a Brahminical view-point in 'Stri Dharma Niti' regarding women's nature and role to a cohesive feminist perspective in *The High Caste Hindu Women* (1888) was mediated by 'The Cry of Indian Women'. Even a casual reading of 'The Cry of Indian Women' showed that Ramabai had outgrown social liberalism of her erstwhile reformist supporters. Fuming with patriotic indignation over the East India Company's ruthless exploitation and impoverishment of India and the subjection of her countrymen, she demanded:

You ought not to treat us with contumely. The help that we ask from you ought not to be considered by you as a gift. We take ... all assistance from you as a matter of right....[12]

Financial assistance was required from the Government for the maintenance of thousands of widows, destitutes and hapless famine victims. Her grievance against the British Government turned into an attack upon its policy when the female victims of famine were returned to the Princely States. The adverse judgement in the Rakhmabai case confirmed Ramabai's assessment of the colonial state as mercenary, exploitative and patriarchal. By 1887, when she had no like - minded friends left, and Anandibai Joshi had died Rakhmabai withdrew into self-imposed seclusion. Henceforth, she still mounted a single-handed offensive against patriarchy whether colonial or Indian.

[10] Ibid., p.92.

[11] 'The Cry of Indian Women', in Meera Kosambi comp., ed. & trans., op. cit., pp.105-14. It was Ramabai's letter to Sir Bartle Frere, dated 11 June, 1883.

[12] Ibid., p.112.

The high - point of her feminist consciousness is reflected in *The High Caste Hindu Women* which had been deeply influenced by the achievements of women's movement in the West particularly America. Primarily addressed to the non-Indian audience, this book is an insightful account of the actual status of women in the high-caste Hindu families and thereby provided a fairly good idea of contemporary Indian society from the feminist angle. Ramabai's personal reminiscences, coupled with quotations from the sacred texts, pinpointed the contradiction between religion and social custom and the latter's hold over the people's daily lives.

In *The High Caste Hindu Women,* Pandita Ramabai has given a vivid account of a woman's life through three stages: childhood, marriage and widowhood. Each stage was marked by a worsening of the cruelty and oppression suffered daily by her. Beginning her analysis with a pregnant mother's fears and anxiety regarding the sex of the unborn child, she deplored how the birth of a girl was treated in Hindu homes (p.14).

Despite her belief that discrimination against the girl-child was widespread, she gave due weightage to the influence of social custom and an individual's capacity to resist it in determining its extent. She also recognized the psychological compulsion of mothers in oppressing their daughters owing to the internalization of patriarchal values during their (mother's) impressionable years (pp. 17-18).

Ramabai ended her section on childhood by drawing attention to the adverse sex-ratio between males and females recorded in the Census of 1881. She attributed it to the prevalence of the practice of female infanticide among high-caste families, especially in Rajasthan and in the Punjab. Another major reason for the disproportionate numerical difference between the two sexes was *"...the imperfect treatment of the diseases of women in all parts of Hindustan, together with lack of proper hygienic care and medical attendance".*[13] The fundamental cause, then, was the social devaluation of women, underpinned by patriarchal ideology.

The issue of social oppression is further elaborated in Ramabai's comparison of the girl-child with a "young colt whose days are spent in complete liberty" and the beginnings of her endless misery when "the ban of marriage is pronounced and

[13] Pandita Ramabai, *The High Caste Hindu Women,* p. 28.

the yoke put on her neck for ever".[14] The child-bride was brought to the women's court, situated at the back of the house, where "darkness reigns perpetually". Occupying the lowest position in her affinal family, the young bride was put under their complete control. *"Breaking the young bride's spirits is an essential part of the discipline of the new abode"* where she remains confined for ever. Ramabai also referred to the vicious practice of wife-beating. However, she conceded that many happy and loving couples could still be found in India.

Widowhood, according to Ramabai, was the most dreaded period of a high-caste woman's life. Contemporary society regarded widowhood as a retribution for sins committed in an earlier life. Without a son, a widow's life was degraded. Worse was the position of a childless widow upon whom "heaven's judgement has been pronounched".[15] Ramabai castigated Manu for prescribing different codes of conduct for widows and widowers. The law-giver had advised widows to "emaciate her body by living on pure flowers, roots and fruits, but she must never mention the name of another man after her husband has died". The mandatory tonsure of widows implied their sexual death. By dubbing them as inauspicious, society debarred them from participation in any family celebrations. It signified their social death. However, for the high-caste men, Manu had given a command to live well:

A twice-born man, versed in the sacred law, shall burn a wife of equal caste (and) having at the funeral given the sacred fires to his wife who dies before him, he may marry again, and kindle the nuptial fires.[16]

The traumatic experience of widowhood was further compounded by the legitimization and glorification of *sati* which Ramabai described as the creation of a "wicked priesthood".[17] Why did widows commit sati? In Ramabai's view, the momentary agony of suffocation in the flames was nothing compared to her lot as a widow. Besides, her daily humiliation, disfigurement and exploitation as a drudge in the family, the young widow was regarded as a *rand* (loose woman) whose sexuality ought to be

[14] Ibid., p. 42.
[15] Pandita Ramabai, op. cit., p.70.
[16] Ibid., p. 72.
[17] Ibid., p. 73.

kept under control to protect family honour. While appreciating the male reform project, she could not ignore its limited reach and failure as a practical means of ending a widow's miseries. These social reformers, who had pledged to marry widows, ended up by marrying "pretty little maidens".[18]

As legitimization of oppression and erasure of women was based on religious scriptures, more specifically on the *Manusmriti,* Pandita Ramabai illustrated her analysis of the position.of the Indian woman as a child, bride and mother, as well as a widow with apt quotations from religious texts, proverbs and catechisms. It is ironical that women as mothers were honored but condemned as females. Even today strongly entrenched in the social imagination of the urban elite and the rural folks, these pithy generalizations are used in daily parlance to belittle women. For example, let us read the following proverbs:

Q.What is cruel ?
A.The heart of a viper.
Q.What is more cruel than that?
A.The heart of a woman.
Q.What is the cruellest of all ?
A.The heart of a soulless, penniless widow.[19]

It is an endorsement of *Manusmriti's* observations regarding women's nature:

Through their passion for men, through their mutable temper, through their natural heartlessness, they become disloyal to their husbands, however, carefully they are guarded in this world.[20]

Pandita Ramabai perceived a crucial link between the low estimate of *strisvabhava* and seclusion of women including strict control over their sexuality leading to the reduction of their status as a commodity. She reserved her harshest remarks for the marital rights of men over their wives. Equated with "cows, mares, female-camels, slave-girls, buffaloes, she-goats and cows"in *Manusmriti,*[21] women were persecuted by social, religious and state-laws. The British law-courts, instead of providing relief to women, reinforced man's "conjugal rights" over his wife. The

[18] Ibid., p. 91.
[19] Cited in Ramabai, op. cit., p. 57.
[20] Ibid., p.53
[21] *Manusmriti* IX, pp. 48-51

shared agenda of the Indian male and the colonial patriarchy was implemented in the classic case of the highly educated Rakhmabai, who had been married as a child to a boy who grew up as a worthless dunce. Unlike husbands, wives have not been given any rights by scriptures to abandon a blemished, diseased, impotent or evil man.[22]

The aggressive opposition of some of the "Orthodox" nationalists[23] to the support of liberals for Rakhmabai disillusioned Ramabai completely. Reacting to the utter failure of the reformers and colonial judges to change the reality of women's lives, Rakhmabai had written to Ramabai:

> .... There is no hope for women in India, whether they be under Hindu rule or British rule.[24]

Thus, a number of women, caught between the politics of orthodox nationalists and the manouvres of the British rulers, felt cheated and despondent. When Ramabai and Rakhmabai refused to bow to orthodox commandments, they were marginalized in upper-caste society.

Ramabai's earlier loyalty and fascination for the ideal of sanskritized Bhartavarsha in 'Stri Dharma Niti' was now eroded and replaced by a total distancing from Hinduism[25] (partly owing to her American connection) as reflected in 'The Condition of Women'.[26] The hysterical reaction of the conservative Hindu leaders to her conversion to Christianity was symptomatic of their fears for the weakening of national identity.[27] It was underpinned by their anxiety over the loss of male control over

[22] Ibid., p.72. According to Manu, "Though a man has accepted a damsel in due form he may abandon her if she be blemished or diseased, and if she have been given with fraud."

[23] B. G. Tilak dubbed it as a defiance of shastras. Defending Rakhmabai's husband's right to co-habitation, he observed, "If a woman does not go to her husband, she should be punished by the king. And if she disobeys the King's order she should be imprisoned." Cited in Stanley Wolpert, *Ranade and Gokhale,* Berkeley, 1962, p. 38.

[24] Cited in Ramabai, *The High Caste Hindu Women*, p. 66.

[25] Meera Kosambi, op. cit., p.16.

[26] For the text of 'The Condition of Women' in the USA (translated from *United Stateschi Lokasthiti ani Pravasavritta*, 1889), see Meera Kosambi, op. cit., pp. 195-246.

[27] Pandita Ramabai, 'A Short History of Kripa Sadan or Home of Mercy (1903)', reproduced in Meera Kosambi, p. 293, Established in 1903, Kripa Sadan functioned as a rescue-home for the destitute women, child-widows and deserted wives who had been exploited by lustful men and flesh- traders.

woman's sexuality.

It is evident from the foregoing discussion that Ramabai was not only deeply concerned with the hopeless condition of women in Indian society but had also unravelled its relationship with the decrepit state of the nation. She argued that Hindu men were weak because their mothers had been kept weak, sickly and submissive. Further on, she observed:

> They are glad to lean upon anyone and be altogether dependent, and thus it has come to pass that their sons as a race, desire to depend upon some other nation and not upon themselves.[28]

Her argument runs counter to that of Swami Dayanand who maintained that strong women produced a strong race of men. Ramabai gave more importance to psychological strength than to physical strength and thereby implied that a slavery-loving womanhood could only produce a subject nation.

Not content with her bold critique of the high caste Hindu society, Pandita Ramabai formulated an action plan to create a more egalitarian social environment through the establishment of four major institutions: Arya Mahila Samaj (1882), Sharda Sadan (1889), Mukti Mission and School (1896) and Kripa Sadan (1903). As has already been suggested, her social vision was inspired by her experiences of the progressive democratic system in the USA, by the more equitable gender-relations in the English and American societies and her close contacts with the Christian missionaries and activists of women's movements.[29] She had been greatly impressed by the gender-egalitarian message of Christianity and its compassionate attitude to sinners especially 'fallen women', which was the motivating force behind the establishment of Kripa Sadan. Even more influential in shaping her social reform efforts during the period 1883-88 was her personal friendship with Dr. Rachael Bodley, Dean of Women's Medical College of Pennsylvania and Frances Willard, President of Women's Christian Temperance Union. They were also the office-bearers of Ramabai Association of Boston. Later on, these two American women and their institutional networks

[28] Pandita Rambaii, *The High Caste Hindu Women*, p.98.

[29] Pandita Ramabai's views regarding the working of the democratic system in the USA, Christianity and women's movement have been abstracted from the chapter 'Condition of Women' in Meera Kosambi, op. cit., pp.195-244. It is part of Ramabai's book *United Stateschi Lokshthiti ani Pravsavritta* (1889).

would support Ramabai's programme of improving the quality of lives of 'fallen women' and of other female victims of social oppression and deprivation.

The American society was portrayed as the brave new world of the late nineteenth century by Pandita Ramabai in the chapter on 'The Condition of Women' in her book on the U.S.A. Her description of the educational and employment opportunities of American women, grant of political rights to them as well as their crusade for saving their sisters from domestic cruelty and sexual violence had broadened their vision and strengthened their feminist inclinations.

The complex response of readers, especially, women, to the apparently utopian social order in America was captured by Kashibai Kantikar, the reviewer of the book *United Stateschi Loksthiti ani Pravasavritta* (1889). She observed :

> It would be hardly surprising if everyone of our countrywomen who reads this book mutters dejectedly that such a golden day will never dawn for us. However, we will have to swallow these words hastily before they reach anybody's ears for fear of committing "treason against men" just as our men are afraid of committing treason when they discuss the government.[30]

Inspired by the American example, Ramabai's alternative vision of Indian society was not only qualitatively different from that of the male social reformers but also a rallying point for the growing number of educated women in Maharashtra. The ideas expressed in her book on the United States indicated her empathy with the country and problematic relationship with Britain where she was conscious of being a colonial subject. Despite her admiration for America's seemingly greater achievements in political, economic and cultural including religious spheres than those of England, she could not ignore the racial prejudice against Indians among its people including her friends and supporters for the women's cause.[31]

[30] Cited in Sarojini Vaidya, *Shrimati Kantibai Kanthkar Atam Charitra Ani Charitra,* Bombay, 1991, 2nd edition, pp.235-36.

[31] For the representative American response to Ramabai's exotic looks, despite her being an Indian, see Caroline Healey Dall, *The Life of Dr. Anandi Bai Joshi: A Kin Women of Pandita Ramabai*, Boston, 1888. She remarked, "Ramabai is strikingly beautiful. Apart from her white widow's saree, here is nothing else about her to suggest the Hindoo (i.e. Indian). Her sharp intelligence, proficiency in English coupled with her high caste identity, facilitated her entry into elite circles in America."

III

My second example is drawn from Rameshwari Nehru's life and career. Her brief life-sketch may be helpful in pinpointing the stimulii, which propelled her to seek a qualitative change in the self-image, social vision and intellectual outlook of Indian women, particularly, the Hindi-educated women in the north. Born in 1886, she belonged to a Kashmiri Brahmin family which had settled in the Punjab during the reign of Maharaja Ranjit Singh. Her father, Raja Narendra Nath, despite his leanings towards the Arya Samaj, disapproved of its campaign for female education. After being given a somewhat elementary instruction in reading and writing and more intensive schooling in domestic arts as befitted the woman of a purdah family, Rameshwari was married to Brij Lal Nehru, an officer in the Accounts Department.[32]

Soon after, the newly married Rameshwari shifted to Anand Bhavan (Allahabad), where her husband had been brought up by his western-educated and liberal-minded paternal uncle Pandit Motilal Nehru. As a result of her constant exposure to new ideas, discussions about current socio-political trends in Europe and heated debates on the extensive involvement of women in the ongoing national struggle for freedom, she was transformed into an articulate woman with a critical mind. Later, she would emerge as one of the early crusaders of the Indian women's movement and as the founder-editor of *Stree Darpan* (1909-1924), a monthly Hindi magazine, published from Allahabad.[33]

Apart from the formative role of the intellectual stimulation gained in the Anand Bhavan, the influence of Mahatma Gandhi is manifest in her book *Gandhi is my Star* (1950) which contains a collection of her speeches and writings. She tended to view all problems of Indian society and find their solutions through

[32] Information regarding Rameshwari Nehru's early career and life in this and the following paragraphs has been drawn from Om Prakash Paliwal, *Rameshwari Nehru : Patriot and Internationalist*,New Delhi, 1986; Somnath Dhar, ed,. *Rameshwari Nehru; Gandhi is my Star*, Patna, 1950; *Rameshwari Nehru Papers* 1928-1959, New Delhi; and T. N. Jagdis and Shyamlal, eds., *Thakkar Bapa: Eightieth Birthday Commemoration* Volume, Madras, 1949.

[33] For a detailed discussion regarding aims and objects of *Stree Darpan* and its role in sculpting new models of Indian women see Kamlesh Mohan, 'Fashioning Minds and Images : A Case-study of *Stree Darpan* (1908-1928)', in Aparna Basu, ed ., *Breaking Out of Invisibility* : *Women in Indian History*, New Delhi, 2002, pp.232-77.

Gandhian ideology and precepts. Her life-long involvement in the 'Constructive Programme'[34] with objects such as removal of untouchability, prohibition and women's mobilization for their own emancipation from social oppression, discrimination, economic deprivation and political slavery may be attributed to her close association with Gandhi. Her mentor. A.V. Thakkar, affectionately called 'Thakkar Bapa,' also inspired Rameshwari Nehru to take up work for eliminating caste discrimination, violence and exploitation of Harijans or Dalits.

Unlike her senior compatriot Pandita Ramabai, Rameshwari followed a conciliatory path for mobilizing indigenous talent and spark of protest among her educated sisters, whether wives and mothers or young girls from middle-class families in order to organize a strong women's movement in northern India. While the Prayag Mahila Samiti (established in 1909) was its nucleus, *Stree Darpan* was intended to enable its readers to engage in a dialogue with the holders of opposite view-points and to forge ideological and emotional bonds among women.

Even after shifting from Allahabad, Rameshwari Nehru continued her efforts for giving a positive direction to public opinion regarding women's rights and for the abolition of the evil social practices of child-marriage, purdah, doli, palki, etc., when she became the founder-president of Delhi Women's League in 1926. Closely associated with the All-India Women's Conference, she carried on the campaign for female education and for equal rights for men and women through her speeches and writings during the period 1932-40. Apart from representing the All-India Women's Conference in 1931 at the Commonwealth of India League, she also served as the Chairman of its women's committee. Her visit to the USSR in the same year brought a revolutionary change in her views and outlook. On her return, she addressed meetings and contributed articles narrating the

[34] In his *Constructive Programme: Its Meaning and Place*, Ahmedabad, 1983, Gandhi defined it in these words: "The Constructive Programme may otherwise and more fittingly be called as construction of Poorna Swaraj or Complete Independence by truthful and non-violent means", Being flexible, it went on evolving with the passage of time as the formal number of items under it were increased. For instance, from 1921 to 1925 Gandhi described it as three-fold namely, Khaddar, Hindu-Muslim unity and removal of untouchability. Later on, one more item (Prohibition) was added, making it a four-fold programme upto 1939. But by August 1940, it had thirteen items and by 1946, eighteen items, when five more items, i.e, Kisan, labour, Adivasis, lepers and students were included in it.

impressions, which she had gained abroad.

'Indian Home ', 'The Happy Home Wife', 'Home and Society', 'Ideal home', 'Reflections on Women's Conferences', are the titles of some of the many articles published by her in Hindi, Urdu and English journals. The well-known Hindi journals of those days, viz. *Chand, Saraswati, Madhuri* and *Roshni* published her articles,[35] which show her perception of the linkages between women, family and nation as well as the cause of world-peace.

In the wake of partition, Rameshwari Nehru was entrusted with the responsibility of evacuating women and children from Pakistan and rehabilitating them.[36] Henceforth, the efficiency of the Government of India was to be measured by its success in providing a secure future for all its citizens. The task of national development was to be accomplished through their integration with the mainstream polity, economy and society where the role of women was of crucial significance.

In the course of her long and varied public career, Rameshwari Nehru communicated her perception of the existing Indian society and location of women as well as her vision of a gender - sensitive and just society and polity through her writings and speeches. The *Stree Darpan* was an effective forum for cultivating women's minds and recasting their image which inevitably involved pruning, re-interpreting and perhaps even 'inventing' Indian tradition. It is not an undifferentiated past which leaps up from its issues. In its reconstruction, voices of women emerge as more radical, stronger and more significant than the liberal or orthodox male voices. The latter had tended to carve role-models for women within the frame-work of the glorious Vedic tradition and patriarchal value system. The ideal of 'competent domesticity' for wives and nurturing of a healthy progeny for mothers, regarded as the basic constituents of Indian womanhood, was now stretched to include their public roles as agitators and pickets in the national struggle for freedom.

Like Pandita Ramabai, a number of contributors, especially women, rejected the assumption regarding the high status of

[35] For the text of these articles see Somnath Dhar, ed., *Rameshwari Nehru : Gandhi is my Star.* Her article entitled 'Home and Society' was critical of overemphasis on family loyalties leading to indifference to developments in the country and the world at large .

[36] *Rameshwari Nehru Papers :* Report of the work done by Rameshwari Nehru in the Women's Section of the Ministry of Rehabilitation 1946-1959. Report no I, November 1947, New Delhi, p.2.

women in the glorious past.[37] They distinguished between illusions of status, real authority and empowerment. For example, pre-fixing the wife's name to that of husband such as Sita-Ram or Radha-Krishan was regarded as a deceptive courtesy.[38] Impelled by their urgent desire to understand the historical past in the light of their present problems as British subjects they questioned the idealization of Sita who suffered such indignity at her husband's hands. While evaluating the romantic images of gods and goddesses in new contexts, these radical women deplored the dangerous tendency of using examples from classics to shape expectations from women and justifying prejudices against them.[39] In view of their dissatisfaction with the mythological models, they faced a dilemma whether to adopt westernized, somewhat anti-male woman or the nationalist construct of superwoman as their ideal.

These middle class women could not fully comprehend the working of the new legal system and of the imported institutions for organizing and controlling rural as well as urban economy in colonial India. However, they were obliged to experience its impact on their social universe, i.e. family relationships, new models of house-keeping, child-rearing, and the changed expectations and demands of their western-educated husbands. By providing them with a forum, Rameshwari Nehru helped them 'to cope with change'.

Related to this was the ticklish issue of resolving the growing dichotomy between the inner sanctum (equated with spiritual / feminine) and the public domain (the exclusive site for contest of political power and wealth) as a result of the extension of British rule to the various parts of India at different points of time.[40] The nationalist and reformist leadership, dominated by the Bengali intelligentsia in the early and mid-nineteenth century had found their answer in crystallizing and highlighting the difference between the Indian tradition and western modernity. Countering the successful colonial ploy of transforming Indian women into signifiers of the inherently oppressive and unfree nature of the entire cultural tradition of the country, the Indian

[37] See for example Uma Nehru, 'Hamare Samaj Sudharak' in *Stree Darpan,* March 1918.

[38] Ibid.

[39] Dharampatni Kalindi Narayan Verma , 'Pativrata Dharam aur Swatantrata', in ibid., August 1921.

[40] Cf., Partha Chatterjee, *The Nation and its Fragments*, pp.119-20.

intelligentsia iconized her as the guardian of the spiritual values and national culture through food, dress and behaviour.[41] Hence, women were sought to be located in the home, far removed from the arena of political contest with the colonial state.

Contrary to the prevalent view that there was unquestioned acceptance of the patriarchal resolution of the cultural crisis and tensions in gender-relations, Rameshwari Nehru and her associates in India's Hindi heartland kept the debate alive. As a believer in the conciliatory path, Rameshwari Nehru did not totally reject the values of the new patriarchy which advocated mobility within the existing framework. Her radicalism, despite its sting, did not arouse male hostility as she often emphasized that the suffragette movement in India was against orthodoxy, reaction and ignorance, not against men.[42]

Broadly speaking, Rameshwari Nehru's generation seems to have internalized the values of new patriarchy which facilitated the co-option of women as the help-mate in the fulfilment of socio-political and economic aspirations of middle-class men under colonial rule. In order to discharge their dual responsibility of acting as the guardian of the 'inner spirituality of the indigenous social life',[43] women were urged to cultivate the virtues of chastity, modesty, meekness, patience, devotion, love for self-less sacrifice and service. After 1919 onwards, Indian women's consciousness underwent qualitative change through Gandhi's positive projection of their inherent qualities and his empathy with their problems. Their discomfort with patriarchy was diluted to some extent.

It must be pointed out that a large number of women such as Raj Kumari Amrit Kaur, Sushila Nayar, Rameshwari Nehru, Bibi Amtus Salaam, Mani Behn Patel and Rehana Tayyabji acknowledged Gandhi's powerful role in moulding their personal lives, attitudes and aspirations. Instead of reiterating the reformist equation between education and uplift of women, Gandhi valued women's potential contribution as practical thinkers and actors in nationalist politics.[44] That was why he was able to mobilize

[41] Ibid.

[42] *Rameshwari Nehru Papers* : Copy of her speech delivered at a Women's College in England, New Delhi.

[43] I have borrowed this expression from Partha Chatterjee, *The Nation and its Fragments*, p.26.

[44] Kamlesh Mohan, 'The Jallianwala Bagh Tragedy and its Impact as a Catalyst of Indian National Consciousness', in the *International Journal of Punjab Studies* (London), vol.3, no.2, 1996, pp.155, 159-60.

educated as well as illiterate women in his non-violent struggle for Purna Swaraj. Rameshwari Nehru cannot be called a blind follower of Gandhi as she differed on the question of professional employment of women. She also rejected Gandhi's selective approach to the issue of widows' remarriage and their 'desexualistion'.[45]

By locating the issue of widow remarriage in the broad context of the improvement of women's position in Indian society, Rameshwari Nehru assisted the contributors to the *Stree Darpan* for evaluating the male agenda for social reform. To this end, implications of oppressive social customs (particularly, child-marriage) for the socio-economic status of women as well as gender-relations with reference to the historical and contemporary situation, were critically analysed in the columns of the journal from 1909 onwards through the technique of juxtaposition of liberal, orthodox and feminist view-points. For example, Hukma Devi, Principal of Girls' School, Dehradun, advocated the formulation of new social norms which gave equal rights to widows with widowers to resume conjugal life.[46] While discussing this issue, she also drew attention to the gap between the scriptural status of women and the harsh reality of the patriarchal Indian society. 'Paon ki Jooti' an expression used by Hukma Devi in her article 'Ardhangni ya Paon ki Jooti' in the issue of March 1918, became a recurring symbol of shame and humiliation for Indian women. The metaphor of 'dumb cattle' referred to the image of Indian women as passive creatures.

One positive outcome of the debate around the issue of widow-remarriage and mismatched marriages of young girls with old men, moderated by Rameshwari Nehru through her editorials, was the heightened sensitivity about gender discrimination, which was voiced through poems, articles and stories in the monthly issues of *Stree Darpan* throughout the period. For example, an anonymous writer in her personal account entitled 'Ek Vidhwa ki Jiwani' presented a comparative view of the privileged position

[45] An extract from *Stree Darpan,* June 1919, clarifies her stand on the issue of widows' remarriage: "...but the problem arises in the case of those widows who fail to control their sexual desire. Among them are included the teenaged girls and young adults. We cannot understand our leaders' logicwhen they sanction remarriage for one category and prohibit it for the other. Widows, belonging to both categories, fall in different age - groups but they suffer from the same mental sickness."

[46] Hukma Devi. 'Stri Unnati Kaise Ho', in *Stree Darpan*, August 1917.

of a widower and the abject status of a widow. While denigrating society for practising discrimination against women, she lashed out at the latter for submitting to injustice and oppression. She queried:

"... Why did they not assert their individuality and right? Women share more responsibility for their own degradation".[47]

Rameshwari Nehru carried on the campaign against evil social customs as an activist of the Indian women's movement. She maintained that problems of early marriage, purdah, dowry and widow-remarriage all came within the purview of the women's movement.[48] As a movement of sufferers of exploitation and social and economic disabilities, the women's movement, she pointed out, shared common goals with the labour and socialist movement.[49]

Acutely conscious of the formal education that had been denied to her as a female member of a purdah-bound high caste family, Rameshwari Nehru emerged as a fierce advocate of female education. From 1911 onwards, *Stree Darpan* launched a vigorous drive for mobilizing public support for this cause. In its January issue, Rameshwari Nehru's article 'Stri Shiksha se Desh-unnati' referred to the contribution of the educated Japanese women to every aspect of Japan's national life in order to reinforce her argument for the necessity of schools, colleges and vocational institutions for women. Regarding young girls as a nation's asset, she advised them to be 'useful wealth'. She believed that education did not end with getting degrees. At a student gathering in Lahore on 19 June 1941, she observed, "...The real education begins afterwards, and I want you to prepare yourself for that, right from now onwards."[50]

The process of learning ought to be continued through every phase of life. Rameshwari Nehru sensitized Indians, particularly, women, regarding the role of education in recasting gender relations, balance of power and authority in the institutions of home and family[51] and thus hastening the process of social

47 Anonymous, 'Ek Vidhwa Ki Jiwani', in ibid., December 1915.

48 *Speeches and Writings of Rameshwari Nehru* (in general category) 'Nistoli Kanya Pathshala', List no. 26, Sr. no.1, New Delhi, p.l.

49 Rameshwari Nehru 'Women's Movement in India', *Hindustan Times* (Delhi), Special edition, 20 December 1929.

50 *The Tibune* (Lahore), 20 June 1941.

51 Kamlesh Mohan, 'Fashioning Minds and Images: A Case-study of *Stree-Darpan*', in Aparna Basu ed., op. cit., p. 239.

change. Daily lives of women, their food, dress, and manners had already been recomposed on the basis of new social and moral principles by the reformers in the early mid-nineteenth century Bengal.[52] Three decades later, the Arya and Singh reformers subjected Punjabi women to similar experiments.[53] Instead of asking for replication of these social projects and division of masculine/feminine qualities or inner/outer domains, Rameshwari Nehru emphasized the urgency of formulating new norms and code of conduct for both men and women as the earlier ones were out-dated and discriminatory.

The most compelling argument for the spread of female education was the growing demand for the educated girls as brides by the western-educated young men of middle-class families who wanted drawing-room companions and not tradition-bound illiterate wives. As a result illiterate women were subjected to daily insults and humiliations at the hands of educated men in many homes.

Surya Devi's poem 'Nari Vilap', published in the December 1918 issue of *Stree Darpan,* gave a heart-rending description of an illiterate wife's mental agony. Its English translation reads as follows:

> The husband is a B.A., M.A. and the wife is utterly illiterate. In such a home, there is no love but bickering and tension. His wife toils the whole day, yet the gentleman is unhappy. A little delay in her task rouses his anger. Many an educated husband honour their women in this way. Why blame women for lapses when they are illiterate!

A number of women also directed their ire at these so-called educated husbands who "hide their narrow and reactionary views about women behind their civilized appearance. It is their heartiest desire to keep women under their control."[54]

It is obvious that a substantial number of readers and contributors to the journal were drawn into the fray as a result of the editor's crusade through the publication of their articles

[52] Partha Chatterjee, *The Nation and its Fragments,* pp. 124-25; Himani Bannerji, *Inventing Subjects: Studies in Hegemony, Patriarchy and Colonialism*, New Delhi, 2001, pp. 99-134.

[53] For an interesting discussion on the upgrading of women for a life suitable to high caste, modernist middle class in this region see Arshu Malhotra, *Gender, Caste and Religious Identities: Restructuring Class in Colonial Punjab*, New Delhi, 2002.

[54] Kailash Rani Baatal, 'Istrion ka Mahatva tatha Purushon ka Kartavya', in *Stree Darpan*, December 1915.

and poems in the various issues of *Stree Darpan,* especially, the May–June 1911 issue. The majority of writers advocated an intensive campaign for education on three counts: efficient motherhood, acquisition of new skills for better performance of wifely duties and pativrata dharma. In its August 1918 issue, Rameshwari Nehru's editorial 'Desi aur Vilayati Shiksha' added to the list of benefits saying that it would enable women to develop a sense of pride in being Indian. A more liberal angle surfaced in Vishwanth Prasad Gupta's article 'Stri Shiksha' in the November 1928 issue which underlined the similarity between the aims and objectives of the lives of both men and women. Hence, the real purpose of education was to develop physical, mental and moral potentialities and capabilities of all Indians irrespective of their sex.

After the achievement of freedom on 15 August 1947, the Indian Government faced the gigantic task of rehabilitating the uprooted people from Pakistan and revitalizing the country's economy. Equally important was the need to remove social discrimination and exploitation on the basis of caste and sex. Rameshwari Nehru participated actively in facilitating the painful birth and growth of new India. As the Director of the Women's Section in Ministry of Relief and Rehabilitation, she helped a large number of evacuated and destitute women and orphans to become economically self-sufficient. Joined by many social workers including Mrs. Hannah Sen and Mrs. Mathur, Women's Section was developed into a Women's Voluntary Service under the executive authority of the Government of India.[55] As the leader of this group, Rameshwari Nehru undertook to inculcate a sense of duty towards the country among its members and sympathizers. While addressing them, she wrote:

> .... You women have more responsibility than men to change the country's economic and social background. So, to fulfil your duty towards your country, you should increase your capability and knowledge.[56]

Apart from her role in the social emancipation of the wives of the rulers of Princely States, she worked for the political

[55] *Rameshwari Nehru Papers*: Reports on work Done by Her in the Women's Section of the Ministry of Rehabilitation 1946-1959, Report No. 1, November 1947, New Delhi, p.2.

[56] *Correspondence Files of Rameshwari Nehru* (All-India Congress Committee Papers), 1953-1960, General Correspondence by the Women Advisory Section of the

empowerment of women by persuading Prime Minister Jawahar Lal Nehru to make more and more women eligible as voters in their own right as citizens. Through her intervention, mass disenfranchisement of women was averted when the Chief Election Commissioner was advised to withdraw the notification or order by which the names of women given as 'wife of' or 'Mrs. so and so' were declared invalid.[57]

Another aspect of her signal contribution towards the transformation of the patriarchal Indian society into a gender-sensitive social order was her vigorous support for reforms of Hindu law. From early 1940s onwards, she advocated radical changes in personal laws in favour of women and demanded that in matters like inheritance, marriage, divorce and guardianship of children the law should deal equitably with men and women.[58] The battle for the legislation of the Hindu Code Bill into law continued through the 1950s. Divided into five separate Acts, the Hindu Code was enacted in this chronological order: Hindu Marriage Act (1954), Hindu Succession Act (1954), Hindu Minority and Guardianship Act (1956)[59] and Hindu Adoption and Maintenance Act (1956). The last important measure, enacted during Rameshwari Nehru's time, was the Dowry Restraint Act (1961). It must be pointed out that Rameshwari Nehru was not actively involved in the prolonged fight for legal equality during the 1950s owing to her engagement with peace and solidarity movement at the international level. Women's organizations, too, became increasingly passive with the passage of this spate of legislation. In fact, achievement of legal equality in the matter of marriage and inheritance rights for women through the legislation of Hindu Code Bill, howsoever truncated, was made possible by Jawahar Lal Nehru's commitment to the cause despite stiff opposition from orthodox Hindus.[60]

The preceding discussion should make it abundantly clear that Pandita Ramabai and Rameshwari Nehru looked at

Ministry of Rehabilitation, 27 April, 1953, File No. 25, List no. 26, New Delhi, p.25.

[57] Ibid., 1924-59, A letter by Rameshwari Nehru to Smt. Urmila Mehta, 29 March 1954, File no. 4, List no.26, New Delhi, p.12.

[58] Jana Matson Everett, *Women and Social Change in India,* New Delhi, 1985, p.97.

[59] J. Duncan M. Derrett, *Hindu Law : Past and Present*, Calcutta, 1957, pp. 319-401.

[60] For more information on his role in the legislation of the Hindu Code Bill see Kamlesh Mohan, *Jawahar Lal Nehru on Democracy and Women,* Chandigarh : Public Reations Department, Punjab Government, 1990.

contemporary Indian society mainly, though not exclusively, from the perspective of high-caste or middle-class women. Their perceptions, observations and contestation of male representations of women's nature, her duties, roles and essential qualities as mother and wife were motivated by a two-fold commitment. The first was a commitment to remove social blindness to domestic cruelty, oppression and exploitation of women's labour and sexuality. The second was to mobilize women to fight for their own emancipation and rights with the ultimate goal of creating a gender-sensitive and more egalitarian society.

Both Ramabai and Rameshwari Nehru saw Indian society as patriarchal. Its customs, cultural practices and code of conduct for men and women were undergirded by double standards of morality and behaviour. On the basis of her thorough knowledge of Shastras as a proficient Sanskrit scholar, Ramabai attributed gender-discrimination to the social legitimation of religious scriptures. However, she noted regional variations in the degree of subjugation and marginalization of women, owing to the weight of social customs among various castes. Rameshwari Nehru's insights regarding the role of Hindu religion were not marked by any first-hand knowledge of scriptures. Her keen sensitivity coupled with sharp powers of observation regarding its negative implications for the daily lives of women were the source of her strength.

The strategies, chosen by Pandita Ramabai and Rameshwari Nehru, partly reflected their different experiences as women. Ramabai adopted the path of confrontation with society and the colonial state. Believing in the efficacy of the conciliatory method, Rameshwari Nehru preferred to engage in a dialogue and debate with both the camps: liberal and orthodox. While Ramabai was isolated and marginalized in the last phase of her life, Rameshwari Nehru was able to enlarge the number of her sympathizers, supporters and fellow-crusaders for a better social universe for women and other underprivileged segments. This also brings us to the second factor for change. Rameshwari Nehru worked in a period of the upsurge of the National Movement with an inflow of radical including socialist ideas into it and a firmer belief in the efficacy of popular (including women's) mobilization.

In order to recast the self-image of Indian women, Pandita Ramabai and Rameshwari Nehru tried to spread awareness about the prejudiced representations of Strisvabhava in the epics,

Manusmriti and *Stree Dharampadhiti.*[61] As a result of their persistent campaign, the educated women were enabled to challenge the patriarchal assertion of a woman's inherent evil nature. The characterization of an ideal woman's virtues as servility, chastity, obedience, devotion and self-sacrificing spirit, too, was rejected. Flowing from this was the radical woman's dissatisfaction with the traditional definition of *Istri Dharma* i.e. the Woman's Code in terms of worship and service of the husband as god. The emergent band of thinking women also questioned the reformist model of Indian womanhood that had made it mandatory for them to be ideal *pativratas* and also to cultivate traits associated with modernity. Her education, emergence from *purdah* while retaining 'lajja' (modesty) and new house-keeping skills, marked her as a modern woman. These feminists underlined the inherent tensions and contradictions in this unilateral construct by Indian men who exhorted woman to emulate Sita-Savitri ideal when they were busy acquiring western education, life-styles and values. An extract from Uma Nehru's article (1918) echoes Ramabai's militant views on the issue:

> The task of producing model women like Sita and Savitri seems incongruent with a social situation which does not oblige men to become a Ram Chandra, a Krishna, a Bharat or a Yudhishter. Dressed in a coat, pant and necktie and inebirated with the ambition to emulate western economic ideals, Indian men's craving for such ideal women is akin to search for the proverbial mythical flower.[62]

Obviously, contributors to *Stree Darpan* remained seriously engaged in the onerous task of rejecting the legitimacy of recovering mythological models as well as of dispelling popular notions about a woman's weak moral nature. As an effective counter-measure, a more humane and positive image of Indian woman was now projected. In their view, a truly modern woman like man ought to acquire qualities of alertness, independent thinking, courage, truthfulness, experience in worldly affairs, organizational skills and an intelligent as well as enlightened outlook in order to perform their social roles more efficiently. Through their personal examples, Pandita Ramabai and

[61] Doranne Jacobson and Susan Wadley, *Women in India : Two Perspectives,* New Delhi, 1977, p.127. It has been drawn from two separate though related sources: Brahminical (also called classical) literature and folk tradition..

[62] Uma Nehru, 'Hamare Samaj Sudharak', in *Stree Darpan,* March 1918. Translation mine.

Rameshwari Nehru demonstrated what a modern woman with independent thinking and forceful personality could achieve.

It may also be noted that Rameshwari's innovative use of media made ordinary women 'seize speech' and intervene in male discourse on issues of social reform and the national movement. A new sense of pride and self-respect in their identity as women and awareness of their power in the roles of mothers and wives exuded from their writings. The substitution of the feeling of helplessness and dependence by an action-oriented outlook marked a real turning point in the transformation of women's consciousness. It had positive implications for the making of India not only an independent but also a just nation.

As a result of this radical change in their self-image and exposure to new currents of thought, women began to review their location in society and role in the struggle for freedom and social reform from the angle of active agents. Departing from male agendas, these critical women argued that the social reform process and programme ought to be related to the nature and pace of political and economic change in the contemporary world. Even before Gandhi had formulated his vision of *Purna Swaraj* through the restructuring of social institutions and strengthening of community networks, these ideas were being floated and implemented in a rudimentary form in Ramabai's Mukti Mission and School, and in the columns of Rameshwari Nehru's *Stree Darpan*.

The process of activating middle class women to 'seize speech' and become active agents in socio-political change also implied the redefinition of masculinity as of femininity. While carrying forward Pandita Ramabai's mission, Rameshwari Nehru and contributors of *Stree Darpan* rejected the association of masculinity with brute physical strength, aggressiveness, competitiveness and rationality. In their view, men ought to cultivate a catholic outlook, generous and affectionate disposition as well as intellectual and emotional compatibility with their wives. Only such men, in collaboration with autonomous but sensitive women, would be able to demolish the existing gender and caste hierarchies in order to facilitate the birth and growth of a democratic India. It must be conceded that the number of these courageous feminists like Pandita Ramabai, who openly challenged the patriarchal customs and laws as well as social institutions, was small. Rameshwari Nehru belonged to the second category of women, who realized that the confrontational perspective for the Indian women's movement had a limited relevance for colonial India. Factually speaking, the Indian social system lacked the basic input for a militant feminist movement — an urbanized middle class with a large number of educated women trained in professional skills and unwilling to waste their talent in domestic drudgery.

Fully sensitized to the accommodating social mood, Rameshwari Nehru effectively used the columns of *Stree Darpan* for bringing a qualitative change in the consciousness and social as well as intellectual outlook of Indian women particularly in the Hindi zone. They were equipped to forge new bonds and loyalties beyond their kinship network in the course of their ideological interaction either as readers or contributors, or as members of Prayag Mahila Samiti, National Federation of Women and All India Women's Conference. Pandita Ramabai's work had, on the other hand enabled destitutes and 'fallen' women to develop empathy for each other. The most significant part of her contribution was to give dignity and social space to widows, the most repressed group among women. Thus, both of them were instrumental in bringing about the emergence of a rudimentary intelligentsia among women who would gradually become an important factor in India's political development from the 1940's onwards.

It must be pointed out that the efforts of both Pandita Ramabai and Rameshwari Nehru, who had adopted different strategies altered the perception of some middle-class Hindu women without however affecting a total break with the past or the existing social system. The transformation of middle-class women was necessarily uneven. The associates, supporters and sympathizers of both these remarkable activists failed to fully comprehend the heterogeneity of women's oppression, which was complicated and mediated by caste, religion and economic conditions.

Nevertheless, the significance of these two women's contribution should not be underestimated. Ramabai inspired a substantial number of destitute and 'fallen' women as inmates of Mukti-Mission School and Kripa Sadan to emulate the Christian way of life. It was a harsh comment upon Hindu society whose aggrieved members found solace and shelter elsewhere. Rameshwari Nehru's more conciliatory strategy enabled a number of educated and socially committed women to work for reducing gender discrimination and oppression and to combine their roles as mothers and wives with participation in public life without leaving the Hindu fold.

16

India as "Hindusthan"
Elements of the Ideological Structure of Hindu Communalism

MRIDULA MUKHERJEE

Hinduise all politics and militarize Hinduism
(Savarkar in his birthday message in 1941)[1]
As a matter of fact we have in Hindusthan a triangular fight. We, Hindus are at war at once with the Moslems on the one hand and British on the other.
(Golwalkar, the Sarva Sanghachalak of the RSS, in *We*, p.9)[2]
It is useless simply to declare the Muslim League communal. That is no news. The fact is that the whole Moslem community is communal, including the Congressite Moslems.[3]
(Savarkar in Presidential Address, Hindu Mahasabha, 1938)

In this chapter we essay to analyse the critical elements in the ideological discourse of Hindu communalism. There is no doubt that there remain basic similarities between the ideological framework constructed by its early ideologues such as Savarkar and Golwalkar and the more recent articulation in the political practice of the BJP and its allied organizations, the RSS, VHP, Bajrang Dal, etc. The basic question, to begin with, is:

What is India?

Savarkar defines India in the following manner:[4]

The land which extends from the Indus to the Southern Seas is Hindusthan—the land of the Hindus and we Hindus are the Nation that owns it. If you call it an Indian nation it is merely an English synonym for the Hindu nation. To us Hindus, Hindusthan and India mean one and the same thing.

Thus in the very description of the country, communal notions are introduced. The use of the suffix *sthan* instead of *stan* in

[1] Quoted in Dhananjay Keer, *Veer Savarkar*, Bombay, 1988, p. 295.
[2] M.S.Golwalkar, *We or Our Nationhood Defined*, 4th edition, 1947 (first published in Nagpur, 1939), p. 19.
[3] Savarkar, *Hindu Sangathan*, Bombay, 1940, p. 76.
[4] Savarkar, Presidential Address, Akhil Bharatiya Hindu Mahasabha, Nagpur, 1938, in Savarkar, *Hindu Sangathan*, p.83.

'Hindustan', as commonly used, is itself communal because it is a way of rejecting what is perceived as the Persian form of the name and so unacceptable. Also the notion that Hindus have some kind of ownership rights over this land is a very important one in Hindu communal thinking (however archaic it may sound to us today) as it is the basis for denying equal claims to members of other religious groups.

In fact, Savarkar clearly says that 'India must be a Hindu land, reserved for the Hindus.'[5]

He unambiguously asserts that Hindus should be 'masters in our own house, Hindusthan, the land of the Hindus.'[6]

Who are the Hindus?

A Hindu means a person who regards this land of Bharat-Varsha from the Indus to the Seas as his Fatherland as well as his Holyland, that is the cradle land of his religion.[7]

This statement of Savarkar is of utmost importance as it automatically excludes the Indian Muslims and Christians from any claims on this country, as their holy lands are outside India. It also enables the inclusion of members of what could be called breakaway religions, such as Jainism, Buddhism, Sikhism, etc., in the ranks of Hindus. This definition is repeated by Golwalkar as well, thus signifying its acceptance by the RSS.

Who constitute the nation(s) in India?

One answer to this is that there are two nations in India. In Savarkar's words, 'India cannot be assumed today to be an unitarian and homogenous nation, but on the contrary there are two nations in the main, Hindus and Moslems, in India.' He refers to 'centuries of a cultural, religious and national antagonism between the Hindus and the Moslems'. The title of the section in which the above statements are made is : 'As it is there are two antagonistic nations living side by side in India.' For Savarkar India is not a nation but is the name of the state in which these two nations live. He even envisages in one place that they could continue to exist within 'an Indian state in which none is allowed any special weightage or representation'.[8]

There was, however, discomfort with the idea of equating Hindus and Muslims as nations. Perhaps this was because

[5] Ibid., p. 92.
[6] Ibid., p. 83.
[7] Savarkar, cited in D. Keer, op.cit., p.143.
[8] Savarkar, Presidential Address, 1937, in *Hindu Sangathan*, pp.32-33.

accepting Muslims as a nation would mean accepting their right to parity or even a country of their own. Thus Savarkar himself put the thesis of two nations in a modified form at his next Presidential Address to the Hindu Mahasabha. Any parity between Hindus and Muslims was now dismissed as absurd. Hindus were not a community, they were the nation. Other religious groups (minorities) were communities. 'It is absurd to call us a community in India. The Germans are the nation in Germany and the Jews a community. The Turks are the nation in Turkey and the Arab or the Armenian minority a community. Even so the Hindus are a nation in India—in Hindusthan, and the Moslem minority a community.'[9]

The Hindus were a nation because they had always been so, from time immemorial. '...in Hindusthan we have the ancient Hindu nation.... The word Rashtra, which expresses the whole of the idea contained in the English word "Nation", is as old as the Vedas.'[10] The last claim shows that there had now to be a deliberate invention of the country's past.

What is the History of India?

Indeed, this is an extremely important component of communal ideology since communalisms rest very heavily on their versions of the past to justify their projects for the future. In fact, if you take away history from communal ideology, there will be very little substance left. The first thing that the communal ideologues do is to assert the antiquity, greatness and indigenous origins of Hindu ('Indian' being equated with Hindu) civilization. As an example, witness the following statement of Golwalkar:[11]

> ...we cannot say when...we in Hindusthan discarded the state of nature and started an ordered, civilized, national existence. It seems as if we never were uncivilized. The Vedas, the most ancient literature extant today, embodies ideas too noble except for a highly organized and cultured people to express....And when the Vedas came into existence, we are at liberty only to conjecture in vain.

The greatness of Hindu civilization being established, he then moves on to establishing its antiquity. In what was to become typical of Hindu communalists, he pushes the origins of this civilization back into the past by at least five thousand years. He calculates (on what basis, we do not know) that Hindus were in

[9] Savarkar, Presidential Address, 1938, in *Hindu Sangathan*, p. 84.
[10] Golwalkar, *We*, p.60.
[11] Ibid, pp 8-9.

undisturbed possession of this land for at least 8- or even 10,000 years before any invasion by a foreign race.[12] It is clear that he does not accept the separate existence of the Indus Civilization and considers it as part of Hindu or Vedic Civilization.

Golwalkar dismisses the theory of Aryan immigration as a Western ploy to claim that the Europeans had as much right as Hindus over India since both are outsiders, and also to deny the antiquity and superiority of Hindu culture.[13] However, there was a serious problem here, since the great Lokmanya Tilak, had written that the Aryans came from the Arctic Zone. Since Tilak was a renowned scholar of Hinduism, and a popular national leader, it was not possible to dismiss him out of hand. The solution was found in the following ingenious formulation, which is a lasting testimony to the inevitably pathological state of the communal mind:[14]

> Modern Paleontologist researches demonstrate that the North Pole is not stationary and quite long ago it was in that part of the world, [which] we find, is called Bihar and Orissa at the present; and then it moved north-east and then by sometimes westerly, sometimes northward movement, it came to its present position. [If Tilak had known this he would have agreed that the] Arctic home in the Vedas was verily in Hindusthan itself and that it was not the Hindus who migrated to that land but the Arctic Zone which emigrated and left the Hindus in Hindusthan.'

It was also necessary to assert the superiority of Indian [read Hindu] culture over all other cultures. It was therefore declared that, despite the degenerative impact of the Muslims and Europeans on it, it 'is still the noblest in the world.'[15] 'Not only has this culture been most markedly effective in moulding man after the picture of God, but in the field of learning...it has produced...intellectual giants, outshining the greatest savants of the modern scientific world.'[16]

It is fascinating to note the remarkable similarity between the versions of history found in the writings of the Hindu communal ideologues such as Savarkar and Golwalkar and the NCERT's new syllabus and the new school textbooks brought out under the aegis of the BJP government. In both these, there is an attempt to push back the Vedic period to 5000 or 6000 BC

[12] Ibid, p 10.
[13] Ibid., p 11
[14] Ibid. p. 12
[15] Ibid., p. 49
[16] Ibid.

It is suggested that Buddhism weakened India with its emphasis on non-violence, and that Asoka's adoption of non-violence led to the decline of the Maurya dynasty. The early communal ideologues referred to the coming of the Muslims as invasions by the murdering hordes, the new text books seek to justify this characterization. As in the version of the founding fathers, so in the new syllabus, there is then a gap of a few centuries and Indian history reappears as resistance to 'Muslim' rule in the form of Rana Pratap and Shivaji which finally results in Maratha victory over the Mughals.

In the modern period, the emphasis is on 'Hindu renaissance', which is how the social reform movement of the nineteenth century is described and on 'Hindu militant nationalism' or cultural nationalism, which is how the Extremist phase of the Indian national movement is sought to be appropriated. Reading this version of history, one would find it difficult to imagine that Dadabhai Naoroji, Gokhale, Ranade, Pherozeshah Mehta, Surendranath Banerjee, G.Subramania Iyer and so many other leaders and activists of the Moderate phase, who in fact founded the national movement, and evolved an elaborate economic critique of colonialism played any positive role at all!

The early communal ideologues were very sharply critical of Gandhian leadership, calling the Congress anti-national and pro-Muslim, and asking all Hindus to vote against it. The new NCERT history books do not take a directly critical position *vis a vis* Gandhi but try to minimize his role and that of the Congress under his leadership from 1919 to 1947 by giving very little space to it and by giving exaggerated emphasis to other political trends which played a relatively minor role in the freedom struggle.

Sanskrit

The mind-set of the communal ideologues is very well illustrated by their discussion of Sanskrit. It is not treated as a language of mortals, but as 'Devabhasha, the dialect of the Gods':[17]

There is but one language, Sanskrit, of which these many languages are mere offshoots, the children of the mother language. Sanskrit, the dialect of the Gods, is common to all from the Himalayas to the ocean in the South, from East to West and all the modern sister languages are through it so much inter-related as to be practically one. It needs but little labour to acquire a going acquaintance with any tongue.

[17] Ibid., p.51.

One reason for asserting the central position of Sanskrit and the commonality between it and other Indian languages appears to be the need to establish that India fulfilled what was regarded in the contemporary liberal discourse as one of the essential criteria of nationhood, i.e. a common language. Unlike the leaders of the national movement who believed that India was not a nation from time immemorial but a nation in the making and that it was the common struggle for freedom that provided a major engine for the process, the communal ideologues had to keep searching for the essential attributes of the nation which they imagined to be Sanskrit, projected as India's one great cementing bond. Thus, such palpably false notions that Sanskrit was the mother of all Indian languages and that it requires little effort to acquire a working knowledge of any Indian language if you know Sanskrit, are asserted as truths. It is indeed remarkable that the syllabus brought out by the NCERT in 2000 reflects almost to the last dot the communal ideologues' understanding of the position of Sanskrit. A prominent linguistic expert with BJP links said on TV that over 40 per cent of Tamil words were of Sanskrit origin! As for Savarkar—

> In the India of Savarkar's dreams, Sanskritized Hindi would be the national language and Nagari the script, not Hindustani in Urdu script. He even led a movement to remove Urdu and Persian words from Marathi.[18]

On Minorities

How do Hindu communalists view the minorities? What is the place of minorities in the future Hindu Rashtra?

The Parsis are certified fit as 'they have been loyal to India and made her their only home'. The Jews are too few and they are alright. But a proposal to invite Jews persecuted by the Nazis to settle in India and work for India's development brought forth vehement opposition and an almost hysterical outburst: 'India must be a Hindu land, reserved for Hindus.'[19] The Christian minority 'is civil, has no extra-territorial political designs against India. Only in religion they differ from us and are a proselytizing church. So on that matter alone Hindus must be on their guard and give the missionaries no blind latitude to carry on their work beyond voluntary and legitimate conversion'.[20]

[18] D.Keer, op.cit., p.198.

[19] Savarkar, Presidential Address, 1938, *Hindu Sangathan*, p. 92.

[20] Ibid., p. 91.

It is the Muslims for whom the real venom is reserved. The 'Moslem' community is so dangerous that 'We must watch it in all its actions with the greatest distrust possible....Not only while we are engaged in our struggle for liberating India but even after India is free we must look upon them as suspicious (*sic*) friends and take great care to see that the northern frontiers of India are well-guarded by staunch and powerful Hindu forces to avoid the possible danger of the Indian Moslems going over to the alien Muslim nations across the Indus and betraying our Hindusthan to our Non-Hindu foes.'[21]

Thus it is clear that even before Pakistan came into being there was this notion of a threat from 'our Non-Hindu foes', 'the alien Muslim nations across the Indus'. Even then, Indian Muslims were thought to be a danger by their propensity to go over to the side of the Muslim nations 'to the north'. All this long before India was partitioned and it could be argued that Muslim loyalty is suspect because many of them had been supporters of the Muslim League and by implication of Pakistan, and because Muslim families were found on both sides of the border.

Why are Muslims communal? Why can they not be treated like other minorities?

'It is useless simply to declare the Muslim League communal. That is no news. The fact is that the whole Moslem community is communal, including the Congressite Moslems', says Savarkar.[22] He then asks why are they so communal? The answer given is that they have not yet outgrown the stage of intense religiosity and the theological concept of the state (which by implication Hindus have outgrown). There is a clear notion of Muslims being barbaric or at least backward in comparison to Hindus. Also, it is said that Muslims cannot be loyal to non-Muslim power, since Islam considers it to be an enemy, which should be conquered by a Muslim power. They are also said to especially look down upon Hindus as they are kafirs and not kitabis ('People of the Book') like the Jews and Christians.[23]

The notions about the extra-territorial loyalties of the Muslims were used to spread a fear psychosis among Hindus. In fact, a

[21] Ibid., p. 93

[22] Savarkar, Presidential Address, 1938, *Hindu Sangathan*, p. 76.

[23] Ibid, pp. 76-8.

major problem for the Hindu communalists was how the majority was to be made to fear the minority, because without such fear communal feelings could not grow. Therefore they liberally took recourse to allegations of extra-territorial loyalties, and references to their disproportionate presence in the army and police and the stereotype of the aggressive Muslim brute or goonda who specialized in sexual aggression against Hindu women. It is amazing how Savarkar could even raise the bogey of the re-establishment of a Muslim Empire in India, as in the following statement:[24]

> ...in the Indian Army and the armed police, they (the Muslims) in spite of their being in minority are already the predominant factor holding some 60% jobs, with all these factors in their favour they are fully confident... that in case the British are over-powered in some big world war, the Moslems with the help of the non-Indian Moslem powers bordering our country may snatch out (*sic!*) the political sovereignty of India out of the British hands and re-establish a Moslem empire here.

Golwalkar too seeks to emphasize that it is in the nature of Islam to be intolerant and oppressive of other faiths. Alleging the persecution of Jews and Parsis by Islam, he refers to 'The same old tale of Islamic invasion, with its attendant massacres, devastation, destruction, loot and arson....'[25]

Savarkar also warns the Muslims that they could meet the same treatment that Jews were getting in Germany. Alleging that the Muslim League was threatening to play the role of Sudeten Germans, he says, 'if we Hindus in India grow stronger, in time these Moslem friends of the League type will have to play the part of German-Jews instead'.[26]

Nationalists as Enemies

It is erroneously thought that communalists are mainly interested in curbing or eliminating the rights of the 'other' communities, and in defending those of their own. In fact, communalists are interested in the other community only in so far as they are impediments to their project of casting the entire society in their own image. Their ultimate objective is to make members of their own religion conform to the communalists' notion of what is the correct path in life. Non-communal, liberal

[24] Ibid., p. 81.

[25] Golwalker, *We*, p.25.

[26] Savarkar, Presidential Address, 1938, *Hindu Sangathan*, p. 85.

elements in their own community are as much enemies as the members of the other community, sometimes even more so. Therefore, we see Hindu communalists had as much venom in store for the Congress as they had for the Muslims. The Congress was characterized as anti-national, anti-Hindu, pro-Muslim, and non-violent, all of which had negative meanings in the Hindu communal lexicon. Witness the following quotes:

Congress as anti-national

The Indian National Congress only condemns itself as an anti-national body when it calls in the same breath the Hindu Mahasabha and the Moslem League as bodies equally communal in the reprehensible and treacherous sense of the term.[27]

Congress as anti-Hindu

We Hindus made the Congress what it is today but it has now suddenly turned against us. It looks today like 'a veritable anti-Hindu tower of strength'.[28]

Savarkar refers to this 'anti-Hindu and anti-National policy of the Congress',[29] which has to be opposed by the Hindu sangathan. He also castigates it for adopting an 'anti-national pro-Moslem attitude'.[30] 'The Congress has compelled us to disown it'.[31]

Savarkar warns Hindus of serious consequences if they do not vote against the Congress:

and if you Hindus do not do even that much and determine to commit a cultural and political and racial suicide by voting for an anti-Hindu and anti-National organization as the Congress has grown today into one—not even Brahmadeva can save you.[32]

Congress leaders referred to as traitors

'Strange, very strange that traitors should sit enthroned as national heroes, and patriots heaped with ignominy.'[33]

Those who do not glorify the Hindu race and nation are 'traitors and enemies to the National Cause' or 'mere simpletons, misguided,

[27] Ibid., p. 87.
[28] Ibid., p. 94-95.
[29] Ibid., p. 103.
[30] Ibid.
[31] Ibid., p. 96.
[32] Ibid, p. 108.
[33] Golwalkar, *We*, p. 6.

ignorant fools.'[34]

In addition to the abuses heaped on the Congress, Gandhiji was especially singled out for attack for his advocacy of non-violence. In Savarkar's view, absolute non-violence (as advocated by Gandhi) was not only sinful, but also immoral. It was because of the influence of Buddhism, and its belief in non-violence, he said, that India was devastated by barbarians like the Huns and Scythians.[35]

The Hindus are exhorted repeatedly that they should 'openly and separately take up our stand as Hindus and support, oppose or take every step in the interests of Hindudom alone.'[36] This could go to absurd lengths, such as when Savarkar asked Hindus to help only the Hindu victims of the Bengal famine of 1943: Hindu leaders and organizations were to help, rescue, feed, clothe and shelter Hindu sufferers alone. The reason given was that Muslim organizations were helping only Muslims and were using surplus food to convert Hindu women and children![37] The dehumanizing impact of communal thinking is so evident here — even in the face of such an overwhelming tragedy as famine, the communalist is found counting the numbers of the dying and the dead in categories of Hindus and Muslims.

The Hindus were also told that they should not vote for the Congress, but only for confirmed 'Hindu nationalists,' which is how Hindu communalists liked to describe themselves. If the Hindus did so, they would have real Hindu ministries and Hindu Mahasabha would be 'raised to the position of dictatorship in shaping the political destiny of India.'

And what will then happen in this India of Savarkar's dreams?

Every Hindu will raise his head high and erect [Echoes of 'Garv se kaho hum Hindu hain'?]....If a Hindu girl is molested in any part of the land by a Moslem gunda such a condign punishment will promptly be inflicted on him as to render all Moslem gundas tremble to touch any other Hindu girl as fearfully as they do in molesting an English girl. If any riot on the part of the Muslim fanatics seeks to force the Hindus to forgo their civil rights, the armed police and the military forces will be so promptly and vigorously made to function...that Moslem riots will be a thing of the past and they will learn to tolerate Hindu music... as kindly as they do now the Government and English

[34] Ibid., p.52.
[35] Keer, op.cit., pp.274-75.
[36] Savarkar, Presidential Address, 1938, *Hindu Sangathan*, p. 88.
[37] Keer, op.cit., pp. 343-4.

bands and processions. The peasants and labourers will get what is due to them....Hindu language will be safe. Hindu script will be safe, Hindu religion will be safe, no illegitimate or forceful conversion of a Hindu to non-Hindu faiths will be tolerated for a minute.... If the Moslems pass an act, say in Bengal, to reserve 60% services for Moslems, our Hindu national ministries will at once get an act passed in Hindu majority provinces to reserve 90% services for Hindus even when we are only 80% of the population...The Moslems will come to their senses in a day...will learn to behave as good boys ....We shall in Punjab and the Frontier districts have an allied party with our Sikh Hindu flank [thus the RSS cry: *Sikh Hindu hain*!]. Our Sikh Hindus .... have a separate electorate and rightly so under the present circumstances.'[38]

It is also inevitable that communalists soon begin to assert their version of their religion as the only valid one, thus denying the right to their own co-religionists to practise their religion in their own different ways. Savarkar's call to 'Hinduise all politics and militarize Hinduism' was in tandem with this.[39]

Hindu communal ideologues had no belief in democracy as a virtue. In foreign policy, for example, 'no empty slogans of democracy or Nazism or Fascism can be the guiding principle of our foreign policy. Hindu interests alone will be our test.'[40]

(Re)definition of Indian Nationalism

It is very necessary to note that the Hindu communal ideologues took great pains to redefine Indian nationalism. They were not merely asserting the rights of the Hindus as a community, they questioned the freedom struggle's definition of nationalism by asserting that Indian nationalism is really Hindu nationalism, that Muslims cannot be Indian nationalists, that Hindu nationalism is an age-old phenomenon, that the Congress has an erroneous notion of territorial nationalism, etc. They accused the Congress of pseudo-nationalism (a precursor to 'pseudo-secularism'). They pointed out the weaknesses of territorial nationalism, and alleged that it had failed in Europe. They asserted that the Congress was not a national organization but was formed as a safety-valve and, except for the Extremist phase, played that role. The Moderates or early nationalists and Gandhi and his colleagues are not accepted as nationalists by Hindu

[38] Savarkar, Presidential Address, pp. 100-01, 104-06.
[39] Savarkar in his birthday message in 1941, cited in Keer, p. 295.
[40] Savarkar, Presidential Address, 1938, *Hindu Sangathan*, p. 90.

communalists. In Golwalkar's long list of illustrious Indians, Gandhi, Nehru, and Patel, for example, find no place.[41] The Congress is criticized for believing that 'we are a nation in the making and had never enjoyed National life before.'[42]

It is very clear that what irked Hindu communal ideologues the most was the refusal of the Congress to treat the Muslims as enemies and second-class citizens. The Congress leaders were accused of committing the sin of 'hugging to our bosom our most inveterate enemies and thus endangering our very existence.'[43] The reference was very obviously to Muslims. To be a nationalist, you had to be anti-Muslim, such was the belief. Golwalkar at least remembered to formally include the British among enemies but just! 'As a matter of fact we have in Hindusthan a triangular fight. We, Hindus are at war at once with the Moslems on the one hand and British on the other.'[44] But Savarkar actually justified the decision of the Hindu Mahasabha and the RSS to stand aside from the Quit India movement in 1942 on the ground that it would lead to the division of India and that energies must be preserved for the battle for the integrity of India (against Muslims). What is most striking is that, in fact, neither in Golwalkar's nor in Savarkar's writings (after his release from jail) is there any discussion of British Imperialism or the struggle against it. The only references are to cultural suppression, denationalization, cultural nationalism, etc. In his Presidential Address to the Hindu Mahasabha in 1938, Savarkar ended with the following passage. He spoke of heralding an:

> Independent and strong and mighty Hindu nation which is but tantamount with a mighty Indian Nation based on perfect equality of citizenship for all loyal and faithful Indian citizens irrespective of race and religion from Indus to the Seas.... Raise the standard of a Hindu Nation! See to it that India must remain a Hindusthan for ever; never a Pakisthan! — an Anglisthan, never never!! And let all India resound with - Hindu Dharma ki Jay! Hindu Rashtra ki Jay!! Vande Mataram!!![45]

[41] Golwalkar, *We*, pp., 49-50.
[42] Ibid, p.72.
[43] Ibid, p.73.
[44] Ibid, p.19.
[45] *Hindu Sangathan*, pp.109-110.

17

Nehru's Economic Vision for India: The Road to Fulfilment

ADITYA MUKHERJEE

Planned development with self-reliance and equity was the cornerstone of Nehru's economic vision of India. This implied to him the path at once of independence and socialism. At the same time, in his conception democracy (which was for him an absolute and critical goal in itself) and people's participation were to be at the heart of the process of development. In this chapter I attempt an outline how these these multiple perceptions led to the articulation of the individual goals in a particular manner and try to evaluate to the extent some of the goals were achieved in relation to how they had been envisioned.[1]

As any reader of his *Autobiography*[2] would find for himself, Jawaharlal Nehru was deeply influenced by Marxism and was especially greatly attracted by the Soviet experiment of economic planning very early in his political career. By the mid-1930s (as his presidential address at the Lucknow session of the Indian National Congress in 1936 makes clear), he had fully imbibed the then dominant current in Marxism where the Soviet pattern of development was taken as the model. Within the praradigm, the emphasis on 'democratic freedom' was sometimes seen by him as only a mechanism to safeguard private property and other privileges of the ruling classes. He believed that the effort towards social change or socialism was not to be diverted by the bogey of 'socialist coercion' or 'totalitarianism' raised by the ruling classes. He, therefore, envisaged "the ending of private property" and the abolition of the "profit system", and had no "illusion" that it could be achieved in any other way but by exercising

[1] See Bipan Chandra, *Jawaharlal Nehru in Historical Perspective*, D.D. Kosambi Memorial Lecture, Bombay, 1990. In my interpretation I have drawn heavily from this work (which is significantly different from the earlier writings of the same author in the 1970s) particularly in trying to interpret the change in Nehru's conception of socialism.

[2] Jawaharlal Nehru, *An Autobiography*, London, 1936. It was written in prison between June 1934 and February 1935. A new edition came in 1942 with an additional chapter.

"effective pressure amounting to coercion".[3]

Nehru gradually resiled from this position. He began to think it possible to abandon part of the Soviet paradigm without abandoning the goal of socialism. He emphasized the centrality of democracy to socialism, though inevitably it was seen by many as a dilution of his commitment to socialism for reasons such as the influence of Gandhiji and the pressures of governance. But what is here urged is that it is possible to see the change in a totally different light once we assume his sincerity of purpose.

Most of Nehru's efforts towards introducing planning in India, both before and after independence, were made within the framework of the National Movement, a coalition of classes, where in any case the pursuit of a Soviet-style economic development was not possible. Planning for Nehru had thus to be *consensual,* and not a unilateral exercise, even if it meant watering down many of his own objectives. The National Planning Committee (NPC) set up in 1938, of which Nehru was the Chairman, functioned within the new perspective of social change that Nehru gradually evolved. His new perspective in the context of planning was evident when he wrote from prison in the 1940s: "...it became clear to me that our plan (NPC), as it developed, was inevitably leading us towards establishing some of the fundamentals of the socialist structure. It was *limiting* the acquisitive factor in society... It was based on planning for the benefit of the common man, raising his standards greatly, giving him opportunities of growth... And all this was to be attempted *in the context of democratic freedom and with a large measure of cooperation of some at least of the groups who were normally opposed to socialist doctrine. That cooperation seemed to me worthwhile even if it involved toning down or weakening of the plan* in some respects."[4] Evident here is the notion of taking *steps* in the socialist direction (rather than establishing of socialism by the immediate *overthrow* of the existing structure), and of doing so within the democratic framework.

The NPC deliberations which continued over about a decade (the final report and the reports of numerous subcommittees were published by 1949) occurred with the active cooperation of

[3] Ibid., pp.543-44. Cf., Bipan Chandra, 'Jawaharlal Nehru and the Indian Capitalist Class, 1936', in *Nationalism and Colonialism in Modern India*, New Delhi, 1981.

[4] See Jawaharlal Nehru, *The Discovery of India*, 4th ed., London, 1956, pp.400-409: emphasis added.

persons of varied opinions including a broad spectrum of Indian capitalists. The adoption of this approach, on carrying even the propertied classes along in the effort at social or economic change enabled the evolution of a societal consensus, at the time of independence, on what was to be the nature and path of development to be followed by India. The successful evolution of such a consensus was one of Nehru's major achievements. The insistence on the democratic path for bringing about social change moreover ensured that democracy itself survived in India and was not seriously challenged by any internal dissent.

The consensus that was arrived at was broadly progressive and may be seen now to reflect the balance of class forces at Independence as a result of the radicalization that the Indian national movement had undergone, particularly since the 1920s. The Gandhians, the Socialists, the capitalists as well as the Communists (barring a brief phase, 1948-51), were all more or less agreed on following a multi-pronged strategy of economic development based on self reliance, with expansion of public sector in capital goods industries; industrialization based on import substitution; prevention of domination by foreign capital; and land reforms involving abolition of zamindari, tenancy reforms, promotion of cooperatives, for marketing, credit, etc. Growth was thus to be attempted along with equity, i.e., the growth model was to be reformist with a welfare, pro-poor orientation; positive discrimination or reservation for a period in favour of the most oppressed in Indian society, viz. the scheduled castes and tribes; the state to play a central role in promoting economic development largely through direct state participation in the production process, i.e., through the public sector.

Most important, there was a consensus that India was to make this unique attempt at planned industrialization within a democratic framework. All the industrialized countries of the world whether they be the advanced capitalist countries of the West or the socialist countries, considerably restricted the rights and liberties of certain classes during the initial period of their transition to industrialism. Nehru and others including the capitalists were acutely aware that they had chosen an uncharted path with no examples from history to follow. It is clear that such measures as enclosure movements (Britain), collectivization (Soviet Union), high land tax (Japan), slavery (USA), and colonial surplus extraction (what Britain, for example, received as unilateral transfers from colonies in Asian and West Indies was a stupendous 86 per cent of its Gross Domestic Capital formation or 6 per cent of the British GDP in 1801),[5] etc., were not open to India. Yet, there was faith that within the democratic framework enough capital could yet be generated mainly through state investments and a home market enlarged through land reforms.

In other words, India has not industrialised in the same manner as most of the industrially advanced countries today. Nor was the alternative of growth pursued through becoming a junior partner or satellite of a metropolitan country, a path later chosen by certain East Asian countries, for example. In Nehru's scheme of things, there was no scope for a trade-off between political democracy and civil liberties, on the one hand, and growth on the other. Nobody in India even argued for a variant of the model followed in parts of Latin America, East Asia, etc., where authoritarian governments in partnership with the capitalists at home and/or with a semi-dependant relationship with the advanced capitalist countries, would push through a process of rapid development in a hot-house fashion. In many respects, then, India's industrialisation, with its undoubted limitations, has been a unique process.

The consensus on development with democracy and economic independence may have somewhat slowed down development but by no means prevented considerable success especially if it is measured against the abysmal initial conditions that two hundred years of colonialism had created and if compared to the achievements of many other countries at a comparable stage of initial development. I have shown elsewhere that how, judged against these parameters India achieved impressive growth in agriculture, industry, investments, infrastructure, and education, after independence.[6]

Particularly successful was the strategy of reducing the near total dependence on the advanced countries for basic goods and capital equipment, which was necessary for investment or creation of new capacity. At the time of Independence, there

[5] See Utsa Patnaik, 'New Estimates of Eighteenth Century British Trade and their Relation to Transfers from Tropical Countries', in K.N. Panikkar, Terence J. Byres and Utsa Patnaik, eds., *The Making of History, Essays Presented to Irfan Habib*, New Delhi, 2000, pp.388-89.

[6] See Bipan Chandra, Mridula Mukherjee and Aditya Mukherjee, *India After Independence*, New Delhi, 2000, chapter 25.

was practically no machine tools industry and to make any capital investment necessitated the import of virtually the entire equipment. Thus in 1950, India met 89.8 per cent of its needs for industrial equipment through imports. In contrast, the share of imported equipment in the total fixed investment in the form of equipment in India had come down to 43 per cent in 1960 and a mere 9 per cent in 1974, whereas the value of the fixed investment in India increased by about two and a half times over this period. In other words, by the mid-1970s, India could meet indigenously more than 90 per cent of her equipment requirements for maintaining her rate of investment. This was a major achievement, and it considerably increased India's autonomy in relation to the advanced countries. It was this, and the food security that India was able to achieve once the process of the Green Revolution took off, which explains India's ability to retain an independent foreign policy through the thick of the Cold War and notwithstanding enormous external pressures. It was this key success of Nehru's strategy which now makes it possible for India to somewhat liberalize her economy externally and participate in the globalization process with some degree of success.

While in the course of the National Movement a reasonable consensus on democracy and sovereignty had emerged, the consensus on the objective of equity remained quite vague. A certain pro-poor orientation in the formation of government policy was generally acceptable, but how this orientation was to be translated into precise policy prescriptions was not so easily to be arrived at. There had certainly not emerged any consensus around socialism as an objective especially in the Marxist sense.

Nehru was acutely aware of this and while energetically trying to shift the consensus in the direction of socialism never pushed his own position beyond what was reasonably acceptable to all sections of society and never insisted on a precise definition of socialism, leaving it sufficiently vague, so as to accommodate a wide variety of elements. In a deeply divided and diverse society like India such a perspective of moving ahead only with democratic consensus seemed to him necessary for not only the maintenance of democracy but also the preservation of national unity.

An example of this tension between Nehru and the forces opposed to his social vision, is seen in the way the capitalists and Nehru negotiated over the framework of the institutions of planning and the public sector.[7] While Nehru and the Left nationalists (Nehru's "near-Communists"), on the one hand, and the capitalists, on the other, were agreed on this issue of the need for the public sector to reduce external dependence, they differed on the scope and extent of the public sector. Nehru saw planning and the public sector as a step in the socialist direction and argued for progressive nationalisation whereas the businessmen saw it as complementary to the private sector, and so an instrument of promoting capitalism. The capitalists were alarmed when Nehru appeared to be taking a position too much to the left, and began to adopt a multi-pronged strategy to contain the Left while seemingly appropriating those elements of the left programme which could be accommodated within the limits of the capitalist system. Nehru on his part in order to be able to carry the capitalist class with him had to go out of his way periodically to reassure them. For example, in 1938 he stated that the Congress was for revolutionary changes in the present economic and social structure of the country so that gross inequalities could be removed and the condition of the masses could be ameliorated. However, though the Congress expressed "general approval" of "socialistic theories", this did not mean that "*the Congress (had) ... in any way accepted socialism*".[8] Again in 1940, while talking of a "socialist planned structure" in which "state control" and "socialization of national activities" would increase rapidly, Nehru assured every one that "private enterprise has certainly not been ruled out but it has to be strictly controlled and coordinated in the general plan".[9]

However while making concessions to ensure that the planning exercise could mobilise as broad a section of society as possible, Nehru continued to believe that planning and the public sector should aim at "establishing some of the fundamentals of the socialist structure". He quite unequivocally told the FICCI in March 1947, "nobody wants any group or class to suffer as a class, but if there is conflict between the interests of one group and the larger community obvioulsy the interests of the larger community must prevail, and it is for this group or class to say

[7] See Aditya Mukherjee, *Imperialism, Nationalism and the Making of the Indian Capitalist Class, 1920-47*, New Delhi, 2002, ch.11.

[8] Chairman's (Nehru's) note on Congress Policy, 21 December 1938, *National Planning Committee Report*, Bombay, 1949, p.35.

[9] Note by Nehru, Chairman, National Planning Committee, 5th session, 30 Aug. 1940, *Jawaharlal Nehru Papers*, fl.no.N-38.

how what it wants done is to the interest of the larger community."[10] While including all classes in it, Nehru obviously hoped to tilt the balance in favour of the poor and the labouring masses through planned development.

The tension between Nehru's aims and the capitalist approach was to become patently visible in the early years after Independence. In 1947, for example, the Economic Programme Committee appointed by the AICC and headed by Jawaharlal Nehru not only laid down the areas, such as defence, key industries and public utilities which were to be under the public sector, it also added that "in respect of existing undertakings the process of transfer from private to public ownership should commence after a period of five years".[11] The capitalists were alarmed and much press criticism ensued. Signs of accommodation were seen in the 1948 Industrial Policy Resolution (IPR) which, while delineating specific areas for the public and the private sectors, added that the question of nationalising any existing industry would be reviewed after ten years and dealt with on the basis of circumstances prevailing at that time. Even after Parliament in December 1954 accepted "the socialist pattern of society as the objective of social and economic policy"[12] and the Congress in its Avadi session (1955) elaborated a Leftward swing on these lines, the 1956 IPR and the Second Plan, while considerably expanding the scope of the public sector, made no mention of nationalising existing industries. In fact the model projected was of a 'mixed economy' where the public and the private sectors were not only to co-exist but were to be complementary to each other, and the private sector was to be encouraged to grow with as much freedom as possible within the broad objectives of the national plan. It is another matter that the great emphasis on heavy and capital goods industries in the Second plan by itself led to a major shift towards the public sector as these were areas which, it was commonly agreed, could be basically developed only by the public sector, because of the limited capacities for capital generation in the private sector.

[10] Nehru's speech at the Federation of Indian Chambers of Commerce and Industry, (FICCI), Mar. 1947, FICCI, *Annual Report*, New Delhi, 1947, pp.16-27, 147.

[11] *Indian National Congress: Resolutions on Economic Policy Programme and Allied Matters 1924-1969* (hereafter INC Economic Resolutions), New Delhi, p.29, emphasis mine.

[12] *Second Five Year Plan*, New Delhi, 1956, p.44.

On the other hand, given the class configuration and the structure of the state apparatus it was unavoidable that the public sector in India was bound to reinforce private indigenous capitalism in India, an aspect I have discussed in detail elsewhere.[13]

On the question of land reforms there was a distinct policy of pushing them forward without reaching the point of a breakdown of the consensus. In the immediate years preceding Independence, reflecting the long history of the peasant movement, a consensus on the agrarian question seemed to have emerged among a broad spectrum of Indian political opinion and on some issues among a wide section of the peasantry. For example, the National Planning Committee (formed in 1938 with Jawaharlal Nehru as Chairman and deliberated through the 1940s), the Bombay Plan (A Plan of Economic Development for India 1944-45, prepared by the leading representatives of the Indian capitalists), and the Election Manifesto issued by the Congress Working Committee in 1945 were more or less agreed on the following basic issues: An urgent reform of the land system to be undertaken which involved the abolition of intermediaries between the peasant and the state, i.e., the Zamindars and Talukdars, who could be paid compensation that was considered necessary and desirable; problem of rural indebtedness to be addressed and cheap credit made available; while individual farming or peasant proprietorship was to continue in large parts of the country, cooperative farming on privately owned lands and collective farming on state lands was to be encouraged.[14]

While on Zamindari abolition the consensus in the countryside (barring, naturally, the Zamindars) was clear, it was not so on issues like cooperativisation or land ceilings. The careful wording of the Congress election manifesto (December 1945) on this issue is significant: "while individualist farming or peasant proprietorship should continue, progressive agriculture as well as the creation of new social values and incentives require some system of cooperative farming suited to Indian conditions.

[13] See Aditya Mukherjee and Mridula Mukherjee, 'Imperialism and the growth of Indian capitalism in the Twentieth Century', *EPW,* 12 March 1988, reprinted in Ghanshyam Shah, ed., *Capitalist Development: Critical Essays*, Felicitation volume in honour of Prof. A.R. Desai, Bombay, 1990.

[14] See *National Planning Committee Report*, Bombay, 1949, Purshotamdas Thakurdas, *et al.*, *A Plan for Economic Development for India*, (Bombay Plan), Harmondsworth, 1945, and *INC Econ. Resolutions*, pp.15-18.

Any such change can however be made only with the goodwill and agreement of the peasantry concerned."[15] A certain disjunction between the agrarian programme of cooperatives put out by the political leadership or the Congress and the preparedness of the peasantry at whom it was aimed was as yet absent.

In November 1947, the All India Congress Committee (AICC) appointed a special committee to draw up an economic programme for the Congress. The programme was to be based on the December 1945 Election Manifesto and a set of stated principles which should meet the great challenge of building "real democracy in the country... based on equality and social justice", enable central planning along with decentralisation of political and economic power; [and] provide "an alternative to the acquisitive economy of private capitalism and the regimentation of a totalitarian state."[16] This was indeed a complex agenda without any pre-existing model to follow. The committee which was to draw up such a programme was headed by Jawaharlal Nehru and included among its members Maulana Azad, Jai Prakash Narain, N.G. Ranga, G.L. Nanda, J.C. Kumarappa, Achyut Patwardhan and Shankarrao Deo — a fair mix of 'Gandhians' and socialists.

The Committee (also called the Economic Programme Committee) made a twenty-point recommendation for agriculture.[17] Some of the points may be highlighted here. Clause 2 of the recommendations read: "All intermediaries between the tiller and the state should be eliminated and all middlemen should be replaced by non-profit making agencies, such as cooperatives." While the first part of the clause clearly referred to the abolition of Zamindari, the second part about middlemen was rather ambiguous. Some have read it to mean "elimination of all private money lenders and traders."[18] While this strand of argument was perhaps present among some Congressmen, the Economic Programme Committee did not seem to be taking such an extreme position. All that was agreed to at this stage was the setting up of multipurpose cooperatives, which would "cut down the costs of agricultural credit, processing and marketing" and

[15] *INC Econ. Resolutions*, p.16, emphasis mine.

[16] "Objectives and Economic Programme", AICC, Delhi, November 1947, *INC Econ. Resolutions*, p.19.

[17] *INC Econ. Resolutions*, pp.20-22.

[18] See e.g., Francine Frankel, *India's Political Economy 1947-77*, Delhi, 1978, p.68.

presumably thus replace the moneylender and trader in course of time.

As for cooperative farming or production cooperatives the Committee recommended that "the state should organise pilot schemes for experimenting with cooperative farming among small-holders and should set up cooperative colonies on Government unoccupied... lands, and should also directly own and run farms for purposes of experiment and demonstration." No compulsion was visualised either for production or service cooperatives.[19]

The Committee also introduced the notion of land ceiling. It now seems for the first time to have been accepted as an official Congress position. The Committee held that. "The maximum size of holding should be fixed. The surplus land over such a maximum should be acquired and placed at the disposal of the village cooperatives." Apart from this some of the other recommendations were: the present land revenue system to be replaced by progressive agricultural income tax, remunerative prices for agricultural produce and equitable terms of trade between agriculture and industry, the consolidation of small holdings and the prevention of further fragmentation. It was also recommended that "Statutory Village Panchayats should be organised... for self governing purposes with well defined powers and adequate financial resources, and with supervisory jurisdiction over all other institutions in the locality."[20] It is significant that an effort to create a situation for proper implementation of such recommendations ultimately required an amendment to the Constitution (73rd amendment in 1993) nearly half a century later.

As we shall see, many of the other clauses especially those regarding cooperatives, ceilings, etc., did not have an easy passage and some like agricultural income tax have not been adopted to this day. Key subjects relating to the rural sector such as land reforms, agricultural credit, land revenue assessment, taxation of agricultural income, etc., were all included in the State list, i.e., it was not the central government but the state governments which were to act on these issues and implement them. This meant that the nature of programme legislated and especially

[19] *INC Econ. Resolutions*, p.22, emphasis mine. Frankel (see note 17), however, maintains that compulsory membership of service cooperatives was visualised.

[20] *INC Econ. Resolutions*, p.23.

the manner of its implementation was left to state governments where the will to carry it out varied according to the strength of radical elements within the Congress and outside at the State level.

A dichotamy soon began to emerged between the recommendations made by the Central government and what the States and the various administrative bodies were willing or able to implement. This occurred particularly when recommendations emanating from the Centre, for example, those made by the Congress Agrarian Reforms Committee (Kumarappa Committee) in July 1949 or by the 1959 Nagpur Congress, on many issues, went way beyond what was acceptable to many of the State leaders of the Congress party itself. These were issues such as the introduction of a degree of compulsion for promoting cooperative farming and for replacing private trade and money-lending with state or cooperative organisations, implementing land ceilings, and so on. Resistance to such programmes occurred in various ways, some overt and others subterranean but equally effective.

It is keeping in mind this tension – the stuff of any democracy — as a backdrop that any evaluation can be made of the actual success and failures of the land reform effort in India.

Nehru was deeply aware of the areas where no consensus had emerged and moved cautiously and slowly. This approach is clearly seen in the context of two bitterly disputed issues in the process of land reforms, namely, land ceilings and cooperation. After the first mention of land ceilings by the 1947 Economic Programme Committee headed by Nehru, the idea was reiterated in 1949 by the Congress Agrarian Reform Committee headed by J.C. Kumarappa, in the First Plan,[21] and in a number of other forums in the early 1950s without actually working out details and setting immediate deadlines.

In the meantime, opposition to ceilings built up in large parts of the country, in the press, in Parliament, in the State Legislatures and within the Congress party. A threat to the right to private property was perceived by the rural landowners and rich farmers as well as by urban interests. Matters came to a head at the Nagpur Session of the Congress in January 1959. Despite opposition from prominent Congressman at the AICC

[21] See *INC Econ. Resolutions*, pp.37ff. and the *First Five Year Plan*. Planning Commission, New Delhi, pp.188-91.

and the Subjects Committee meeting preceding the open session, the Nagpur Congress (January 1959) passed a resolution stating that "in order to remove uncertainty regarding land reforms and give stability to the farmer, ceilings should be fixed on existing and future holdings and legislation to this effect... should be completed in all States by the end of 1959." Further, the land declared surplus, i.e., above ceiling limits, was to "vest in the panchayats... and (be) managed through cooperatives consisting of landless labourers."[22]

A wave of criticism followed in the months after the Nagpur Session. N.G. Ranga, Secretary of the Congress Parliamentary Party who had already, in December 1958, sent to Nehru a letter signed by a hundred Congress Members of Parliament, opposing the idea of ceilings, resigned from the Congress in February 1959. The Nagpur Resolution contributed considerably towards the consolidation of the Right wing forces both in the rural and urban sectors of the country. N.G. Ranga and C. Rajagopalachari now joined hands with Minoo Masani, an important leader of the Forum for Free Enterprise, which campaigned against the any form of nationalisation, and formed the Swatantra Party in June 1959, with Ranga as President. Some of the beneficiaries of Zamindari abolition, the large tenants who had now become landowners, also ranged themselves against this next step in land reform, the attempt at redistribution of land ownership through imposition of land ceilings.

The opponents of the ceilings legislation were to have their partial victory at the State level, as it was the States which had to formulate and implement the legislation. The State legislatures, which met shortly after the Nagpur Session, showed no haste in implementing the Nagpur resolution. The ceilings issue thus dragged on and most States passed the enabling legislation only by the end of 1961.

The effort to persist with the implementation of ceiling laws continued even after Nehru's death (1964) and in fact intensified during the second spurt of land reforms in the 1970s despite the strong opposition it faced. However the implementation remained so full of loopholes that little land was actually found to exceed the ceilings. The total area declared surplus as late as the 1990s and distributed among the landless constituted only about 2 per cent of the cultivated area. Again, while it is true that more than four and a half million people, mostly landless, did receive some

[22] *INC Econ. Resolutions*, p.121.

land (however poor its quality and however small the size of the holding) the inequities in Indian agriculture, which the ceiling laws were intended to address, remained unaffected. Yet an important result of the ceiling laws, and perhaps in the long run the most critical one, was that these killed the land market and prevented an increasing concentration in landholdings through de-peasantisation. As the eminent scholar of Indian agriculture, C.H. Hanumantha Rao, has put it, "The law discouraged concentration of landownership beyond the ceiling level and thus prevented the possible dispossession of numerous small and marginal holders which would probably have occurred through a competitive process in the land market in the absence of a ceiling on landholdings."[23]

Also, though the opportunity to acquire large areas of surplus lands for redistribution was missed because of defective and delayed ceiling laws, in the long run the high population growth and the rapid subdivision of large holdings over several generations (in the absence of the practice of primogeniture for inheritance in India) led automatically to reductions of size of individual holdings. In fact the number of holdings and the operational area under the category of large holdings, 25 acres or above (even 15 acres and above) kept falling in the decades after Independence right upto the 1990s. Except in certain small pockets in the country, very large landholdings of the semi-feudal type became things of the past. Inequality among landowners was no longer a key issue, as it was not very skewed any more. By one estimate, by 1976-77 nearly 97 per cent of the operational holdings were below 25 acres and 87 per cent were below 10 acres.[24]

Regarding cooperatives, the Congress under Nehru's leadership kept campaigning in favour of cooperatives, carefully avoiding any talk of coercion till the break which came with the Nagpur resolution of the Congress in January 1959. The Nagpur resolution clearly stated that "the organisation of the village should be based on village panchayats and village cooperatives, both of which should have adequate powers and resources to discharge the functions allotted to them." Further, the resolution

[23] C.H. Hanumantha Rao, 'Agriculture: Policy and Performance', in Bimal Jalan, ed., *The Indian Economy: Problems and Prospects*, New Delhi, p.118.

[24] D. Bandyopadhyay, 'Land Reforms in India: An Analysis', *EPW*, Review of Agriculture, June 1986. For a detailed discussion of the ceiling issue that I have engaged in elsewhere see Bipan Chandra, Mridula Mukherjee and Aditya Mukherjee, *India After Independence*, New Delhi, 2000, chapter 29.

stated:[25]

The future agrarian pattern should be that of cooperative joint farming, in which the land would be pooled for joint cultivation, the farmers continuing to retain their property rights, and getting a share of the net produce in proportion to their land. Further, those who actually work on the land, whether they own the land or not, will get a share in proportion to the work put in by them on the joint farm.
As a first step, prior to the institution of joint farming, service cooperatives should be organised throughout the country. This stage should be completed within a period of three years. Even within this period, however, wherever possible and generally agreed to by the farmers, joint cultivation may be started.

A big leap was involved here. Not only did the Nagpur resolution visualise an agrarian pattern based on joint cooperative farming in the future, it specified that such a pattern was to be set in motion within three years. The proposal for introducing cooperatives, which was being made since the mid-1940s, could no longer be treated as just another radical recommendation with no concrete programme for its implementation. A wave of opposition both within and outside the Congress rapidly emerged as a result of this recommendation of the Nagpur resolution, as much as about land ceilings and the introduction of state trading in wholesale trade in foodgrains.

Parliament, which was convened shortly after the Nagpur session, brimmed with sharp criticism of the Nagpur resolution. It was argued that the resolution was the first step towards ending private property and eventual expropriation of the landed classes. Senior Congress leaders like C. Rajagopalachari, N.G. Ranga and Charan Singh mobilised opinion in the party and outside and mounted an open attack saying that a totalitarian, Communist programme was being thrust upon the country.

Faced with such strident opposition Nehru struck a conciliatory note, assuring Parliament in February 1959 that there was no question of using any coercion to introduce cooperatives and that no new law was going to be passed by Parliament on this question. He only reiterated his personal conviction that cooperative farming was desirable and vowed that he would continue to try and convince the peasants, without whose consent the programme could not be implemented.

Thus even more than in the case of ceiling legislation Nehru's moves towards cooperativisation were severely muted and while

[25] *INC Econ. Resolutions*, pp.120 ff, emphasis mine.

hardly any progress occurred in the direction of production cooperatives, even the service cooperatives which grew rapidly suffered from many shortcomings, serving much more the interests of the well-to-do than the rural poor. Yet the effort to correct these distortions continued, particularly during the 1970s. Over time the service cooperatives, particularly the credit cooperatives, came to perform a critical role in Indian agriculture. While in 1951-52 the Primary Agricultural Credit Societies (PACS), which were village level cooperative societies, advanced loans worth only about Rs.23 crores, in 1960-61 about 212,000 such societies disbursed nearly Rs.200 crores. By 1992-93 these societies were lending as much as Rs.4,900 crores.[26] Moreover, one positive result of the concerted effort in the early seventies to make institutional benefits reach the rural poor was that a much larger proportion of cooperative and bank credit started becoming available to the small and marginal farmers. In 1979-80 about 34 per cent of the short-term loans given by scheduled commercial banks went to households with less than 2.5 acres each, when such households constituted only 33 per cent of the total households. Similarly, 57 per cent of the loans went to households owning up to five acres, while the number of households in that category was only 49 per cent of the total. No longer was institutional rural credit the preserve of the rural elite. Policy initiatives were to follow which led to the rural banks giving a much higher proportion of credit to the weaker sections. As for the cooperatives (PACS), those with holdings up to 5 acres received 34 per cent of the credit and those holding above 5 acres received 62 per cent. The situation of the landless however remained the same: only 4 per cent of the credit went to them.[27]

It is thus evident that service cooperatives started to play a very important role in rural India. Their role in making available a much increased amount of cheap credit to a wider section of the peasantry was critical. They immensely helped in bringing improved seeds, modern implements, cheap fertilisers, etc., to the peasants. And, in many areas they also helped the poorer peasants to market their produce. In fact in many ways they provided a necessary condition for the success of the "Green

[26] I have discussed this issue in greater length in Bipan Chandra, Mridula Mukherjee and Aditya Mukherjee, *India After Independence*, New Delhi, 2000, chapter 30.

[27] The figures in this paragraph are from Rudolph and Rudolph, *In Pursuit of Lakshmi*, Table 42, p.373.

Revolution" strategy launched in the late 1960s, which was based on intensive use of modern inputs in agriculture. It is not surprising then that Wolf Ladejinsky, who was fully aware of all the shortcomings of the cooperative movement in India, recorded in his annual note to the World Bank in May 1972 that "millions of farmers have benefited from them (cooperatives) and rural India without this landmark is hard to visualise".[28]

In sum then we see that the agrarian redistributive and anti-poverty aspects of Nehru's programme experienced the maximum social dissensions and so were the most difficult to implement. The success in this direction was limited though, as we saw, not insignificant. Yet it is this aspect of equity, which proved to be the major weakness of the Indian planning effort under Nehru. The major weakness was not, as is often mistakenly argued, on the question of independent development. India against heavy odds successfully avoided the path of dependent or neo-colonial development. Its economy grew independently, but essentially along bourgeois lines, an aspect Nehru himself was acutely aware of. The brave attempt to tilt the balance in favour of a socialist perspective, on the other hand, met with only limited success.

It may be noted that institutions like planning, public sector, democracy, cooperatives are not intrinsically class specific. By itself, the introduction of these did not mean either a step in the direction of socialism or of strengthening capitalism, whatever may be the wishes of those who promoted them. Which direction these institutions actually came to be used for was a function of the balance of class forces and the various parts of the state apparatus (including the government, legislatures, bureaucracy, judiciary and the educational system). The capitalists attempted to use these institutions to promote in industrial development, while ensuring that it occurred within the capitalist framework. Nehru hoped to use them too for India's industrialisation but in such a way as would take India towards socialism. Both sides were trying to use the same instruments for opposite purposes. The fact that the capitalists accepted some elements of the nationalist programme did not alter their hostility to socialism. Similarly, Nehru's agreeing to 'tone down' the programme to carry along the capitalists with him in the developmental effort did not amount to his adopting the simple objective of building capitalism.

[28] Louis J. Walinsky, ed., *Agrarian Reform as Unfinished Business, The Selected Papers of Wolf Ladejinsky,* New York, 1977, pp.505-06.

What needs emphasis is that, contrary to a view among come of his criticis on the Left, the weakness of Nehru's economic programme did not lie in his making so many concessions to the capitalists as undermined its basic objectives. Rather the limitations were due to his high regard for democratic norms. He could not carry coercion and breach of consesus to a particular point. On the other hand, far from being an obstacle to the cause of equity, democracy emerged as its chief protector. While in India the transition to industry had necessarily to be built on forced savings, through deficit financing and inflation, yet there a series of measures to protect the workers and peasants to retain popular support. The working class made major advances through collective bargaining and there was by and large a net transfer of resources to agriculture after Independence rather than vice-versa. Even inflation had to be contained. The early fifties saw falling prices and the rate of inflation did not exceed 8 per cent per year between 1956 and 1990 despite two oil shocks and several droughts. Even when necessary stabilisation and structural adjustments were undertaken during the post-1991 reforms, these being measures which make the poor particularly vulnerable through contraction of public expenditure, democracy ensured that they were not entirely left high and dry. Anti-poverty measures were expanded and a quick reversal of the rise in poverty that occurred during the first two years of reforms was secured. In the dilemma between fiscal prudence and egalitarian commitment (a dilemma which, as Amartya Sen points out, is not a choice between good and bad, but a genuine dilemma between two goods),[29] democracy ensured that it did not get resolved without adequate weight to the latter.

The cause for the failure to implement the socialist programme as originally envisioned perhaps lay elsewhere. From the very beginning the Nehru-Mahalanobis strategy of growth with equity had assumed that popular mobilisation from below would be necessary to implement it effectively. There was no dearth of initiatives from the top: the government introduced some of the most radical legislations, including those in the sphere of land reform, and created several institutions capable of being transformed for the service of people such as cooperatives, panchayati institutions, public sector etc., were created. But so long as the balance of class forces at the ground level and within

[29] Amartya Sen, 'Social Commitment and Democracy', *New Thinking Communist*, 1 November 1998.

the state apparatus the bureaucracy, police, media, judiciary, etc., remained unfavourable, these institutions tended to strengthen the vested interests.

The problem was in locating an 'agency' which was going to perform this task of mobilisation. With Independence, the Congress party with Nehru at its head got transformed from a party of struggle and movement to a party of governance. Efforts to make the Congress workers perform the former role rather than try to learn the ropes of the latter proved essentially unsuccessful. (Gandhiji anticipating this denouement had called for the disbanding of the Congress at Independence and forming of a separate organisation, distinct from the one which governed, that would struggle for the people's cause.) Nehru, however, hoped that the Congress would produce from within its ranks both rulers and volunteers, those who governed and those who mobilised. This proved an illusory hope. Antagonisms with Nehru from 1942 onwards meant that Communists could make only limited use of the space provided by the democratic set-up (Kerala, West Bengal), while the Left within Congress was swallowed up in the mere tasks of governance. Nehru tried to fill the void by creating a developmental bureaucracy from the local village worker to the highest level, unwittingly creating a byzantine institution whose main purpose increasingly appeared to be that of multiplying and feeding itself.

The political space for mobilisation in favour of the poor thus largely remained untapped – though simple democratic arithmetic has secured the poor several concessions as all political formations have to seek their votes.

Jawaharlal Nehru died in 1964. As we have seen the appeal that his vision made to the minds and hearts of the Indian people continued to keep successive Congress governments at the centre largely loyal to it and measures continued to be taken in the realms of industry, agriculture and poverty alleviation within the framework that he had constructed, down to the 1980's. There is no doubt that this groundwork is responsible for much of the economic strength that India possess today. But if we go back to Nehru's dream for India, he would certainly have not wished to see so much of this strength concentrated in the hands of corporate magnates, nor accepted the replacement of the cause of equity by the mantra of the market. It is time we remember this as much as we ought to remember the secular legacy he has bequeathed to us, which too is being so steadily undermined by our rulers today.

Index